The End Game

SURVIVAL HANDBOOK
FOR THE END TIMES

Constantine I. Nightingdale

The End Times Apostle to the World from Hawaii

TRILOGY CHRISTIAN PUBLISHERS

TUSTIN, CA

Trilogy Christian Publishers
A Wholly Owned Subsidiary of Trinity Broadcasting Network
2442 Michelle Drive
Tustin, CA 92780

The End Game

For information, address Trilogy Christian Publishing

Rights Department, 2442 Michelle Drive, Tustin, Ca 92780.

Trilogy Christian Publishing/ TBN and colophon are trademarks of Trinity Broadcasting Network.

For information about special discounts for bulk purchases, please contact Trilogy Christian Publishing.

Manufactured in the United States of America

10 9 8 7 6 5 4 3 2 1

Library of Congress Cataloging-in-Publication Data is available.

ISBN 978-1-68556-813-9

eISBN 978-1-68556-814-6

A Very Important Letter to Our Lord Jesus

Dear Jesus:

My hope and prayer are that people around the world reading this book never see me, Lord, but see You, Lord Jesus. I initially thought not to give my name as the author, nor did I wish to publish my photo as the book's author, but You showed me I needed to include my name and photo to bear testimony of You.

Lord Jesus, You recall that in 2005, it was prophesied to me that I would write these books. I wrote these books out of obedience and love for You, Lord Jesus. Let every word glorify Your holy name, not mine.

Let every soul touched by reading this book Lord, give You honor and pluck them out of hell into Your loving arms in Heaven. Lord Jesus, never let us lose sight of You. Amen.

In His service,

Constantine I. Nightingdale

The End-Time Apostle to the World from Hawaii

Special Thanks and Acknowledgements

The Army of the Lord—5 Distinct Roles (Ephesians 4:11)
My Friends, Christians and Born Again
John and Linda Keough, The Healing Rooms of Honolulu
Pastor David and Virginia, The Prayer Center of the Pacific (prayercenterofthepacific.org)
Joe and Prophetess Phyllis Ramia and Prophetess Michelle Ramia
Hawaii Dream Service Center
Hawaii Christian Community Land Trust
Hawaii Pacific Christian Community Foundation
Pastor Wade Boo Soares, Hawaii Coalition of Christian Churches
Chaplain Dennis Yokota, Good News Prison
Lyn, JoAnn, Karlyn,
Island Women Empowered By God
Pastors Glenn and Sandy Shimabukuro
Prophetess Charene Davis, Editor
Irene Shiroma
Christine Carson

And to Many Other Friends and Servants of the Lord

Many Thanks To:

Founding Pastor Wayne Cordeiro, NHI (enewhope.org)

New Hope Christian Fellowship Oahu, Hawaii

John Tilton, Senior Pastor of New Hope Oahu (enewhope.org)

Pastor Donovan Sabog (enewhope.org)

Pastor Keola Richards (enewhope.org)

Pastor Pua Palakiko (enewhope.org)

Pastor Gavin Tsuda (enewhope.org)

Pastor Elwin Ahu (newhopemetro.org)

Pastor Brandon Ahu (enewhopemetro.org)

Paul and Cheryl Okimoto

Matt and Laurie Crouch (tbn.org)

Dr. Lester Sumrall (familybroadcastingcorporation.com)

Marcus and Joni Lamb (daystar.com)

Edward G. Atsinger III (salemmedia.com)

Prophet Morris Cerullo (mcwe.com)

Evangelist Reinhard Bonnke

Evangelest Nick Vujicic

William Lile and My Cell Group (pearlside.org)

Greg Tavares

Norman Nakanishi, Sr. Pastor of Pearlside Church (pearlside.
org)

Pastor Parris Hayashi (pearlside.org)

Pastor Billy Lile (pearside.org)

Pastor/Apostle Cal Chinen (mgmchawaii.com)

George and Murle Milles

Prophetess Helena Cochran

Pastor/Apostle Eric Hurd
Prophet Nathan Pakai
Apostle Ed and Ruth Silvoso (edsilvoso.com)
Terlie Joy Perceda
Ravi Zacharias International Ministries
Nabeel Qureshi
Pastor Mike and Lisa Kai (inspirechurch.live)
Dawn O'Brien (dob4GOD@gmail.com)
Billy Graham Evangelistic Association (billygraham.org)
Kathryn Kuhlman (YouTube)
Dr. Pat Zukeran (evidenceandanswers.org)
Evangelist Elijah Pierick
Evangelist Kanoe Morihara (cru.org)
Dr. James Kwong
Dr. Corey Miller (ratiochristi.org)
Pastor Randy and Louise Manley (molokaibaptist.com)
Sandra Young, Attorney (hawaiichristianfoundation.org)
Thomas A. Rulon, Attorney (hawaiichristianfoundation.org)
Messianic Rabbi Daniel Yeshurun Vargus (bethisraelministries.com)
Colonel Donna Gamboa
PragerU.com
Dr. Leon Watson
Pastor Richard and Vicky Knox
Charlie Kirk—Turning Point USA
Podcast—Charlie Kirk Show
(KTIE Radio)
Michael J Lindell (mypillow.com)
Pastor Jack Hibbs (JackHibbs.com)

Bob Fopma, TBN
Tom Newman, TBN
Shane Harwell, TBN
Bryan and Misty Norris, TBN
Ashley Welch, TBN Trilogy Publishing
Allison Dyer, TBN Trilogy Publishing
Shelley Jobe, TBN Trilogy Publishing
Jeff Summers, TBN Trilogy Publishing

Contents

Foreword

It isn't hard to see that the times we are living in are indeed a call to wake up. Wake up to the truth, search for a solid foundation, and search for things in which to believe. Turn off mainstream media, do your own research on what's really going on—socially, economically, and politically and consider what's happening spiritually.

The author, Mr. Constantine Nightingdale, has spent years literally searching for the truth. When he found it, he couldn't hide it under a rock or stay silent. That's why you are now reading this book, ***End Game***. Years have been spent by Mr. Nightingdale gathering information on the times in which we live.

Once you read this book, it is the author's hope and prayer that you'll emerge with a sense that you're a bit more prepared for what's coming than before reading this book.

Are you ready for the *End Game*?

Introduction

A Note from the Author

I remember praying to God to reveal to me the scripture verse found in Ephesians 4:11 (KJV),

And he gave some, apostles; and some prophets; and some, evangelists; and some, pastors and teachers;

I asked God, "What are You calling me to do as a Christian?" No one knew; not one single soul knew that I was praying about this. God answered my prayer in sets of threes. Three is a divine number in confirmation in the Christian faith.

First, Prophetess Helena Cockran called me, then secondly, Prophet Nathan Pakai called me, and third, Apostle/Pastor Eric Hurd called me. All three basically said, "Constantine, the Lord has called you to be an Apostle."

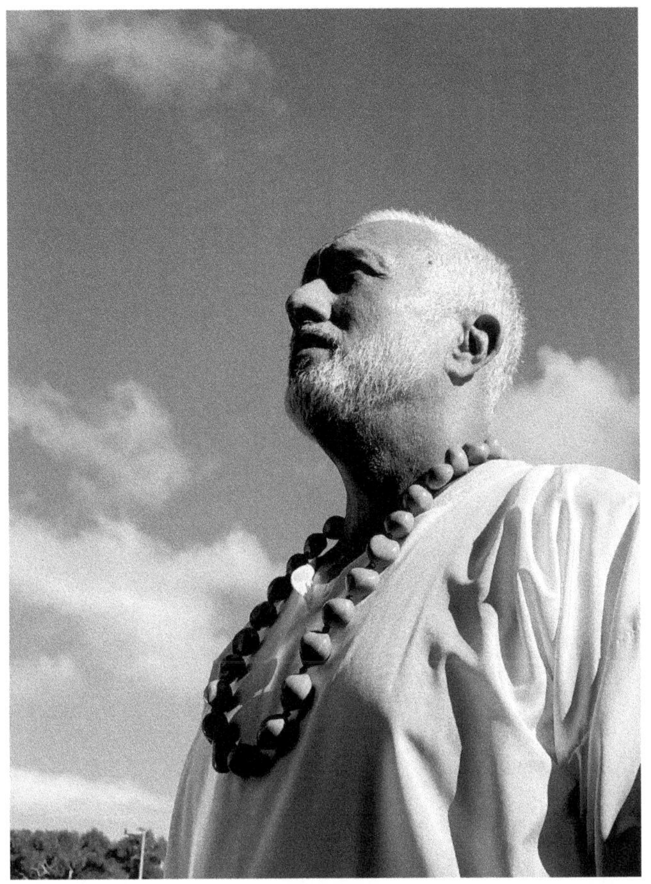

End-Time Apostle Constantine Nightingdale is pictured here looking up to God, Jesus Christ, and the Holy Spirit. He is wearing the gown he wore when he was baptized on March 20, 2018 (while on a TBN tour led by Matt and Laurie Crouch) in the Jordan River, Israel. Notice the lei, which is a Hawaiian kukui nut lei. Fifteen kukui nuts on each side represent grace—five for a total of fifteen. A total of thirty nuts symbolizes the *Trinity*—three times ten equals thirty—the number of *completion*. As Mr. Nightingdale travels around the world to preach the Gospel of Jesus Christ and the *End Game* with those who have an open heart—this signifies completion as an Apostle of Jesus Christ.

CHAPTER 1

Are We Living in End Times, or Are These Socio-Political Events as Usual?

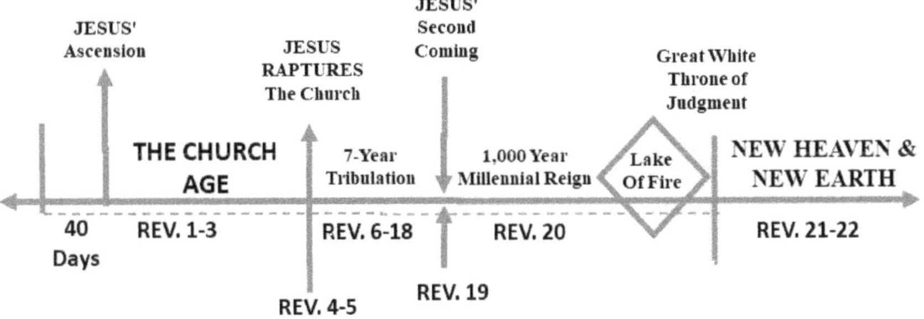

This end-time events timeline shows that we are currently living in the "Church Age". The next event to occur is the "Rapture" of God's people—which could be coming at any second! (1 Corinthians 15:52).

Other Timelines Floating Around Out There

According to the International Union of Geological Sciences (IUGS), the professional organization in charge of defining Earth's time scale, we are officially in the Holocene ("entirely recent") epoch, which began 11,700 years ago after the last major ice age.[1] However, with the advent of the Mount St. Helens eruption in 1980, science revealed startling facts to show that the earth is not as old as IUGS suggests.[2] Mount St. Helens practically single-handedly debunks the science of carbon dating. Even with the scientific data we have as a result of the Mount St. Helens eruption, Scientists were unwilling to change what has been written or understood about carbon dating, and thus we have an ongoing debate when it comes to intelligently discussing the age of the earth.[3]

The Information Age began around the 1970s and is still going on today. It is also known as the Computer Age, Digital Age, or New Media Age. This era brought about a time period in which people could access information and knowledge easily.[4]

However, Christians with a biblical worldview recognize that the most important era to label, if one needs to label the era we are living in, is the **Church Age**. Revelation 1–3 talks about the Church Age.

---

1 Joseph Stromberg, *What Is the Anthropocene and Are We in It?* Smithsonian Magazine, January, 2013, https://www.smithsonianmag.com/science-nature/what-is-the-anthropocene-and-are-we-in-it-164801414/

2 Brian Thomas, "30 Years Later, the Lessons from Mount St. Helens," The Institute for Creation Research, 2010, https://www.icr.org/article/a-30-years-later-lessons-mount-st-helens.

3 "History of Technology," History of Technology, Accessed August 22, 2022, https://historyoftechnologyif.weebly.com/

4 "Information Age," History of Technology, 2014, https://historyoftechnologyif.weebly.com/information-age.html.

I am a proponent for Young Earth Creation. I believe that in Genesis 1, the creation of our world as we know it—the separation of the heavens and the earth—literally occurred in six days and that a day is a twenty-four-hour period.

Young Earth Creationists believe that the earth is approximately 6,000 years old,[5] the flood occurred 4,400 years ago,[6] and Jesus came to earth about 2000 years ago.[7] For example, "carbon, which dissipates in just tens of thousands of years, is present in diamonds and fossils. Carbon-14 calls the whole Old Earth paradigm into question."[8] In other words, biology textbooks in educational institutions do not support the current view of science.

5 Bodie Hodge, "How Old Is the Earth?" Answers in Genesis, 2007, https://answersingenesis.org/age-of-the-earth/how-old-is-the-earth/.
6 David Wright, "Timeline for the Flood," Answers in Genesis, 2012, https://answersingenesis.org/bible-timeline/timeline-for-the-flood/.
7 Bodie Hodge "From Genesis to the Gospel," Answers in Genesis, 2010, https://answersingenesis.org/jesus/from-genesis-to-the-gospel/.
8 Andrew Snelling, "Geology | The New Answers," Answers in Genesis, 2022, https://answersingenesis.org/geology/.

CHAPTER 2

The Importance of Israel and the Jews

God is working out man's salvation through the nation of Israel. We cannot question the authority of God and why He designed salvation as such. We can only try in earnest to understand the mind and heart of God by being in fellowship with Him and studying His Word.

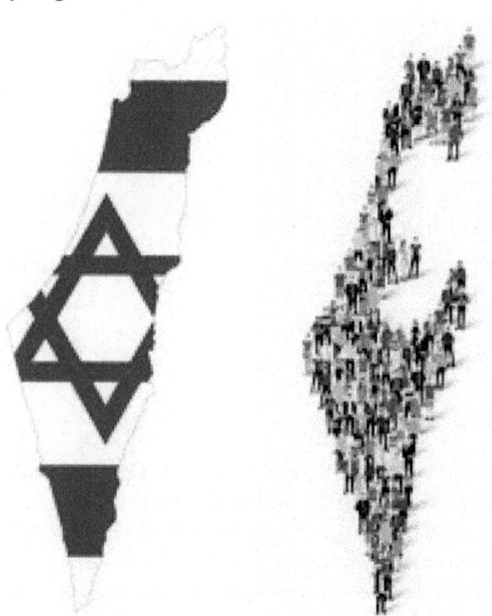

Playing With Fire: God is working out man's salvation through the nation of Israel—even today.[9]

9 Walt Russell, Playing With Fire.

Since God is working out man's salvation through the nation of Israel, it should behoove Believers around the world to pay attention to the Jewish Calendar dates of their customary feasts and festivals.

In 733 BC, the Assyrian Empire destroyed Israel, and the Dispersion of the Jews began, which scattered these people all over the world.[10] Nothing short of a miracle brought the Jews back from the ends of the earth to their homeland.

One man, Eliezer Ben Yehuda (1858–1922), known as the father of modern Hebrew, brought the Hebrew language back to life.[11] Hebrew is the only language to be revived from extinction among the 7,000 languages spoken in the world.[12] Eliezer Ben-Yehuda was truly God's instrument to revive the Hebrew language, which is now the spoken language of Jews in Israel.

Since May 14, 1948, when Israel became a modern state, seventy-four years have passed, bringing us to 2022.[13] The next six years will bring us to 2028, which will be eighty years since Israel became a modern state (Zechariah 8:2–3, 12:1–9; Isaiah 11:12, 52:8; Daniel 11:45; Deuteronomy 30:1–5).

---

10 Assyrian Empire Builders - Israel, the 'House of Omri,'" History Department, University College London, 2013, https://www.ucl.ac.uk/sargon/essentials/countries/israel/.

11 "Eliezer Ben Yehuda," Your Dictionary, 2022, https://biography.yourdictionary.com/eliezer-ben-yehuda.

12 "The Greater Sum Presents 7000 Languages," 2020, YouTube: The Greater Sum Foundation. 2020, https://www.youtube.com/watch?v=WI9h_cJOf7c.

13 "State of Israel Proclaimed," History Channel: A&E Television Networks, LLC., 2022, https://www.history.com/this-day-in-history/state-of-israel-proclaimed

I feel that once Israel became a modern state in 1948, this began God's countdown for the Rapture of the Christian Church. And yes, the Bible says no man knows when—not even Jesus Christ (1 Thessalonians 4:17).

Bible prophecy that has indeed come to pass concerning Israel is that massive numbers of Jews have returned to Israel once becoming a modern state in 1948. More than three million Jews have moved to Israel from around the world since 1948.[14] In 1948 there was an estimation of 25,000 Christians.[15] However, 50% of the Christian population lost their homes, and some areas of Israel reported up to 85% of Christians exited Israel.[16] Statistics project that at least 175,000 Messianic Jews in the U.S. alone believe in Jesus, while estimates worldwide range from 350,000 to 1.7 million.[17] If you take the statistics to percentages, it would be... 2.5% to 12.14% of Jews worldwide believe in Jesus Christ.[18] There are approximately 6 million Jews in the U.S. and approximately 6.9 million Jews scattered around the world.[19]

14 Timothy Jones, "Jewish Immigration to Israel Increases in 2018," Deutsche Welle (DW) News, 2018, https://www.dw.com/en/jewish-immigration-to-israel-increases-in-2018/a-46905719.

15 "Demographics of Israel: Population of Jerusalem (1844-Present)," Jewish Virtual Library: A Project of AICE, 2022, https://www.jewishvirtuallibrary.org/population-of-jerusalem-1844-2009.

16 "Jerusalem's Christian Population Dwindles Further," Al Monitor, 2021, https://www.al-monitor.com/originals/2022/04/jerusalems-christian-population-dwindles-further; "Christians in the Holy Land: Under (Israeli) Siege," Institute for Middle East Understanding [IMEU], 2012, https://imeu.org/article/christians-in-the-holy-land-under-israeli-siege.

17 "Why Do Most Jewish People Not Believe in Jesus?" Jews for Jesus, 2021, https://jewsforjesus.org/learn/why-do-most-jews-not-believe-in-jesus.

18 Ibid.

19 "Jewish Population by Country 2022," World Population Review, 2022, https://worldpopulationreview.com/country-rankings/jewish-population-by-country.

Israel will continue to bloom despite the fact that a significant portion of the country is in an arid or desert climate. Israel, a country the size of New Jersey, produces enough fruits and vegetables to feed all of Europe. This country has the third highest number of citizens with a college education, physicians, Nobel Peace Prize recipients, scholars, and scientists.[20] Israel also ranks number thirteen for high-tech and start-up companies in the modern world.[21] Israel was also the first country in the modern world to vaccinate most of its citizens with the COVID-19 vaccines.[22]

Desalinization is extracting salt from the ocean so that it is fit to drink. Israel leads the world in this critical ability to provide water for its citizens.[23] Israel is the eighth most powerful military in the modern world (there's no military school in the world that can learn from Israel's military because history shows that God is at the helm and fights their wars (Joshua 10). For solar power energy, Israel ranks number two in the world.[24]

"While farmworkers made up only 3.7% of the work force, Israel produced 95% of its own food requirements."[25] Eighty-five

---

20 "Most Educated Countries 2022," World Population Review, 2022, https://worldpopulationreview.com/country-rankings/most-educated-countries.

21 "Startup Index of Nations & Regions," University of Southern California Marshall School of Business [USC], 2022, https://www.marshall.usc.edu/faculty-research/centers-excellence/center-global-innovation/startup-index-nations-regions.

22 Isabel Kershner, "How Israel Became a World Leader in Vaccinating Against Covid-19," The New York Times, 2021, https://www.nytimes.com/2021/01/01/world/middleeast/israel-coronavirus-vaccines.html.

23 Max Kaplan-Zantopp, "How Israel Used Innovation to Beat Its Water Crisis," Israel21c, 2022, https://www.israel21c.org/how-israel-used-innovation-to-beat-its-water-crisis/.

24 Daniel Madar, "Israel Not yet World Power in Renewable Energies," The Jerusalem Post, 2020, https://www.jpost.com/opinion/israel-not-yet-world-power-in-renewable-energies-634747.

25 Wikipedia Contributors, "Agriculture in Israel," Wikipedia, The Free Encyclopedia, 2022, https://en.wikipedia.org/wiki/Agriculture_in_Israel.

percent of wastewater is purified and used for farming.[26] The cows in Israel produce more milk and meat than anywhere else in the world.[27] Israel is the inventor of drip irrigation, which greatly aids in farming.[28] Another high-tech accomplishment that Israel is renowned for is the ability to extract water from the atmosphere.[29]

"Israel ranks 23rd worldwide in its total number of millionaires, and by 2024 is expected to have 173,000 millionaires, representing a growth rate of 32 percent, the annual Global Wealth Report found."[30] One article entitled in the Daily Business newspaper, "Israel has seventy-one billionaires as of 2021, with one of the highest per capita rates in the world, at 6.7 billionaires for every million people."[31] Some of the wealthiest people in the world are from Israel.

In the very beginning, God said in Genesis 12:3 ESV,

> "I will bless those who bless you, and him [any nation or any president or any ruler] who dishonors you I

---

26 "How Israel Recycles Roughly 90% of Its Wastewater," YouTube: ILTV Israel News, 2016, https://www.youtube.com/watch?v=zMoVHYsoDc4.

27 "The Israeli Dairy Industry Is the Word Leader in Milk Production per Cow," Israeli Dairy School, 2022, https://www.dairyschool.co.il/the-israeli-dairy-industry-the-highest-milk-production-in-the-world/

28 Ruth Schuster, "The Secret of Israel's Water Miracle and How It Can Help a Thirsty World," Science & Health - Haaretz.Com., 2017, https://www.haaretz.com/science-and help-a-thirsty-world/0000017f-e095-df7c-a5ff-e2ffb6540000.

29 Zachary Keyser, "Israeli Tech Company Producing Water from Air Gets Top Honor in Las Vegas," Israel News: The Jerusalem Post, 2020, https://www.jpost.com/israel-news/israeli-tech-company-producing-water-from-air-earns-honor-in-las-vegas-613623.

30 Luke Tress, "Israel Has 131,000 Millionaires, and Its Wealth Is Growing Quickly, Report Finds," The Times of Israel, 2019, https://www.timesofisrael.com/israel-has-131000-millionaires-and-wealth-is-growing-quickly-report-finds/.

31 Wikipedia Contributors, "List of Israelis by Net Worth," Wikipedia, The Free Encyclopedia, 2022, https://en.wikipedia.org/wiki/List_of_Israelis_by_net_worth.

> will curse, and in you [Israel] all the families [everyone else on this earth] of the earth shall be blessed."

For a time, Jewish children will play in the streets of Jerusalem (Zechariah 8:4–5). However, the Bible also clearly states that in the end times, the nations will align themselves against Israel (Ezekiel 38; Revelation 16:16–21, 19:11–16).

- Ezekiel 38:2 Gog—Czar*
- Ezekiel 38:2 Magog—Russia
- Ezekiel 38:5 Cush—Ethiopia
- Ezekiel 38:5 Put—Libya
- Ezekiel 38:6 Gomer—Eastern Europe, Germany, Poland)
- Ezekiel 38:6 Togarmah—Turkey, Armenia, and Georgia)

**Vladimir Putin has lied and deceived many.*

Putin is reportedly the richest man in the world with an impregnable net worth.[32] I highlight Russia because Putin will be leading the attack on Israel soon, Putin has already taken control of Crimea, and he is working on taking over Georgia and Ukraine (2022).[33] Putin is becoming more insulated and more erratic. There are 150,000 Russians stranded around the world due to canceled and blocked flights to Russia. Putin is reportedly a changed man since countries around the world have is-

32 "Russia Becomes to Most Sanctioned Country After Invading Ukraine (Has More Sanctions Than Iran and North Korea)," LatestNGnews, 2022, https://latestngnews.com/russia-becomes-to-most-sanctioned-country-after-invading-ukraine-has-more-sanctions-than-iran-and-north-korea/.
33 Tucker Reals and Alex Sundby, "Russia's War in Ukraine: How It Came to This," CBS Interactive Inc., 2022, https://www.cbsnews.com/news/ukraine-news-russia-war-how-we-got-here/.

sued sanctions against Russia. He sees that the rest of the world is gaining momentum against his policies.[34]

These countries will question Russia and Iran for attacking Israel:

- Ezekiel 38:13, Sheba—Saudi Arabia, Sudan
- Ezekiel 38:13, Tarshish—England

Plunder of Israel by Other Countries

Ezekiel 38:11-13 clearly states that when Russia and Iran lead the attack on Israel in the final battle against Israel, a number of countries will question Russia and Iran about these attacks.

> And thou shalt say, I will go up to the land of unwalled villages; I will go to them that are at rest, dwell safely, all of them dwelling without walls, and having neither bars nor gates,
> To take a spoil, and to take a prey; to turn thine hand upon the desolate places that are now inhabited, and upon the people that are gathered out of the nations, which have gotten cattle and goods, that dwell in the midst of the land.
> Sheba, and Dedan, and the merchants of Tarshish, with all the young lions thereof, shall say unto thee, Art thou come to take a spoil? hast thou gathered thy company to take a prey? to carry away silver and gold, to take away cattle and goods, to take a great spoil?
> (Ezekiel 38:11–13 KJV)

34 Tucker Reals and Alex Sundby, 2022.

The chart below shows Israel as among the third highest Gross Domestic Product (GDP) in the region. The attacking countries mentioned in Ezekiel 38 are not going to attack out of sheer hatred for Israel. They will attack because they would like to capture and control Israel's resources. Some of Israel's resources "include potash, copper ore, natural gas, phosphate rock, magnesium bromide, clays, and sand," cut diamonds, gold, and silver.[35]

GDP: The Middle East and North Africa

Region	GDP in Billion U.S. Dollars
Iran	1426.30
Saudi Arabia	833.54
Israel	481.59
United Arab Emirates	409.97
Egypt	402.84
Iraq	209.51
Qatar	179.57
Algeria	164.56
Kuwait	135.35
Morocco	131.47
Oman	83.66
Tunisia	46.48
Jordan	45.35

35 G.P. Thomas, "Israel: Mining, Minerals and Fuel Resources," AZO Mining, 2012, https://www.azomining.com/Article.aspx?ArticleID=234

Bahrain	38.87
Libya	32.35
Yemen	22.02

MENA region: Gross domestic product (GDP) in 2021, by country (in billion U.S. dollars).[36]

In Deuteronomy 33:19 (KJV), the Lord speaks of the "abundance of the seas" and "treasures hid in sand" for the Promised Land of Israel. According to Isaiah 45:3 (KJV), the Lord said He would bless Israel,

> And I will give thee the treasures of darkness, and hidden riches of secret places, that thou mayest know that I, the LORD, which call thee by thy name, am the God of Israel.

Modern-Day Peace Treaties with Israel

The U.S. and Egypt signed a peace treaty with Israel in 1979. Jordan signed a peace treaty with Israel in1994. Syria's economy will collapse (Isaiah 17:1–4). NO country will defend Israel in the end times. Only God Himself! No other country! China, North Korea, Japan, Pakistan, India, and Afghanistan will join Russia and Iran in the second phase of the attack on Israel.

Fast Facts: The Six-Day War

- June 1967 war between Israel and Arab neighbors changed the map of the Middle East and transformed the region for decades.

36 Aaron O'Neill, "Gross Domestic Product of the MENA Countries in 2021," Statista, 2022, https://www.statista.com/statistics/804761/gdp-of-the-mena-countries/

- Egypt's leader, Nasser, vowed to destroy Israel in May 1967.
- Combined Arab nations massed troops to attack Israel.
- Israel struck first with devastating air raids.
- The ceasefire ended the conflict after six intense days of fighting. Israel gained territory and redefined the Middle East.
- Casualties: Israeli: approximately 900 killed, 4,500 wounded. Egyptian: approximately 10,000 killed, an unknown number wounded (official numbers never released). Syrian: approximately 2,000 killed, an unknown number wounded (official number never released).[37]

The Yom Kippur War

After the exhilaration of the victory in the Six-Day War of 1967, Israelis became increasingly dispirited. The growing level of terrorism, combined with increasingly ominous threats from Egypt, made peace seem further away than ever. Rather than reconciling themselves to Israel's existence, the Arab states looked for a way to avenge the humiliation of their defeat. The Soviet Union was doing its share to stroke the flames of war by pouring arms into the region. And the Gulf Arab states were also beginning to take greater control of their oil resources and use the revenues to flex their political muscle.[38]

37 Robert McNamara, "Six-Day War in 1967 Reshaped the Middle East," ThoughtCo., 2020, https://www.thoughtco.com/1967-six-day-war-4783414.
38 "The Yom Kippur War: Background & Overview," Jewish Virtual Library: A Project of AICE, 2022, https://www.jewishvirtuallibrary.org/background-and-overview-yom-kippur-war.

Previous Attacks on Israel

Israel was attacked fifty-two times and destroyed two times.[39] The temple in Jerusalem was destroyed in 70 AD, some 2,000 years ago.[40] The third temple on the Islam mount of the rock, Jerusalem, will be built by the Israelites. The Islam Muslims will move their mosque to another site. The antichrist will help in this switch. Then the antichrist will break the peace treaty and claim himself as god in the third temple of Jerusalem over the world.

Attacks on Israel Since Becoming a Modern State in 1948

- 1948—Egypt, Iraq, Jordan, Lebanon, Syria
- 1967—Egypt, Syria, and Arab states
- 1973—Egypt, Arab states (Arab League)

What are the names of the twenty-two states which comprise the Arab League? Algeria, Bahrain, Comoros, Djibouti, Egypt, Iraq, Jordan, Kuwait, Lebanon, Libya, Mauritania, Morocco, Oman, Palestine, Qatar, Saudi Arabia, Somalia, Sudan, Syria, Tunisia, the United Arab Emirates, and Yemen.[41]

Any nation that tries to come against Israel in the form of an attack or battle will not prevail. For example, End-Time prophecies declare that Russia and Iran will lead the battle against Israel in the final battle against Israel. God tells us clearly in Revelation that Israel will prevail because it is actually the Lord

39 Behjamin Elisha Sawe, "How Many Times Was Jerusalem Destroyed?" WorldAtlas, 2019, https://www.worldatlas.com/articles/how-many-times-was-jerusalem-destroyed.html.

40 "70 AD: Romans Destroy Jerusalem and Temple," Aboutbibleprophecy.com., Accessed August 22, 2022, http://www.aboutbibleprophecy.com/e30.htm.

41 "Live: Emergency Arab League Summit Convenes in Mecca," YouTube, 2019, https://www.youtube.com/watch?v=J7gFfVxXUJU.

Almighty who prevails through the nation of Israel (Revelation 19:11–20).

Peace Treaty Symbol[42]

Peace treaties have existed since the beginning of civilizations and have carried on in various forms for various lengths of time. Whether a peace treaty between two or more nations or countries is completely honored, there is one significant peace treaty that will usher in the last days on earth.

Truth silences: The cult lies
and brings about falsehoods.

The flip side of fear or false doctrine
is truth and true understanding.

There is only one way to go, and that's ***up***! When you choose Jesus Christ as your personal Lord and Savior, you are on your way up! No other way but down, otherwise.

What will you choose?

42 © [designtools] 2016 — canstockphotos.com

CHAPTER 3

Why Are Jewish Festivals Significant?

Jewish festivals are significant because, in the Old Testament, God implemented a religious calendar for the Israelites to follow.

> Within each year, there were seven specified feasts (Leviticus 23), four in the spring and three each fall. Through these feasts, the Jewish people celebrated their history, their faith, and the blessings of God. Throughout Jesus' life, the hope of each feast was fulfilled in a dramatic way.[43]

Further, the significance of Jewish Festivals is that God is still working out man's salvation through the nation of Israel, and these festivals will come into play in the end days or end game to come. Please pay attention to the Rosh Hashanah, or Shmita Year, which we are currently in (2021–2022). See the chart below.

---

43 Ray Vander Laan, "That the World May Know | Jewish Feasts," Focus on the Family, 2022, https://www.thattheworldmayknow.com/jewish-feasts.

Festival Begins and Ends Description

Festival	Begins	Ends	Description
Purim	Sunset	Nightfall	Work should be avoided. Celebrates the deliverance of the Jewish people from the wicked Haman in the days of Queen Esther of Persia.
Passover	Sunset	Nightfall	No work permitted, or work permitted with certain restrictions. Celebrates the deliverance of the Jewish people from slavery in Egypt.

Lag B'Omer			Celebrating the anniversary of the passing of the great sage and mystic Rabbi Shimon bar Yochai, author of the Zohar. Commemorates the end of a plague that raged amongst the disciples of the great sage Rabbi Akiva.
Shavuot	Sunset	Nightfall	No work is permitted. Marks the giving of the Torah on Mt. Sinai.
The Three Weeks	Fast of the 17th of Tammuz	Fast of Tish'a B'Av	Work permitted, except Shabbat. Designated as a time of mourning over the destruction of the Holy Temple and the galut (exile).

The 15th of Av			Work permitted. Sages of old proclaimed the 15th of Av as one of the two greatest festivals of the year, yet they ordained no special observances or celebrations for it.
Rosh Hashanah [Also known as Shmita. We are currently in a Schmita year, which is a seven-year period every seven years from ancient Jewish times. We are now in a Shmita year (2022–2023)]	Sunset	Nightfall	No work is permitted. This is the Jewish New Year. It is the anniversary of the creation of Adam and Eve and a day of judgment and coronation of God as King. [Rosh Hashanah is also known as Shmita year. We are currently in a Shmita year.]

Yom Kippur	Sunset	Nightfall	No work is permitted. The holiest day of the year—the day on which we are closest to God and to the quintessence of our own souls. It is the Day of Atonement. For on this day, He will forgive you, to purify you, that you be cleansed from all your sins before God (Leviticus 16:30).

Sukkot	Sunset	Nightfall	No work permitted. The seventh day of Sukkot—celebrated by dwelling in the sukkah, taking the Four Kinds, and rejoicing—the holiday when we expose ourselves to the elements in covered huts, commemorating God's sheltering our ancestors as they traveled from Egypt to the Promised Land. The Four Kinds express our unity and our belief in God's omnipresence. Coming after the solemn High Holidays is a tie of joy and happiness.

Shemini Atzeret & Simchat Torah	Sunset	Nightfall	No work is permitted. Following the seven joyous days of Sukkot comes the happy holiday known as Shemini Atzeret/ Simchat Torah.
Chanukah	Sunset	Nightfall	Work permitted, except Shabbat. Commemorates the rededication of the Temple in Jerusalem after a group of Jewish warriors defeated the Occupying mighty Greek armies.

Fast of Tevet 10	Sunrise	Nightfall	Work permitted. On Asarah B/Tevet, the 10th day of the Jewish month of Tevet, in the year 3336 from Creation (425 BCD), the armies of the Babylonian emperor Nebuchadnezzar laid siege to Jerusalem. Asarah B'Tevet is observed as a day of fasting, mourning, and repentance.
15 Shevat			Work permitted. Marks the beginning of a "new year" for trees.

Jewish Holidays—Begins and Ends Description[44]

There is a wealth of information online that you can research about Jewish holidays and festivals tied to significant historical events.

44 "Jewish Holidays in 2022," Chabad Jewish Center of Oakland Inc., 2022, https://www.jewishoakland.org/holidays/jewish-holidays-in-2019/.

As I mentioned at the beginning of this chapter, believers of Jesus Christ need to pay attention to the Jewish festival called Rosh Hashanah, which is another name for Shmita Year. Since the Shmita Year occurs every seven years. We are currently in a Shmita Year (2021–2022). The next Smita Year will be 2028–2029. It is believed by Bible scholars and modern-day prophets that the Great Tribulation will begin during a Shmita Year—which ultimately points to an end-time war known as *Armageddon*.

Major Points Concerning Shmita (Rosh Hashanah) With Respect to the Signs of the Times (the End Game)

Please read Daniel 12:4 and Leviticus 25:1–5.

Code Red

- Ukraine War (notice Russia will be attacking Israel for its natural gas, oil, gold, silver, and other booties soon).
- COVID-19, Delta, Omicron, B1, B2, and Monkey Pox are viruses that have affected mankind worldwide with in the last three years. Additionally, these viruses will persist in mutating and will continue to affect our society as a whole.
- I had a vision of a washing machine shaking. I will further explain this in another chapter in this book. As we celebrate the Seventh Year of the Shmita (September or October of 2021–2022), God is ready to shake up the world as we know it. The last revival on earth will take place in the next five years. I call it a "tsunami Global

Revival" for the end game. This is it! No more playing around—the time is close! (*The author is interpreting a vision he had about a washing mashing with many colored clothing inside*).

- The Shmita cycle ends on August 20, 2029, and on October 1, 2029, China celebrates its eightieth anniversary. I don't feel that God would want His holy day or a huge and significant event of the Christian Church (such as the Rapture) to coincide with China's eightieth celebration.[45]
- Shmita dates, according to the Jewish Calendar, originally occurred in September and October, and our Triune God (God the Father, Jesus, and the Holy Spirit) has allowed the Shmita month of 2028 to begin in August or one month before the communist eightieth anniversary. Explaining the Shmita in its entirety would be worthy of an entirely separate book, but if you do your research about Shmita, you will find the information relevant and surprising to where we are in the course of humanity today.[46]
- Soon the world will reach 7,000 years from the earth being created by God, Jesus (also God), and the Holy Spirit (also God). Notice all the 7s in God's calendar or 7 in the Bible, meaning "perfection" or "divine completion". The number 7 is one of the sacred numbers in the Bible. The number 7 is found in 7 trumpets, 7 bowls, 7 year Tribulation, 7 years Jacobs trouble, 70th jubilee

45 "Jubilee 2022? Whiteboard Animation," YouTube: RockIslandBooks, 2022, https://www.youtube.com/watch?v=9-j8YpZH9yk.
46 "Jubilee 2022? Whiteboard Animation," 2022.

(October 5, 2022), 7 stars, 7 candle stands/Menorah, 7 seals, 7 eyes, 7 plagues tribulation, 7 thunders, 7 hills and kings, 7 horns, 7 churches, earth's creation in 7 days, 7 day week, a bride circles her future husband 7 times during the Jewish marriage ceremony, Joshua circles the city 7 times, 7 angels, 7 visions, 7,000 years of mankind on earth and much more. Seven, the biblical numeral for perfection, is incredibly astounding! The next biblical number, 8, is symbolic of new beginnings. We will begin to see the number 8 as a significant number to watch for and embrace in terms of new beginnings.

- Notice the number 40. The Israelites spent forty years in the desert looking for the promise land, Jesus fasted and prayed forty days and nights, Jesus spent forty days doing ministry before His resurrection, and there are many more events and concepts with the numeral forty.
- In Judges 6:1–8:35, we find that the enemies of Israel were defeated, and the land had rest for forty years. Throughout the whole Bible, we find numbers having a spiritual and physical meanings. For example, the number forty is used 159 times in the Old and New Testaments of the Bible with a deep and specific meaning. Jesus fasted for forty days. Moses spent forty years in the desert wandering with his 2 to 3 million people. There are also forty suggested days for a woman to rest after giving birth to a child. God flooded the earth for forty days and nights with Noah. Moses fasted for forty days and sought God on the mountain for forty days.

- This is important in the end game or end times because if you look at the time period, which has lapsed since May 14, 1948, it will have been eighty years since Israel became a state or a nation. In 2028 eighty years will have passed to mark Israel's eightieth anniversary. This is numerically 2 times 40 equals 80, which also means 8 (new beginning) or 8 times 10; ten meaning judgment, completion, or fulfillment towards the "rapture of His Christian Church," and the number 888 is the number for Jesus Christ.
- Yes, I get it, ***no one*** knows the day or the hour as to when the rapture of the Christian Church will take place, but forty, eight, and ten mean something? What do you think?
- One year after this, in 2029, China will have its eightieth anniversary as a "Communist" Nation.
- Again, on May 14, 2028, Israel will reach its eightieth anniversary as a modern state or nation. I believe that on May 14, 1948, when Israel became a state, the countdown began toward the "Rapture of the Christian Church". I feel that God, through His grace of a nation's emergence, survival, and thriving, said... For forty years you have suffered, yet I am still desiring that people on earth come to know me and accept me (Jesus) as their Lord and Savior, so I (our Triune God) will give you another forty years as my abundant "Grace" and "Mercy" to receive me (Jesus) so that you could be in Heaven with me and not suffer the other eternal existence—Hell.

- Looking at eighty years, the number 8 in the Bible means "new beginnings". The number 10 in the Bible means "judgment" or "completion". So, 80 equals 8 times 10. If you type in 888 in the search bar from your phone, Google will return countless sites which contend that the number 888 stands for "Jesus". My question to God, which I pose right here in this book: Is 2028 the year that something big will happen?
- Jesus lived 12,585 days on earth, and Adam lived 12,593 days *before he sinned*. I said before he sinned, so 12,585 minus 12,593 equals 8 days difference. Considering that the Bible has several hidden meanings and everything related to God, Jesus, and the Holy Spirit has a hidden significance means... Followers of Christ should be compelled to pray and fast to enter into an intimate relationship with our Lord, calling upon the Holy Spirit. Convening with the Holy Spirit allows you to dig deep. In my heart, mind, and soul, I'm wondering... Is the eight-day difference the last number in 2028, the year of the Shmita? And yet no one knows the day or hour. Jeremiah 33:3 (NIV) says, Call to me and I will answer you and show you great and unsearchable things that you do not know.
- If the Smita is followed by following God's laws or principles and there is a blessing after six years of work, we are going into the seventh year of rest. If God's commandments are not observed or followed and disobeyed in the previous years, then there can be a curse for disobedience. When we try to teach our kids certain family

principles, such as when to go to bed and wake up and eat well and choose friends wisely, etc., and they rebel or don't listen—do they sometimes get punished and have privileges taken away (like staying up late on Friday or Saturday taken away), or be grounded for a period of time. God is very much like Father God, who teaches us certain principles in hopes that we will follow these with our own free will. Scholars say that when "sin" entered mankind or the world from 4005 BC to 3970 BC, it was some thirty-five years.

- Every seven years, the Shmita takes place, and then another seven year-cycle of Shmita begins. However, will the next Shmita cycle usher in the "Tribulation"?
- The ending of the Shmita on God's calendar goes to the "Elul," or the twenty-ninth of the month, and the "Tishri," or the first of the month or the beginning. In the Roman calendar, the months begin in September and end in October. However, keep in mind that October 1, 2029, is the eightieth anniversary of Communist China. I do not think the Lord God will coincide His important date with Communist China. Remember also that May 14, 2028, is Israel's eightieth anniversary for Israel a Shmita year.
- No one knows the day or the hour (of the rapture), but interestingly the tribulation timeline can be determined by major events occurring every seven years. Consider what happened every seventh year since 2001:
  - o 9/11 of the World Trade Center occurred on September 1, 2001.

- o Sub-prime market fallout 2008.
- o 2014 to 2015: In February, the West African Ebola virus epidemic began. Infecting beyond 28,000 people and killing in excess of 11,000 people, the most severe both in terms of numbers of infections and casualties.[47] From February 7 to 23, the XXII Olympic Winter Games were held in Sochi, Russia.[48]
- o What crisis happened in 2015? "**Syria refugee crisis**. Syria's descent into conflict has resulted in the deaths of more than 220,000 people, according to the United Nations, with millions displaced from their homes as President Bashar Assad and his opponents have waged a bitter, bloody war."[49]
- o 2021–2022 Unprecedented, worldwide COVI-19 and variants pandemic, Russian-Ukraine War...

Year of the Jubilee—God Has a Divine Purpose and Plan for Mankind

- Living in the "Church Age" and getting ready for the "Rapture of the Christian Church" and the year of the Jubilee or God's fifty years or 5 meaning "Grace" and 10 meaning "judgment" or "completion" or 5 x 10 equals 50 or Jubilee year.
- Please read Ezekiel 40:1–3.

47 Kathryn Reid, "2014 Ebola Virus Outbreak: Facts, Symptoms, and How to Help," World Vision, 2020, https://www.worldvision.org/health-news-stories/2014-ebola-virus-outbreak-facts.

48 Wikipedia Contributors, "2014 Winter Olympics Medal Table," Wikipedia, 2022, https://en.wikipedia.org/wiki/2014_Winter_Olympics_medal_table.

49 Anmar Frangoul, "Major Global Events That Shook 2015," CNBC World News, 2015, https://www.cnbc.com/2015/12/31/major-global-events-that-shook-2015.html.

- A Jubilee year is very special on God's calendar
- Jubilee (Leviticus 25:10) is separated from the previous forty-nine years.
- Jubilee is about rest and restoration.
- Please refer to 1 Kings 6:1.
- Some scholars and rabbis believe that September 26th to October 5th, 2022 is the seventieth Jubilee year of mankind on earth.
- See John 5:43.
- Many scholars and rabbis are looking at God the Father, not Jesus the Son, coming to redeem them during the month of "Tishri" on the day of atonement, October 5th, 2022, in the "7-year Shmita cycle". Again, I believe that God, Christ, and the Holy Spirit want to give these last five years (2023 to 2028/2029) of additional "grace" upon mankind as a window of opportunity for each person on earth to receive Jesus Christ as their Lord and Savior. As saints (believers of Christ), we have the responsibility of fulfilling the Great Commission (Matthew 28:16–20). Jesus calls on His followers to make disciples of and baptize all nations in the name of the Father, the Son, and the Holy Spirit.
- It is all-important for a new Believer (or Believer who hasn't done so) to be baptized and find a church, and build an intimate relationship with Christ.
- The rest of the people in the world will receive the false christ or the antichrist as their messiah and receive the mark of the beast 666. They will do this to stay alive on the so-called earth with remaining humanity. They will

do this to have food to eat, a place to live, and to avoid martyrdom (See John 10:9).[50]

- March 9, 2022, President Biden signs a Executive Order #14067 section 4 legal - legal surveillance to all Americans! Did I say all Americans! Of your personal information, bank accounts, purchases, flights, etc. Isn't this leading to the "Tribulation" and the anti-christ and false prophet. Already happening in China, Russia, North Korea, Canada, and other countries[51]
- Government legal executive order to silence anyone that argues with them. See Canada[52]
- Project Lithium is a new spyware currency[53]
- Project Hamilton is also a new spyware currency[54]
- The Chinese Communist Party (CCP) will judge you on all aspects of behavior, attitude, social credit, etc. and issue points for good behavior or bad behavior. If you are low on points because you "jaywalked" a cross-walk sign,

50 "Jubilee 2022? Whiteboard Animation," 2022.

51 Executive Order#14067: https://www.google.com/url?sa=t&source=web&cd=&ved=2ahUKEwjo2cTNjbb7AhWaJEQIHfrACwMQFnoECB8QBQ&url=https%3A%2F%2Fen.m.wikipedia.org%2Fwiki%2FExecutive_Order_14067&usg=AOvVaw1-8Sawv1QfpSQa9ZoJDPCy

52 Silencing Citizens: https://www.google.com/url?sa=t&source=web&cd=&ved=2ahUKEwjY4Mi3kLb7AhWfJUQIHY1_DwlQFnoECBAQBQ&url=https%3A%2F%2Fmoney.com%2Fcryptocurrency-legal-status-by-country%2F&usg=AOvVaw1tLhPc_yjN-Z4v5sMt90ONL

53 Project Lithium: https://www.google.com/url?sa=t&source=web&cd=&ved=2ahUKEwi578qXkbb7AhWkK0QIHUwoAxQQFnoECBYQBQ&url=https%3A%2F%2Fwww.soonparted.co%2Fp%2Fproject-lithium&usg=AOvVaw18EiMj4sZCAXLLZjWQQ8M8

54 Project Hamilton: https://www.google.com/url?sa=t&source=web&cd=&ved=2ahUKEwi6nMa0kbb7AhWCMEQIHZPCAvkQFnoECBIQBQ&url=https%3A%2F%2Fwww.forbes.com%2Fsites%2Fvipinbharathan%2F2022%2F02%2F09%2Fproject-hamilton-on-the-report-published-by-the-boston-fed-and-mit%2F%3Fsh%3D75cc40d21d83&usg=AOvVaw1-v0zjoHzQK-Xwma8waANpx

> or didn't pay your bills on time, etc., the government will stop or take away things or privileges you might enjoy, such as taking a plane flight to see friends or loved ones.[55]

Therefore, when considering that God's calendar is the Jewish Calendar and that significant world events are tied to the Jewish holiday, Rosh Hashanah, or the Shmita, we find ourselves looking at what's to come—including the Rapture of the Christian Church, the Tribulation, and the End-Time war against Israel, which is detailed in Chapter 4, *Ezekiel 38 Explained*. The importance of Ezekiel 38 is such that I have included the entire chapter in this book.

55 https://www.google.com/url?sa=t&source=web&cd=&ved=2ahUKEwjl-czgkb-b7AhXRIUQIHZ8ICpwQFnoECA4QAQ&url=https%3A%2F%2Fwww.businessinsider.com%2Fchina-social-credit-system-punishments-and-rewards-explained-2018-4%3Famp&usg=AOvVaw0HyeWLCISLUC1jfRt337EW

CHAPTER 4

Ezekiel 38 Explained

The LORD's Great Victory Over the Nations

The word of the LORD came to me: "Son of man, set your face against Gog, of the land of Magog [*Russia*], the chief prince of Meshek [*Moscow*] and Tubal [Asia Minor]; prophesy against him and say: 'This is what the Sovereign LORD says: I am against you, Gog [*Title of Czar Prince*], chief prince of Meshek and Tubal. I will turn you around, put hooks in your jaws and bring you out with your whole army—your horses, your horsemen fully armed, and a great horde with large and small shields, all of them brandishing their swords. Persia [*Iran*], Cush [*Ethiopia*] and Put [*Turkey, Armenia*] will be with them, all with shields and helmets, also Gomer [*Eastern Europe, Germany, Poland*] with all its troops, and Beth Togarmah [*Libya*] from the far north with all its troops—the many nations with you.

"'Get ready; be prepared, you and all the hordes gathered about you, and take command of them. After many days you will be called to arms. In future years you will invade a land that has recovered from war, whose people were gathered from many nations to the mountains of Israel, which had long been desolate. They had been brought out from the nations, and now all of them live in safety. You and all your troops and the many nations with you will go up, advancing like a storm; you will be like a cloud covering the land.

"'This is what the Sovereign LORD says: On that day thoughts will come into your mind and you will devise an evil scheme. You will say, "I will invade a land of unwalled villages; I will attack a peaceful and unsuspecting people—all of them living without walls and without gates and bars. I will plunder and loot and turn my hand against the resettled ruins and the people gathered from the nations, rich in livestock and goods, living at the center of the land." Sheba [*Saudi*] and Dedan [*Arabia*] and the merchants of *Tarshish* [*England, Gibraltar*] and all her villages will say to you, "Have you come to plunder? Have you gathered your hordes to loot, to carry off silver and gold, to take away livestock and goods and to seize much plunder?"'

"Therefore, son of man, prophesy and say to Gog: 'This is what the Sovereign LORD says: In that day, when my people Israel are living in safety, will you not take notice of it? You will come from your place in the far north, you and many nations with you, all of them riding on horses, a great horde, a mighty army.

You will advance against my people Israel like a cloud that covers the land. In days to come, Gog, I will bring you against my land, so that the nations may know me when I am proved holy through you before their eyes.

"'This is what the Sovereign LORD says: You are the one I spoke of in former days by my servants the prophets of Israel. At that time they prophesied for years that I would bring you against them. This is what will happen in that day: When Gog attacks the land of Israel, my hot anger will be aroused, declares the Sovereign LORD. In my zeal and fiery wrath I declare that at that time there shall be a great earthquake in the land of Israel. The fish in the sea, the birds in the sky, the beasts of the field, every creature that moves along the ground, and all the people on the face of the earth will tremble at my presence. The mountains will be overturned, the cliffs will crumble, and every wall will fall to the ground. I will summon a sword against Gog on all my mountains, declares the Sovereign LORD. Every man's sword will be against his brother. I will execute judgment on him with plague and bloodshed; I will pour down torrents of rain, hailstones and burning sulfur on him and on his troops and on the many nations with him. And so I will show my greatness and my holiness, and I will make myself known in the sight of many nations. Then they will know that I am the LORD.'

(Ezekiel 38:1–23 NIV, emphasis mine)

Notice that there is no mention of Egypt, Jordan, and Syria, perhaps because these nations are not directly involved in this End-Time war.

Where Did Islamic Countries Originate?

The Bible tells us in Genesis 16:15 that Hagar, Sarah's handmaiden, bore Abraham a son. The son of Hagar and Abraham was named Ishmael, and he became the father of the Islamic nations whom we now know as Muslims. The Lord said this about Ishmael in Genesis 16:12 (KJV),

> And he will be a wild man; his hand will be against every man, and every man's hand against him; and he shall dwell in the presence of all his brethren.

Why did the Lord allow this to occur despite the promised son to Abraham and Sarah? Because of free will. Abraham and Sarah, of advanced age, nearly 100 years old, grew impatient or disillusioned when they still had no son in their old age. Sarah gave Hagar, her handmaiden, over to Abraham despite what God had promised them.

Succinctly, Ishmael is a result of free will disobedience to God. Throughout human history, we have one account after another of the consequences of free will disobedience—the birth of a child, death of a child, destruction of an entire nation, worldwide flood, and worldwide pandemic of pestilence and disease.

Medina is located in Saudi Arabia and is called Madinah al-Munawwarah, or the prophet's city. This is one of the Islam

Muslim's sacred spots, which was begun by Muhammed and is known today as the Mosque. Muslims may do a yearly pilgrimage or a once-in-a-lifetime visit to this mosque. The dome is green vs. the gold dome of the mosque in Jerusalem. It is said that prophet Muhammad, Abu Bakr, Umar, and others were told to change the direction of prayer here to Mecca, Saudi Arabia. Mohammad has been said to have set up the Islam Muslim Church here or the "Ummah". Like Mecca and the Kaaba, this mosque is private, and only Islam Muslims may attend.

Although God wants the best for humankind, He loves us so much that He gave us free will to choose to obey Him or not. You have exercised your free will to read this book. The Holy Spirit is therefore working in you so that you may know the truth and that the truth will set you free. Where do you need to be freed from bondage? What decision will you make to seal your eternal destiny?

Every person on this earth must sooner or later (better sooner) accept Jesus Christ as their Lord and Savior—or face a certain eternity outside of Heaven—Hell. I should apologize for sounding fanatical, but if you ended up on the other side of Heaven, that apology would not only be in vain, but it would also be so wrong and completely out of context. My heart and desire are that you and every person on this earth will come to know Jesus Christ sooner than later and later than never.

Lastly, I need to say this again. I need to impart a very real truth and a warning from God Himself. Knowing that humans have free will, God lovingly reminds us about the grand authority and sovereignty of His Word.

While we can read His Word and know His commandments (Exodus 20; Deuteronomy 5) and the Great Commission (Matthew 28:16–20), as humans, we exercise our free will to keep those commandments and fulfill the great commission.

This is why daily prayer and communion (spending time alone with God, Jesus, and the Holy Spirit) are so important. When we draw close to Him, our free will becomes more and more like Jesus' will for all of humanity—to attain Heaven on earth and Heaven for all eternity to be with Him.

For example, if I attend church only on Sunday and my fellowship with other Christians, communion with our Lord, and reading His Word is only limited to Sunday, I may need to ask myself...

- How am I spending the remainder of the week?
- Who am I spending time with, communicating?
- What activities am I involved in?
- What are the most important things in my life?
- Who are the most important people in my life?

Answering those questions may help me see where I am in my spiritual walk with our Lord. Am I staying the same spiritually as five years ago? Am I growing spiritually? Am I falling away?

Answering these questions and doing a self-evaluation helps one to grow and mature in Christ and create a personal relationship with God. So, where do you stand with Jesus?

CHAPTER 5

Seven-Year Tribulation

What Is the Seven-Year Tribulation Period?

After millions of blood-washed saints have been raptured from the earth to be with the Lord, there begins a seven-year period called the Tribulation. The Bible uses various names for this period, such as the Day of the Lord (Isaiah 2:12), The Time of the End (Daniel 12:9), and The End of this World (Matthew 13:40, 49).

The Tribulation Period is divided into three eras, the first era being approximately three and a half years; the brief middle period being perhaps only a few weeks; and the last era, called the Great Tribulation, being approximately three and a half years.

A powerful ruler, led by Satan and referred to as the antichrist, will rise to power. After leading the nations to form an alliance to help preserve the world system, he will break the treaty and be responsible for persecuting the nation of Israel and leading the last great battle against the forces of God in the battle of Armageddon.

During this time, God will be pouring out His wrath upon the earth and mankind unlike anything that has ever taken place before. It will be a terrible time of persecution and suffering.

The antichrist will gain ascendance and will lead into sin the vast majority of the people who were left behind when Christ appeared in the clouds to take out all the Christians.

Those who become Christians will be terribly persecuted. Judgments from God upon the natural elements of the earth and upon the inhabitants of the earth will be severe.

Even in the midst of this tribulation men will still be unwilling to turn to God and will blaspheme Him (Revelation 16:21). See other Scripture passages: Matthew 24: 2 Thessalonians 2:3–9; and Revelation 13:16–18; 14:14–20.[56]

Will the Church Go through the Seven-year Tribulation Period?

The answer to this question is "NO."

Although the word "Rapture" is not found in the Bible, this is indeed an event in prophecy which is taught in the Scriptures. The passage in 1 Thessalonians 4:14–17 is actually the next prophecy that shall be fulfilled (see also 1 Corinthians 15:51–57).

1 Thessalonians 5:9 tells us: God hath not appointed us unto wrath. Revelation 3:10 is also an indication that the church will not suffer the terrible days of the Tribulation.

From the first chapter through the third chapter of Revelation, there are several references to the church. However, from the fourth chapter until the nineteenth chapter, the church is

56 "What Is the Seven Year Tribulation Period?" BibleSprout, 2020, https://www.biblesprout.com/articles/bible/seven-year-tribulation/.

not mentioned at all, as the times of the Tribulation are discussed. There will be many people converted and saved during the Tribulation (Matthew 25:1–13).

These are the Christians who will have to suffer for the Lord during the days of the Tribulation and about whom the Bible speaks of in Revelation 20:4. These Christians will suffer terrible persecution and will have to refuse the mark of the beast. However, this will not affect Christians who are living today.[57]

---

57 Ibid.

CHAPTER 6

The Countdown for Jesus' Rapture of His Church and Second Coming

Again, I feel that once Israel became a modern state in 1948, this began God's countdown for the Rapture of the Christian Church.

The Bible tells us in Matthew 24:36 (BSB),

> No one knows about that day or hour, not even the angels in heaven, nor the Son, but only the Father.

Jesus warns us in 1 Thessalonians 5:2–3 (NIV),

> For you know very well that the day of the Lord will come like a thief in the night.

Jesus was telling us to be aware of the signs and the seasons in which we live.

2 Timothy 3:1–5 (NIV) says,

> But mark this: There will be terrible times in the last days. People will be lovers of themselves, lovers of money, boastful, proud, abusive, disobedient to their parents, ungrateful, unholy, without love, unforgiving, slanderous, without self-control, brutal, not lovers of good, treacherous, rash, conceited, lovers of pleasure rather than lovers of God—having a form of Godliness but denying its power...

An example of having a form of godliness but denying its power would be like attending church with other believers and having fervent worship, and then outside of the church, you may gossip with your friends and unintentionally or intentionally slander someone.

There is an all-important parable of the Ten Virgins in Matthew 25:1–13, which describes ten virgins with oil lamps. And only five have oil in their oil lamps, and the other five do not. God uses ten virgins as a symbol for His churches around the world. The biblical translation of ten means completion; in essence, God is using the parable of the ten virgins to warn His churches all over the world to be ready. However, at the time of the Rapture, the Bible tells us that only half of the churches or believers will be ready—did I say half? It's very heartbreaking but true.

The recent events of political strife, racial unrest, and certainly the worldwide COVID-19 pandemic and economic collapse are not socio-political events as usual—these are signs of the end times.

Ten Plagues in Moses' Time vs. Revelation 15 End-Time Plagues

Past	Future
Blood (Exodus 7:15–24)	Sores
Frogs (Exodus 8:1–15)	Sea of Blood
Live Gnats (Exodus 8:16–19	Rivers and Springs of Blood
Flies (Exodus 8:20–32)	Scorched Earth; Extreme Heat
Pestilence: Plague on Livestock (Exodus 9:1–7)	Famine, Noisome Beast, Pestilence
Skin Disease, Boils (Exodus 9:8–12)	Pestilence of Various Kinds (Ezekiel 14:21, 33:27)
Hailstorm (Exodus 9:13–35)	Earthquakes and Hailstorm (Luke 21:11) *This is already a reality in Afghanistan.*
Locusts (Exodus 10:1–20)	Euphrates River Dries Up
Darkness (Exodus 10:21–29)	Darkness; Void of Sunlight
Death of the Firstborn (Exodus 12:1–30)	

Ten Plagues in Moses' time vs. Revelation 15 End-Time Plagues.

If you don't think that the worldwide Coronavirus Pandemic of 2019–2022 (or whenever it is deemed "over") is not a sign of the end times, think again and do your research on how this pandemic may have occurred in the first place. The Bible talks about signs of the end times as likened to birthing pains, which will grow in intensity (Matthew 24:1–6, Mark 13, and Luke 21).

The Gospel will be preached to the ends of the earth (Matthew 24:24). Ninety-seven percent of the world has some or all of the Bible in their language. This is made possible with the advent of the internet, social media, television, radio, newspapers, books, and other forms of mass media, such as podcasts. Podcasts are recordings of audio discussions on a specific topic, like business or travel, that can be listened to from many devices.

As we are currently living in the Church Age, there is a responsibility that comes with the knowledge of God where we must be prepared and look to what lies ahead—the Rapture of the Christian Church, which I explain in the next chapter.

For some, this era is something exciting, and these people are filled with giddy anticipation since the Rapture of the Christian Church can occur at any time. For others, the thought of millions of people suddenly vanishing in this air strikes them as incredulous. They cannot really believe this could happen. And for others yet, there is a cloud of doom and gloom and fear which manifests in different ways: hoarding, not paying their bills, not nurturing healthy relationships, etc., since they feel that this would mark the end of the world as we know it.

It is my hope and prayer that you will be among the ***elect***, someone excited with anticipation that our Lord Jesus Christ may at any time have us caught up in the air with Him.

CHAPTER 7

Things to Look for in These End Times

1. As consumers worldwide, we are almost completely dependent on our mobile devices. We text, read emails, do business transactions, socialize, and even attend classes and court via our phones or computers. Our mobile devices have a tracking chip called an RFID (radio frequency identification). As we see in the movies, it is true that people can be found because they may have their phone, laptop, or another device with them. As long as the device has an RFID, a person carrying that device can be found.
2. A cashless society or one world order, i.e., cryptocurrency (bitcoin), is a $200 Billion business.[58] Airlines, hotels, and car rental companies are already going cashless. If you travel frequently, a major credit card is a must, as many vendors do not accept cash.
3. Consumers pay for things mostly by credit card via phone, computer, or AppleWatch (i.e., VISA, Mastercard, and debit cards).

58 "How Cash Is Becoming a Thing of the Past | DW Documentary (Banking Documentary)," YouTube, 2020, https://www.youtube.com/watch?v=GbECT1J9bXg.

China, Sweden and many other countries are already becoming a cashless society. The digital yuan or e-CNY is a digital version of China's sovereign currency and has been in the works since 2014. It is not a cryptocurrency like bitcoin but is instead issued and controlled by the People's Bank of China.[59]

4. In the next 4–5 years or sooner, we will be seeing a cashless world.
   a. The IMF (International Monetary Fund)... "has drawn up plans to force a cashless society upon all the people within IMF member nations. In their 'The Macroeconomics of De-Cashing,' it gives the following advice to governments who want to abolish cash against the will of their citizenry."[60]
5. Big Tech invades our privacy and sells our information in the end times—Your personal or family data through Facebook, PayPal (426 million customers worldwide),[61] Oracle, Google, YouTube, Gmail, Apple, TenCent, ByteDance, TikTok, etc. Once you sign up on Amazon, all your information is collected. Even though they say that your personal information is secure, it is not.

---

59 Arjun Kharpal, "China Launches Digital Currency App to Expand Usage," CNBC LLC., A Division of NBC Universal, 2022, https://www.cnbc.com/2022/01/04/china-launches-digital-currency-app-to-expand-usage.html.

60 Lorimer Wilson, "IMF Plans to Force a Cashless Society On World Unfolding - Here's How (+8K Views)," MunKNEE, 2020, https://munknee.com/imf-plan-to-force-a-cashless-society-on-world-unfolding-heres-how/.

61 David Curry, "PayPal Revenue and Usage Statistics (2022)," Business of Apps., 2022, https://www.businessofapps.com/data/paypal-statistics/.

What about Customers' Rights, You Ask?

1. Look at China. A totally monitored society and total state control, everything and everyone are monitored. This is where we are headed.
2. More than 385 million Chinese nationals leave their country every year to celebrate the Chinese Lunar Year.[62] This is why in the early days of the COVID-19 outbreak, the virus was unchecked until the world got wind of it.
3. Facial Recognition. Many organizations or companies are using fingerprints or facial recognition to access your accounts or your whereabouts.
4. The false prophet will rise up in a final world deception. He will implement the Mark of the Beast (666) (John 10:10).
5. The false prophet is satan's puppet, and satan wants to mark you as his for all eternity.
6. Many high-tech proponents believe that the microchip (the size of a rice grain) will be implanted in those left behind. The people left on the earth will not be able to buy or sell without the microchip. Your medical record, mortgage statement, etc., will be embedded on this chip. You will not be able to buy gasoline, food, water, utilities, etc., without it. I encourage you to watch a YouTube video of people getting micro-chipped.
7. Worldwide financial collapse.

---

62 "Chinese New Year Celebrations," KING-TV: King5.Com., 2022, https://www.king5.com/gallery/news/nation-now/chinese-new-year-celebrations/465-6d54bda5-a755-400b-a858-ed4f226b5660.

Truth silences: The cult lies
and brings about falsehoods.

The flip side of fear or false doctrine
is truth and true understanding.

Christians can be comforted and not fear when reading the Bible passage from Romans 10:9 (KJV),

That if thou shalt confess with thy mouth the Lord Jesus, and shalt believe in thine heart that God hath raised him from the dead, thou shalt be saved.

Consider the COVID vaccination card implemented in some states. Despite that it is related to ridding society of the COVID virus, the government has used the mandates (September 2021 under the Biden Administration) as a form of control. Without a vaccination card in Hawaii, for instance, one could not go to a restaurant, the movies, or the gym. Those in the military who decline to be vaccinated are being kicked out of the military under *religious exceptions*, which is *religious discrimination*.

Family, friends, co-workers, and neighbors will turn you in if you don't have the chip or the mark of the beast, and military police will arrest you on the spot. You and your family will not have water (we can survive without water for only three days), food, gasoline, utilities, sewage services, etc., to live on in a one-world government. You and your family will live in a state of fear, confusion, lies, and darkness by receiving the mark of the beast and microchip. Currently, it is a state law in Hawaii that all cats and dogs must be microchipped.

Since we are in the **Church Age**, the next phase on the timeline is the *rapture of the true Christian Church*. Those who did not receive the true Christ will be left behind. At the onset of the rapture, they will only see your shoes, slippers, thongs, and clothing on the floor. If the rapture should occur while you are driving a car, operating a boat, or flying a plane—the vehicle, boat, or plane will suddenly be without a driver or pilot. (Does the possibility of this scenario scare you or alarm you?)

In the end-time scriptures, it mentions the Euphrates River drying up, and this is already occurring today. The End-Time *antichrist* is akin to satan's apostle—he will deceive those who are left behind. He will project the idea that he wants peace, but in his heart, he is moving toward the total annihilation of Israel and God's people (all Christians). He will gain control via the *One-World government* through totalitarianism, socialism, communism, Marxism, etc.

Q: *Are these current end-time events really occurring?*
A: Yes... they are.

1. Cryptocurrency (Bitcoin)

No one knows for sure who first invented coins, but historians believe that metal objects were first used as money as early as 5,000 B.C. Around 700 B.C., the Lydians were the first in Western culture to make coins. Other countries and civilizations soon began to mint their own coins with specific values.[63]

63 Helen Williams, "Ancient India Currency?" Kerala Travel Tours, Accessed July 18, 2022, https://kerala-travel-tourism.com/india/ancient-india-currency.html.

Today, we have currency that exists online in a digital wallet. Sweden and China are **already becoming cashless societies**. Any day now, China will be going cashless or cryptocurrency, and many countries under China's control will switch over to digital currency as well.[64]

2. Islam Wants to Destroy Israel

> It was only perhaps three weeks ago that the president of Iran once again said that Israel should be eradicated off the face of the Earth. As you recall, it was about in 2005 when he [Mahmoud Ahmadinejad] said before that Israel—he would use a nuclear weapon to wipe Israel off the face of the Earth.
>
> —Rep. Michele Bachmann
> (R-Minn.), September 19, 2011[65]

Currently, the thirty-six acres of the Muslim run "dome of the rock" or "the third temple mount future site" done by Muslims in 621 A.D. will be moved by satan, the antichrist, and the false prophet for the antichrist to be worshiped as god in the third future temple. The temple institute in Jerusalem is already ready to build the third future temple. (*For more information on this temple mount future site, visit Bob Cornuke at baseinstitute.org and David Seilaff, at* askelm.com.)

64 "China's Great Leap to Wallet-Free Living | Moving Upstream," YouTube: Wall Street Journal, 2018, https://www.youtube.com/watch?v=75AXINUL47g.
65 Glenn Kessler, "Did Ahmadinejad Really Say Israel Should Be 'Wiped off the Map'?" The Washington Post, 2011, https://www.washingtonpost.com/blogs/fact-checker/post/did-ahmadinejad-really-say-israel-should-be-wiped-off-the-map/2011/10/04/gIQABJIKML_blog.html.

3. Owners of **dogs and cats** worldwide are being **required to microchip their pets**.

4. The **Communist Chinese Party, one world government** society, wants to control its people's finances, utilities, and social structures.[66]

5. The U.S. has companies and their employees already using **microchips**.

6. **Big Tech invades our privacy.** Big tech also sells our information in the end times.

7. Warning from *Healer Kathryn Kuhlman*.[67] [68]

8. **The U.S. is over $30 Trillion in debt**, leaning toward financial collapse. We see this in terms of emergency printing of bills and inflation. **This translates to $92,253 for every single person in America**.[69]

The federal government spends $1,000,000 a minute of taxpayer money, which equals half a billion a day. The federal government gives over $1,000,000 in bonuses to federal work-

66 Ryan Hass, "Assessing China's 'Common Prosperity' Campaign," The Brookings Institution, 2021, https://www.brookings.edu/blog/order-from-chaos/2021/09/09/assessing-chinas-common-prosperity-campaign/.
67 Ian Francis, "Kathryn Kuhlman—A WARNING TO 21ST CENTURY CHARISMATICS," YouTube, 2017, https://www.youtube.com/watch?v=QUVg6vyXH3o.
68 Liam Norris, "Compulsory Dog Micro-Chipping… Do You Agree?" Medium, 2015, https://medium.com/@liamnorris/compulsory-dog-microchipping-do-you-agree-30e13aa7641e.
69 "National Debt Clock: What Is the National Debt Right Now?" Peter G. Peterson Foundation, 2022, https://www.pgpf.org/national-debt-clock.

ers from taxpayer money and has over 400,000 employees who earn over $100,000 per year—over a million and a half (1.6 million). State and local governments make over $100,000 a year of taxpayer money.[70]

9. In 1929, 1987, and 2008 We Saw Forms of Financial Crises

We are leading up to the biggest financial collapse of all time. Are we ready for this as a nation, state, city, neighborhood, family, or individual?

10. Financial Debt Crisis Soon

We are warned through reliable resources that a financial crisis is coming soon, which will lead to the antichrist (satan's apostle) and the false prophet (satan's prophet). These end-time events will create a one-world government and one-world religion because it will be necessary for the end-time rulers to try to control what's left of humanity and one way to control people is to have one system of government and one religion (Revelation 17:1–18).

Unfortunately, the one religion will be to bow to the antichrist. This is truly the end of humanity left on earth when it comes to that.

After years of research on what is happening globally and within the U.S. financial system, I feel that many countries are collapsing, and many countries with collectively over a billion people are currently close to financial collapse. Issues such as the COVID-19 Pandemic and variants Delta, Omicron, and

70 "America's Finance Guide," U.S. Treasury Data Lab, 2020, https://datalab.usaspending.gov/americas-finance-guide/.

Monkeypox and the Russia-Ukraine War are all culminating in the end time events in the last two years (2020–2022). Not to mention exorbitant gas and oil prices, high-interest rates, troubled nations borrowing money, food shortages that will cause inflation in food costs, and other factors.

These countries and many others are now facing a "debt crisis":

- Sri-Lanka
- Egypt
- Tunisia
- Lebanon
- Argentina
- El Salvador
- Deni
- Ghana
- Ethiopia
- Kenya
- South Africa
- Turkey[71]

We need to ask ourselves, among all these end-time facts—what's next for America, the free world, and the rest of the world?

71 Sydney Maki, "Why Developing Countries Are Facing a Debt Default Crisis," Bloomberg Business Week, 2022, https://www.bloomberg.com/news/articles/2022-07-07/why-developing-countries-are-facing-a-debt-default-crisis?leadSource=uverify wall.

11. Consider the American Debt to China

The U.S. debt to China is $1.17 trillion as of August 2018. That's 19 percent of the $6.3 trillion in Treasury bills, notes, and bonds held by foreign countries. The rest of the $21 trillion national debt is owned by either the American people or the U.S. government itself.[72]

12. Many Societies Are in Big Financial Debt

Greece, Italy, Spain, Venezuela, Sudan, Lebanon, and many more countries.

13. Stock Market Decline

See YouTube video: *Why the Stock Market Would Be in Trouble | Steve Forbes.*

14. There Is Instability in the Middle East and Israel

See Gaza the Fight for Israel [Middle East] Documentary Real Stories; Gaza, Hamas, and the New Middle East | Al Jazeera World.

15. "The Army has plans to start promoting by dialect in the near future so that we can grow our Arabic inventory in Iraqi, Levantine, and Egyptian."[73]

---

72 Palki Sharma, "Gravitas LIVE with Palki Sharma| China's Debt Bomb Explodes: How Defaults Worth Billions Impact You," YouTube: Wion News TV, 2021, https://www.youtube.com/watch?v=2SpKxDV6Qog.

73 Meghann Myers, "Army Wants More Iraqi and Egyptian Language Experts, but That Could Affect Pay for Some Arabic Linguists," Army Times, 2018, https://www.armytimes.com/news/your-army/2018/03/13/army-wants-more-iraqi-and-eqyptian-language-experts-but-that-could-affect-pay-for-some-arabic-linguists/.

A note about YouTube. If you'd like more details on any of these end-time subjects, type in what you're searching for, and many documentaries posted on YouTube will be available to you, such as those shared in this book.

CHAPTER 8

Signs in the Sky

Jesus said that when you see certain things begin to happen,

> "...look up and lift up your heads, because your redemption draws near." "...when you see these things happening, know that the kingdom of God is near."
> (Luke 21:28, 31 NKJV)

The sun stood still on October 30, 1207 BCE. Why did Joshua ask God to make the sun stand still?

> Joshua needed more daylight to finish the contest. So, Joshua asked God to make the sun stand still. And God did. On the day the Lord gave the Israelites victory over the Amorites, Joshua prayed to the Lord in front of all the people of Israel.
> He said, "Let the sun stand still over Gibeon, and the moon over the valley of Aijalon."[74]

74 Kristin van Tilburg, "What Joshua's Sun Stand Still Prayer Means For You," Medium, 2018, https://medium.com/publishous/what-joshuas-sun-stand-still-prayer-means-for-you-88cc9af09f50.

Joshua 10:13 (KJV) states,

> And the sun stood still, and the moon stayed, until the people had avenged themselves upon their enemies. Is not this written in the book of Jasher?

Significance of Blood Moons

Blood Moons are associated with lunar tetrads, meaning occurring in four phases. Lunar tetrads occurred in 1909–1910, 1927–1928, 1949–1950, 1967–1968, 1985–1986, 2004–2005, and 2014–2015, and are on target to occur in 2032–2033.[75]

Following Israel's establishment as a modern state in 1948, the Blood Moons were witnessed by the whole world in 1949 and 1950 and then by Jerusalem in 1967 (the eye and heart of God). Lunar tetrads are said to be associated with Israel's socio-economic and spiritual situations, tied to the feasts and festivals of Israel, and often a time period that begins with a tragedy and ends with a triumph for the Jewish people.

In 1967 Jerusalem was restored following the *Six Day War* between Israel and Jordan, Syria, UAR, and Egypt. The U.S. Embassy officially relocated to Jerusalem on May 14, 2018, to coincide with the seventieth anniversary of the Israeli Declaration of Independence. I happened to be in Jerusalem to witness the start of the building of the U.S. Embassy.

The Blood Moon or lunar eclipse of July 27–28, 2018, lasted 103 minutes, making it the longest eclipse of the Twenty-first century, and is said to begin the count down to the "end times". Code Red signs are not necessarily in the sky but all around us

75 John Hagee, Four Blood Moons (Brentwood, TN: Worthy Publishing, 2013).

Code Red—End Game Signs

- It is apparent by what can be described as *hedonistic*—infused cultures in our societies that satan is dominating everyday life in the natural world and pop culture, and he is trying to control the world in the *End Game*. For example, people don't realize or seem to care that President Kim Jong-un of North Korea, President (Czar) Vladimir Putin of Russia, and President Xi Jinping of China have these things in common: money, military might, manpower, nuclear weapons but they all lack the most important element— "Jesus Christ" as their Lord and Savior.
- In July 2022, Iran provided Russia with military drones and military-grade weapons. Russia has the "Satan II" Nuclear Rocket (actual name), which is the deadliest missile in the world. Its height is 35.3m (115.8 feet), weighing 208,100kg (229.39 tons), and its payload is 16 nuclear warheads. Its range is 10,000–18,000 km or 6,213.712–11184.681 miles.[76]
- The devil is putting out all the ammo or pulling the stops to get every soul before the "Christian Rapture of the Church" or "End Game". Are you ready?
- In India, they perform 63 million abortions a year, and around the world, 75% of all abortions are unsafe and

76 "RS-28 Sarmat | Missile Threat | CSIS Missile Defense Project," Center for Strategic and International Studies, 2021, https://missilethreat.csis.org/missile/rs-28-sarmat/.

sometimes involve knitting needles, bicycle spokes, or drinking chemicals or bleach to kill the fetuses.[77]

- Elementary, intermediate, and high schools and colleges are teaching transgender, homosexual and lesbian curricula.[78]
- The forty-sixth President of the U.S. is talking about a "New World Order".[79]
- The separation between sheep and goats has begun (Matthew 25:31–46).
- The antichrist's names are master of intrigue, worthless shepherd, and beast.
- In South Africa, 7.5 million people are infected with HIV/AIDS.[80]
- Pope Frances is the 266 Pope of the Vatican Roman Catholic Church. There are 1.36 billion Catholics around the World.[81] Are they ready for the "Rapture of the Christian Church" and "Tribulation"?
- Diseases, bacteria, and viruses are hitting the world—Ebola, Rabies, Swine Flu, Crimean-Cong Fever, SARS,

---

77 "Canada Province Allows Possession of Some Drugs | BTS Visits White House," YouTube: Wion News TV, 2022, https://www.youtube.com/watch?v=Z8GoOwEEFDE.

78 Virginia Allen, "Are These 7 LGBT 'Kids' Books in Your Child's Classroom, School Library?" The Daily Signal, 2021, https://www.dailysignal.com/2021/08/09/are-these-7-lgbt-kids-books-in-your-childs-classroom-or-school-library/.

79 Steve Forbes and Forbes Staff, "Biden Says U.S. Must Lead New World Order: What America Needs If He's Serious," Forbes, 2022, https://www.forbes.com/sites/steveforbes/2022/03/25/biden-says-us-must-lead-new-world-order-what-america-needs-if-hes-serious/?sh=63b4c4691640.

80 "South Africa: An Ongoing Battle with HIV," Open Access Government, 2021, https://www.openaccessgovernment.org/south-africa-hiv/119993/.

81 CNA Staff, "Vatican: Number of Catholics Worldwide Rose by 16 Million in 2020," Catholic World Report: Catholic News Agency, 2022, https://www.catholicworldreport.com/2022/02/11/vatican-number-of-catholics-worldwide-rose-by-16-million-in-2020/.

COVID–2, COVID–19, DELTA, OMICRON, B1 and B2, BA.2, BA.5, MonkeyPox, and more!

- Kids are going to websites like *backstage* (recently closed) and replaced by *BedPage*. Other sites, *Snapchat, Facebook*, etc., are fertile grounds for pimps to solicit and pick up young ladies (and young men) as prostitutes or human trafficking.

Reports of human trafficking in the United States are on the rise. According to data from the National Human Trafficking Hotline, reports of potential cases of human trafficking in America rose 35.7 percent from 2015 to 2016. The growing number could be indicative of the prevalence of the problem, or it could be the result of growing awareness about this crime.

Under the federal Trafficking Victims Protection Act of 2000, sex and labor trafficking are considered "severe forms of trafficking in persons," and are defined as:

- **Sex trafficking:** A commercial sex act induced by force, fraud or coercion, or in which the person induced to perform such an act is younger than 18.
- **Labor trafficking:** The recruitment, harboring, transportation, provision or obtaining of a person for labor or services, through the use of force, fraud or coercion for the purpose of subjection to involuntary servitude, peonage, debt bondage or slavery. At the federal level, the prosecution of offenders falls under the jurisdiction of the Department of Justice. In 2015, U.S. attorney's offices prosecuted 1,049 suspects for human traffick-

ing-related offenses, according to the Bureau of Justice Statistics.[82]

- Finland, Sweden, and other countries are looking at joining NATO, which will be led one day in the future by the antichrist (satan's apostle) and the false prophet.
- In the world today, there are enough nuclear bombs to destroy the world seven times over.

82 "Prosecuting Human Traffickers," National Conference of State Legislatures [NCSL], 2018, https://www.ncsl.org/research/civil-and-criminal-justice/prosecuting-human-traffickers.aspx.

CHAPTER 9

The Four Horsemen

Significance of the Four Horsemen

(Revelation 6; Daniel 8:15–24, 9:24)

From the day that satan had convinced Adam and Eve to partake of the forbidden fruit, this giving in to temptation by the evil one became the original sin. The original sin is disobeying the Lord God. Every single person after that was sinful, and satan wished they belonged to him and dwelled with him in hell! No ifs, buts, or what ifs! The human race seemed to have no way out! Not one soul was perfect to redeem us from hell!

However, God (Jesus), our creator in Heaven, found a way. The second person of the *Godhead* became human and came to earth (by the way, you can't turn humans into God). A perfect, loving, giving, trustworthy savior—*equally human and equally God* (Yes, a *radical concept* but oh so true!) died on the cross to pay the debt for the sins of all humanity. Why did Jesus do this? So that you, I, and everyone who comes to Him can go to Heaven, not hell. Christians will essentially take the earth (similar to a land deed) back to God

From the beginning, satan tempted Jesus. When Jesus was fasting for forty days and nights at the beginning of His ministry (around thirty years old), satan essentially stated that he owns the earth and its people!

Matthew 4:8–10 (NKJV) says,

> Again, the devil took Him up on an exceedingly high mountain and showed Him all the kingdoms of the world and their glory. And he said to Him, "All these things I will give You if You will fall down and worship me." Then Jesus said to him, "Away with you, satan! For it is written, 'You shall worship the Lord your God, and Him only shall you serve.'"

Revelation Chapter 6

Let's look at the last chapter in the Bible as we cover Revelation 6:1–11 (KJV)...

> And I saw when the Lamb opened one of the seals, and I heard, as it were the noise of thunder, one of the four beasts saying, Come and see.
> And I saw, and behold a white horse: and he that sat on him had a bow; and a crown was given unto him: and he went forth conquering, and to conquer.
> And when he had opened the second seal, I heard the second beast say, Come and see.
> And there went out another horse that was red: and power was given to him that sat thereon to take peace from the earth, and that they should kill one another: and there was given unto him a great sword.

> And when he had opened the third seal, I heard the third beast say, Come and see. And I beheld, and lo a black horse, and he that sat on him had a pair of balances in his hand.
> And I heard a voice in the midst of the four beasts say, A measure of wheat for a penny, and three measures of barley for a penny; and see thou hurt not the oil and the wine.
> And when he had opened the fourth seal, I heard the voice of the fourth beast say, Come and see.
> And I looked, and behold a pale horse: and his name that sat on him was Death, and Hell followed with him. And power was given unto them over the fourth part of the earth, to kill with sword, and with hunger, and with death, and with the beasts of the earth.
> And when he had opened the fifth seal, I saw under the altar the souls of them that were slain for the word of God, and for the testimony which they held:
> And they cried with a loud voice, saying, How long, O Lord, holy and true, dost thou not judge and avenge our blood on them that dwell on the earth?
> And white robes were given unto every one of them; and it was said unto them, that they should rest yet for a little season, until their fellow servants also and their brethren, that should be killed as they were, should be fulfilled.

Let me explain the *antichrist* (satan's apostle) at this juncture. He goes by many names like *the wicked one, man of sin, the beast, son of perdition, little horn* (satan is the big horn), *son of satan, prince of peace.* He will come from Europe and his mission is to exterminate the Jewish people and all those who profess that Jesus is their Lord and Savior. He also wants to try to deceive Christians and have them become lukewarm and fall away from their faith. One-third of the Christian Church has already left because of COVID-19, Delta variant, Omicron, B1, B2, and other variants.[83]

Most likely, this end-times leader will not be a Muslim or Jewish because these nations hate each other, and they would never support a person in charge who would come from these nations. This is why I believe the antichrist will be a leader arising out of the European Union.

The antichrist is a genius. He is prideful and arrogant, and he works for satan only. He hates anything or anyone who loves and follows God or Jesus Christ. The antichrist spirit has always been in existence but is more prevalent today. We see this spirit in the political arena, government, social unrest, pandemics, sickness and disease, poverty, hopelessness, homelessness, and depression. The antichrist acts as satan's apostle—a counterfeit to the true Apostles of Jesus Christ.

Again, the antichrist spirit has been on the earth since Lucifer fell from heaven to earth—and in the *End Game,* he is a human being, a man who is already an adult. When he *takes office* or becomes the ruler of the end times, he will be the evilest man on earth (*far worse* than Hitler).

I've been studying Hitler because he is like the antichrist. Hitler took ten years before he became president. December

83 "Why Are So Many People Leaving the Church?" YouTube: Belief It Or Not, Accessed August 23, 2022, https://www.youtube.com/watch?v=FdU2Bolo4tI.

2022 will mark the halfway mark before the antichrist takes charge, and 2028–29 (Shemitah) will mark ten years for the antichrist.

Also, the Lord showed me just as Auschwitz and Hitler did, the antichrist will have his own Auschwitz for the world, and all those who don't receive the mark of the Beast (666) will die—instead of millions, billions will die.

The antichrist is very rich, has maids and a mansion, has his own private plane, is charismatic, wears suits and a tie, and is well connected to world leaders. His status is due to special demonic powers from satan, and he has bodyguards 24/7. The antichrist will set up a *one-world order, religion,* and *currency*. He will cause a global collapse of the financial world and take control. The antichrist will set up a fake, false treaty between Israel and Islamic nations or Muslims (Daniel 7, 8, 9:26; Acts 17:31; Proverbs 6:17; Revelation 6:1–2; 19, 21:8; Matthew 24; John 4:23, 5:43; 1 John 4:3). The Scriptures speak for themselves and are provided so that you may read them for yourself.

The antichrist will lead ten nations and conquer three of these nations (see current member countries in the table of European Union below) and lead seven nations into a world war (Revelations 13:1).

> The dragon stood on the shore of the sea, and I saw a beast coming out of the sea. It had ten horns and seven heads with ten crowns on its horns, and on each head a blasphemous name.
>
> Revelation 13:1 (NIV)

The following is an explanation of the above verse:

- Dragon—satan's antichrist. He will be evil to the core, bad in all respects—violent, prideful, vain, arrogant. He will not care about human life. He essentially will act in a savage, lawless, and wild manner, and he hates God, Christ, and the Holy Spirit. He (satan) will even appoint him as an apostle (Daniel 7:8; Revelation 13:1–4).
- Satan always copies God and formed the unholy trinity, which is comprised of satan, the antichrist or satan's apostle, and the false prophet in a continuum against Christians, humanity in general, and our Triune God (God the Father, Jesus Christ, and the Holy Spirit).
- The Beast out of the Sea (Mediterranean) —a gentile, worldly man coming quietly from Europe.
- Ten horns—represent ten nations, ten prime ministers, ten presidents, or ten countries (Daniel 2:41; Revelation 17:12) in which satan, the antichrist, and the false prophet will dominate.
- Seven heads—mean seven consecutive leaders out of the ten will be destroyed whereupon satan, the antichrist (satan's apostle), and false prophet will create "one nation" and implement a *one world government, one world religion, one world finance,* etc.

Author's Note:

The Bible does not give a name for the antichrist or false prophet because people will try to kill that person and take him out. The antichrist's name and false prophet's name will come out into the open and be known to the general public once the "Rapture of the true Christian Church" occurs (which marks the end of the Church Age) and the next stage, the "tribulation" begins.

I also feel the Bible has the antichrist, false prophet, and the time and day of the Rapture of the Christian Church and Tribulation coded in it. This insight will entail many years of Bible study, attending prophetic conferences and Bible Study courses, and drawing close to Jesus so that the Holy Spirit may impart knowledge.

The following chapters defend and explain the Christian faith (apologetics) and provide Bible Study tools for personal growth as a Christian in the modern world. Included are interesting facts and figures, personal accounts, and testimonies—all a testament of faith in Jesus Christ, our Lord and Savior. It is my sincere hope and prayer that you come away blessed and super-charged that the End Game is really the beginning of things to come where God Himself and all those who believe upon Him shall prevail in Heaven on Earth and the ages to come.

Get Ready!

CHAPTER 10

Characteristics of the Godhead

Another name for God is our Triune God, which consists of God the Father, Jesus Christ the Son, and the Holy Spirit. We will start by exploring concepts about God the Father.

God the Father

The Bible says that God is Spirit,

> God is a Spirit: and they that worship Him must worship Him in Spirit and in truth.
>
> (John 4:24 KJV)

Also, read Deuteronomy 4: 12.

> God is invisible,
>
> Who is the image of the invisible God, the firstborn of every creature:
>
> (Colossians 1:15 KJV)

> Now unto the King [God] eternal, immortal, invisible, the only wise God, be honor and glory for ever and ever, Amen.
>
> (1 Timothy 1:17 KJV)

John 5:19 (KJV) says,

> Then answered Jesus and said unto them, Verily, verily, I say unto you, The Son can do nothing of himself, but what he seeth the Father do: for what things soever he doeth, these also doeth the Son likewise.

Based on this scripture, the cult believes that what Jesus did on this earth, God did first (e.g., took on human form). But read John 5:20–47, and you'll see that Jesus isn't talking about the incarnation but rather about future events.

Other things the Bible says about God include:

- God, the Father, is Spirit but possesses some form of physical glory that cannot be directly seen by human eyes. Refer to Moses' encounter with the Lord God (Exodus 33:22–23).
- God can experience and relate to human emotions because He created us, after all, with human emotions.

> God is not man, that he should lie; neither the son of man, that he should repent: hath he said, and shall he not do it? or hath he spoken, and shall he not make it good?
>
> (Numbers 23:19 KJV)

- God is unique and set apart from human beings.

For I am the Lord your God: ye shall therefore sanctify yourselves, and ye shall be Holy; for I am Holy: neither shall ye defile yourselves with any manner of creeping thing that creepeth upon the earth.

(Leviticus 11:44 KJV)

Let them praise thy great and terrible name; for it is holy.

(Psalms 99:3 KJV)

For thus saith the high and lofty One that inhabiteth eternity, whose name is Holy; I dwell in the high and holy place, with him also that is of a contrite and humble spirit, to revive the spirit of the humble, and to revive the heart of the contrite ones.

(Isaiah 57:15 KJV)

- God has a heart.

And it repented the Lord that he had made man on the earth, and it grieved him at his heart.

(Genesis 6:6 KJV)

- God has a soul.

Behold my servant, whom I uphold; mine elect, in whom my soul delighteth; I have put my spirit upon him: he shall bring forth judgment to the Gentiles.

(Isaiah 42:1 KJV)

Bible Verses Which Reveal the Characteristics of God

- Deuteronomy 26:17, 30:20—God's voice.
- Exodus 20:3; Deuteronomy 5:7—There is only **one** true God. This means that **no** Buddha, **no** Hindu gods, **no** allah, **no** Mormon god, **no** Jehovah's Witness god, and **no** cult gods can ever be the **one** true God.
- James 1:13—God is Holy and cannot sin.
- Isaiah 42; Joshua 23:14—God has a soul.
- Genesis 6:6—God has a heart.
- Psalms 121:3—God never sleeps.
- Romans 11:33—God's ways are unfathomable.
- Colossians 1:15–16, 19, 2:3, 8:10—God is the highest authority.
- Isaiah 45:5—Only one God.
- Isaiah 40:28–29—God doesn't become weary or tired.
- Psalms 149:5—God has no limit to understanding you.
- Exodus 14:20, 34:5; Numbers 10:34; Psalms 104:3—God travels.
- 1 Kings 19:11–12; Jeremiah 20:9; Romans 8:16—God talks to you today.
- Psalms 103:19; Job 22:12—God lives in the highest of Heaven.
- Leviticus 11:44; Psalms 99:3; Isaiah 57:15—God is unique and set apart from all other human beings.
- Numbers 23:19—God has human emotions.
- John 4:24—God is Spirit.
- Colossians 1:15—God is invisible.
- Psalms 56:8—God counts tears.
- Isaiah 31:2—God does not retreat His words.

- Psalms 14:2—God looks down from Heaven.
- 1 John 5:14—God hears us.
- Isaiah 30:27—God's tongue is a consuming fire.
- Job 36:26—God's age is unsearchable.
- Jeremiah 20:12—God discerns your attitude and spirit daily.
- Ecclesiastes 12:7—God gave spirit.
- Isaiah 55:8—God's thoughts are not our thoughts, and God's ways are not our ways.
- 1 Corinthians 10:13—God never gives you more than you can handle.
- 2 Peter 1:19–21—true prophecy is from God, not men.
- Isaiah 6:1—God's robe fills the temple.
- Numbers 23:19—God does not repent.
- 1 John 4:8; Psalms 103:8—God is slow to anger and abounding in loving kindness.
- 1 Corinthians 1:29—there is no fleshly glory in God's presence.
- Exodus 33:20—no man shall see God and live.
- Psalms 92:5—God's thoughts are very deep.
- Mark 9:7—God is in the clouds.
- Exodus 3:7—God knows our sufferings.
- Exodus 19:8–9, 24:17—God is fire.
- John 6:44—God draws you to Him.
- John 10:3–4—When you know God, you know God's voice.
- Genesis 1:1—God made the universe.
- Psalms 33:6–9—God made the Heavens.
- Psalms 104:5—God made the earth.
- Isaiah 40:26–28; Hebrews 1:1–2—God made all things.

There are seventy-five places in the New Testament where God the Father, His Son, Jesus Christ (fully man and fully God), and the Holy Spirit (God) are mentioned at length. The Bible is the only book that starts from the beginning of the creation of the world and ends with the future. Contrast that to cults like Hinduism, Buddhism, Islam, Mormonism, etc.

The Bible gives God the Father the following names:

- Jehovah/Yahweh—He Is.

> And God said unto Moses, I AM THAT I AM: and he said, Thus shalt thou say unto the children of Israel, I AM hath sent me unto you.
>
> (Exodus 3:14 KJV)

- Jehovah Jireh—The Lord will provide.

> And Abraham called the name of that place Jehovahjireh: as it is said to this day, In the mount of the Lord it shall be seen.
>
> (Genesis 22:14 KJV)

- Jehovah Nissi—The Lord is thy banner.

> And Moses built an altar, and called the name of it Jehovahnissi.
>
> (Exodus 17:15 KJV)

- Jehovah shalom—The Lord is peace (Judges 6).

- Jehovah Shammah— "The Lord is there" (Ezekiel 48:35 KJV).
- Jehovah Tsebaoth—The Lord of hosts.

> And this man went up out of his city yearly to worship and sacrifice unto the Lord of hosts in Shiloh. And the two sons of Eli, Hophni and Phinehas, the priest of the Lord, were there.
>
> (1 Samuel 1:3 KJV)

- Jehovah Elohe Yisrael—The Lord God of Israel (1 Samuel 15).
- Elohim—in Hebrew means the Supreme Being (Genesis 1:1–3), is found 2,500 times in the Old Testament (Deuteronomy 5:9; Genesis 21, 33, 32:28–30; Exodus 6:3, etc.).

Jesus Christ—God the Son

Now let's look at Jesus Christ.

Jesus has many names when referenced in the Bible because of who He is. His amazing and wonderful nature cannot be contained in one name. When we have a personal relationship with our Savior King, we call Him by a special name that describes His Holy attributes.

In the Bible alone, there are more than 150 different titles used in reference to Jesus Christ. However, some titles are much more common than others.

1. **Christ:** The title "Christ" is derived from the Greek Christós and means "the anointed one." It is used in Matthew16:20: "Then he strictly charged the disciples to

tell no one that he was the Christ." The title also appears at the very beginning of the Book of Mark: "The beginning of the gospel of Jesus Christ, the Son of God."

2. **Son of God:** Jesus is referred to as the "Son of God" throughout the New Testament—for example, in Matthew 14:33, after Jesus walks on water: "And those in the boat worshiped him, saying, 'Truly you are the Son of God.'" The title emphasizes Jesus divinity.
3. **Lamb of God:** This title appears only once in the Bible, though in a crucial passage, John 1:29: "The next day he saw Jesus coming toward him, and said, 'Behold, the Lamb of God, who takes away the sin of the world!'" The identification of Jesus with the lamb emphasizes Christ's innocence and obedience before God, an essential aspect of the crucifixion.
4. **New Adam:** In the Old Testament, it is Adam and Eve, the first man and woman, who precipitate the fall of man by eating the fruit from the Tree of Knowledge. A passage in First Corinthians 15:22 positions Jesus as a new, or second, Adam who by his sacrifice will redeem the fallen man: "For as in Adam all die, so also in Christ shall all be made alive."
5. **Light of the World:** This is a title Jesus bestows on himself in John 8:12: "Again Jesus spoke to them, saying, 'I am the light of the world. Whoever follows me will not walk in darkness but will have the light of life.'" Light is used in its traditional metaphorical sense, as the energy that allows the blind to see.
6. **Lord:** In First Corinthians 12:3, Paul writes that "no one speaking in the Spirit of God ever says, 'Jesus is ac-

cursed!' and no one can say 'Jesus is Lord' except in the Holy Spirit." The simple "Jesus is Lord" became an expression of devotion and faith among early Christians.

7. **Logos (The Word):** The Greek logos can be understood to mean "reason" or "word." As a title for Jesus, it first appears in John 1:1: "In the beginning was the Word, and the Word was with God, and the Word was God." Later in the same book, the "Word," synonymous with God, is also identified with Jesus: "The Word became flesh and dwelt among us, and we have seen his glory, glory as of the only Son from the Father, full of grace and truth."
8. **Bread of Life:** This is another self-bestowed title, which appears in John 6:35: "Jesus said to them, 'I am the bread of life; whoever comes to me shall not hunger, and whoever believes in me shall never thirst.'" The title identifies Jesus as a source of spiritual sustenance.
9. **Alpha and Omega:** These symbols, the first and last letters of the Greek alphabet, are used in reference to Jesus in the Book of Revelation: "It is finished! I am the Alpha and the Omega—the Beginning and the End. To all who are thirsty I will give freely from the springs of the water of life." Many Biblical scholars believe the symbols represent the eternal rule of God.
10. **Good Shepherd:** This title is another reference to Jesus's sacrifice, this time in the form of a metaphor that appears in John 10:11: "I am the good shepherd. The good shepherd lays down his life for the sheep."[84]

---

84 Rachel Bruner, "The Many Names and Titles of Jesus Christ," Learn Religions, 2019, https://www.learnreligions.com/names-of-jesus-christ-2159232.

Other Titles for Jesus Christ

The titles above are just a few of those that appear throughout the Bible. Other significant titles include:

1. **Advocate:** "My little children, I am writing these things to you so that you may not sin. But if anyone does sin, we have an advocate with the Father, Jesus Christ the righteous." (1 John 2:1)
2. **Amen, The:** "And to the angel of the church in Laodicea write: 'The words of the Amen, the faithful and true witness, the beginning of God's creation'" (Revelation 3:14).
3. **Beloved Son:** "Behold, my servant whom I have chosen, my beloved with whom my soul is well pleased. I will put my Spirit upon him, and he will proclaim justice to the Gentiles" (Matthew 12:18).
4. **Captain of Salvation:** "For it was fitting that he, for whom and by whom all things exist, in bringing many sons to glory, should make the captain of their salvation perfect through suffering" (Hebrews 2:10).
5. **Consolation of Israel:** "Now there was a man in Jerusalem, whose name was Simeon, and this man was righteous and devout, waiting for the consolation of Israel, and the Holy Spirit was upon him" (Luke 2:25).
6. **Counselor:** "For to us a child is born, to us a son is given; and the government shall be upon his shoulder, and his name shall be called Wonderful Counselor, Mighty God, Everlasting Father, Prince of Peace" (Isaiah 9:6).
7. **Deliverer:** "And in this way all Israel will be saved, as it is written, 'he Deliverer will come from Zion, he will banish ungodliness from Jacob'" (Romans 11:26).

8. **God Blessed:** "To them belong the patriarchs, and from their race, according to the flesh, is the Christ, who is over all, God blessed forever. Amen" (Romans 9:5).
9. **Head of the Church:** "And he put all things under his feet and gave him as head over all things to the church" (Ephesians 1:22).
10. **Holy One:** "But you denied the Holy and Righteous One and asked for a murderer to be granted to you" (Acts 3:14).
11. **I Am:** "Jesus said to them, 'Truly, truly, I say to you, before Abraham was, I am'" (John 8:58).
12. **Image of God:** "In whom the god of this world hath blinded the minds of them which believe not, lest the light of the glorious gospel of Christ, who is the image of God, should shine unto them" (2 Corinthians 4:4).
13. **Jesus of Nazareth:** "And the multitude said, This is Jesus the prophet of Nazareth of Galilee" (Matthew 21:11).
14. **King of the Jews:** "Where is he that is born King of the Jews? for we have seen his star in the east, and are come to worship him" (Matthew 2:2).
15. **Lord of Glory:** "Which none of the princes of this world knew: for had they known it, they would not have crucified the Lord of glory" (1 Corinthians 2:8).
16. **Messiah:** "He first findeth his own brother Simon, and saith unto him, We have found the Messiah, which is, being interpreted, the Christ" (John 1:41).
17. **Mighty One:** "Thou shalt also suck the milk of the Gentiles, and shalt suck the breast of kings: and thou shalt know that I the Lord am thy Savior and thy Redeemer, the mighty one of Jacob" (Isaiah 60:16).

18. **Nazarene:** "And he came and dwelt in a city called Nazareth: that it might be fulfilled which was spoken by the prophets, He shall be called a Nazarene" (Matthew 2:23).
19. **Prince of Life:** "And killed the Prince of life, whom God hath raised from the dead; whereof we are witnesses" (Acts 3:15).
20. **Redeemer:** "For I know that my redeemer liveth, and that he shall stand at the latter day upon the earth" (Job 19:25).
21. **Rock:** "And did all drink the same spiritual drink: for they drank of that spiritual Rock that followed them: and that Rock was Christ" (1 Corinthians 10:4).
22. **Son of David:** "The book of the generation of Jesus Christ, the son of David, the son of Abraham" (Matthew 1:1).
23. **True Vine:** "I am the true vine, and my Father is the husbandman" (John 15:1).[85]

Characteristics of Jesus Christ

- Joh.n 14:6—Jesus Christ is the **only** way to Heaven (not allah, not buddah, not Hinduism, not Islam, no Mormonism, no cult).
- Romans 9:5; Matthew 1:23—Jesus Christ is God.
- John 8:29—Jesus Christ does all things to please God.
- John 15:15—Jesus Christ hears from His Father.
- Galatians 3:13; Mark 15:34; 2 Corinthians 5:21—Jesus Christ knew no sin.
- Revelation 1:14—His head and hair are white like wool.

85 Bruner, 2019.

- Hebrews 1:4–6—Jesus Christ is greater than angels.
- Jeremiah 29:13—seek and search for Jesus Christ, and you will find Him.
- Philippians 2:8—Jesus Christ humbled Himself and became obedient.
- John 7:46—no one can speak like Jesus Christ.
- Colossians 1:28–29—Jesus Christ is working today.
- Revelation 1:17—Jesus Christ's eyes burned like fire, and His feet are like brass.
- John 5:45—Jesus Christ does not accuse you.
- John 21:25—scriptures do not record all things of Jesus Christ.
- Matthew 12:6; John 2:19—Jesus Christ greater them temple.
- Luke 2:25—Jesus grew in knowledge and wisdom.
- Hebrews 7:26—Jesus Christ is of a high priesthood.
- Mark 6:3; 1 Corinthians 9:5; Galatians 1:19; Matthew 13:55—Jesus Christ had four brothers (James, Joses, Judas, and Simon) and unspecified sisters.
- John 10:3–4—He knows God's voice.

Jesus Suffered for the Sins of the World

When Jesus Christ died on the cross for the sins of all of humanity, it was His choice—He didn't have to. He could have taken Himself down from the cross. But this is what Jesus had to go through for you and me. First, Jesus was flogged with a *flagrum*, which was a terrible weapon created during the Roman wars and used to send a message to all who crossed the Roman Empire.

This flagrum was intended to rip off skin and cause much bleeding when used. After *just one lash* with the flagrum, you would be in extreme, writhing pain. After many slashings from this several-tailed whip, you would wish you were dead and put out of your intense misery. You would be fainting, half-dead, with skin and muscle ripped open and hanging from your body in threads.

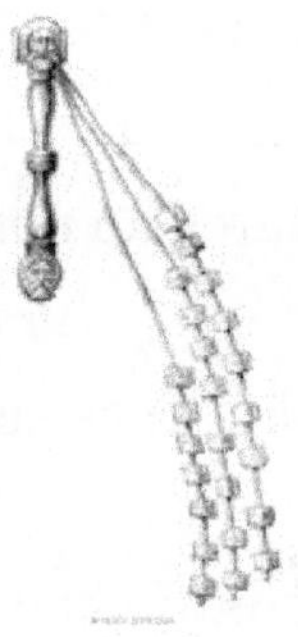

Flagrum[86]

The flagrum pictured here had lead beads on the ends of each strip of leather. The leather whips were long so that it could reach around a human's body, more so if the person had a thin body frame like Jesus. A person's veins would be exposed. In some cases, the victim's guts or intestines would come out. This is truly inhumane torture. After being flogged until nearly dead, you would be nailed to a wooden cross with seven-inch nails. One nail between each of your hands and wrists.

To imagine what Jesus endured for us is a life-changing concept for many. The nails would be driven right into your median

86 © (Flagrum) — stock.adobe.com

nerve, which caused Jesus excruciating pain and destroyed the use of his hands. As if all those cruel and inhumane acts committed on your body weren't enough, seven-inch nails would then be driven through your feet.

After the huge nails are driven into your hands and feet, the cross is set up right into a hole in the ground. When you are erected onto the cross with your hands nailed in a cross fashion, this would immediately cause you to have a hard time breathing. Victims would push up from their feet to take the pressure off their chests in order to gasp for air. The sheer ounce of energy to keep standing with all these nails in your body would cause agonizing pain. You would pray and hope that the breath you are taking in would be your last, as you are totally drained of hope and energy and ready to die of asphyxiation.

History tells us that when the Romans went to check, they found Jesus had died on the cross, but the two men on either side of Jesus needed to have their legs broken to succumb to death on the cross. Jesus was also pierced with a spear to his side to make sure He was dead.

Can you imagine what Jesus went through? My stomach is so upset at writing this all down, but I must relay to you the price Jesus paid on the Cross. Jesus did all this for you and me when He didn't have to! Jesus paid our debt to God for you and me to have eternal life in Heaven and not go to Hell if we receive Jesus Christ as our Lord and Savior in our hearts.

John the Baptist said of Jesus,

> I indeed baptize you with water unto repentance: but he that cometh after me is mightier than I, whose

> shoes I am not worthy to bear he shall baptize you with the Holy Ghost, and with fire.
>
> (Matthew 3:11 KJV)

Jesus Christ came from Heaven, not from the dust of the ground like man or a rib like a woman. He, and He alone, was given the authority to judge the world.

> For we must all appear before the judgment seat of Christ; that every one may receive the things done in his body, according to that he hath done, whether it be good or bad.
>
> (2 Corinthians 5:10 KJV)

> In the day when God shall judge the secrets of men by Jesus according to my gospel.
>
> (Romans 2:16 KJV)

This passage alone shows that Jesus Christ, not any other god, is the supreme being over all humans and earth. Jesus is equally God and equally man. On earth, Jesus Christ had a body, spirit, and soul. When He died, He was resurrected in his earthly body. That same body ascended into Heaven. That same body will come again when He returns for the final judgment.

The Names of Jesus Christ Most Often Heard Are:

- Son of Man: "And Jesus said unto him, Foxes have holes, and birds of the air have nests; but the Son of man hath not where to lay His head" (Luke 9:58 KJV). Also, read Luke 7.

- Messiah: "Jesus saith unto him, Thou hast said: nevertheless, I say unto you, Hereafter shall ye see the Son of man sitting on the right hand of power, and coming in the clouds of Heaven" (Matthew 26:64 KJV).
- Son of God: "And there came a voice from heaven saying, Thou art my beloved Son, in whom I am well pleased" (Mark 1:11 KJV). Also, read Mark 14:62.

Holy Spirit: Member of the Triune Godhead

I thought I knew everything there was to know that's been written about the Holy Spirit, but I had to think again with heartfelt meditation and prayer when I attended a lecture offered through Alec and Bell Waterhouse Lecture Series entitled *The Triune God in Worship, Prayer, and Life.*

With a matter-of-fact style Dr. Rodrick Durst, author and professor of Gateway Seminary, presented this lecture, and my understanding of the Trinity hit an all-new level of understanding. I highly suggest reading Dr. Durst's books.

Did you know that with the Trinity, there are six possible ways that one may address or call upon God in His Triune existence?

TEXT AND CONTEXT IS KING:

Triadic Order	Core Theme	Key Feature, Meaning, Value
Father-Son-Spirit	Missional	Sentness
Son-Father-Spirit	Christological	Service
Spirit-Son-Father	Ecclesial	Oneness/Giftedness (Unity/Diversity)
Son-Spirit-Father	Evangelistic	Acceptance
Spirit-Father-Son	Liturgical	Reverence
Father-Spirit-Son	Formational	Consecration

EXPERIENCING THE TRINITARIAN PRAYER EXPERIMENT

Text and Context Is King: The Triune God in Worship, Prayer, and Life[87]

Referencing the above chart, *Text and Context Is King*, let's say, for example, when you pray to God, you use the Triadic Order **Jesus**, the **Holy Spirit**, and the **Father** (in that order, or awareness in your mind, soul spirit that you are praying to God and that all three are present) you can see from the third row on this chart that the **Core Theme** of your prayer or request falls under *Ecclesial*, and the **key feature, meaning** or **value** in that prayer or request is *Oneness/Giftedness*. If we take the first row as an example, "Father-Son-Spirit," the core theme is "Missional," and the key feature, meaning, or value is "Sentness".

I invite you to experience the Trinitarian Prayer Experiment in the same way Dr. Rick Durst had invited us to experience it during his lecture. Take a moment for heartfelt prayer. Anything you'd like to pray to God (the Triune God) about is pos-

87 Rodrick K. Durst, 2015, *Reordering the Trinity: Six Movements of God in the New Testament*, Kregel Academic & Professional.

sible. Now ask yourself, "Did I call upon any one of the Trinity in any certain order?" Next, refer to the chart above. What was your Triadic Order? Core Theme? What about the Key Feature, Meaning, and Value?

It is my sincere hope that you have come away from this experiment a bit closer to understanding the dynamic nature of the Triune God in worship prayer and as you apply these principles to your life.

According to G.K. Chesterton, a Catholic apologist and mystery writer, most people read the Bible as tourists and not as travelers.[88] Tourists go out to see what they expect to see, while travelers go out to see what's there.

The New Testament has various passages that witness the Trinity when we start to recognize unexpected persons of the three persons in the Godhead. (See 2 Corinthians 13:14 and 1 Corinthians 12:4–6.)

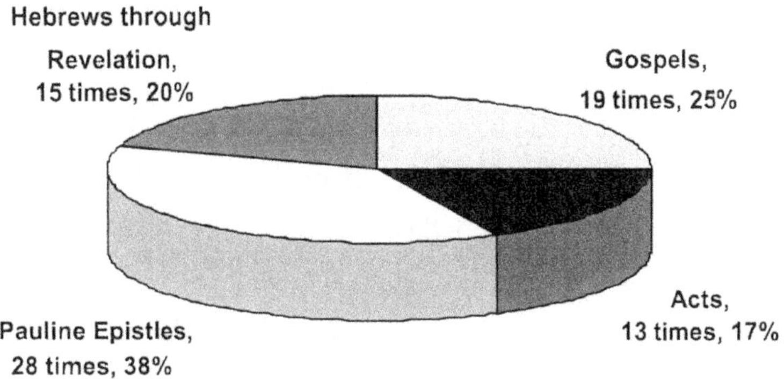

Pie Chart Triadic Occurrences—Spirit, Son, and Father[89]

88 Durst, 2015.
89 Ibid.

There are at least seventy-five scriptural references to the Triune God in the New Testament. The New Testament writers (Luke, John, Peter, James, Jude, and Paul) embraced the Triune God because they walked and talked with Jesus and believed that Jesus was the Son of God. When Jesus ascended to Heaven after rising from the dead, He said He would send His Holy Spirit (John 14:15–31, 16:–7; Acts 2).

As God, the Holy Spirit has existed through all eternity. In the Old Testament, He is also referred to as the Spirit, the Spirit of God, and the Spirit of the Lord. In the New Testament, He is sometimes called the Spirit of Christ. The Holy Spirit first appears in the second verse of the Bible, in the account of creation:

> And the earth was without form, and void; and darkness was upon the face of the deep. And the Spirit of God moved upon the face of the waters.
>
> (Genesis 1:2 KJV)

The Holy Spirit caused the Virgin Mary to conceive (Matthew 1:20), and at the baptism of Jesus, He descended on Jesus like a dove (Luke 3:22). On the day of Pentecost, He rested like tongues of fire on the apostles (Acts 2:3).

> In many religious paintings and church logos, He is often symbolized as a dove.
> Since the Hebrew word for the Spirit in the Old Testament means "breath" or "wind," Jesus breathed on His apostles after His resurrection and said, "...Receive ye the Holy Ghost" (John 20:22 NIV). He also command-

ed His followers to baptize people in the name of the Father, Son, and Holy Spirit.

The divine works of the Holy Spirit, both in the open and in secret, advance God the Father's plan of salvation. He participated in creation with the Father and Son, filled the prophets with the Word of God, assisted Jesus and the apostles in their missions, inspired the men who wrote the Bible, guides the church and sanctifies believers in their walk with Christ today.

He gives spiritual gifts for strengthening the body of Christ. Today He acts as Christ's presence on earth, counseling and encouraging Christians as they battle the temptations of the world and the forces of Satan.

The Holy Spirit's name describes His chief attribute: He is a perfectly holy and spotless God, free of any sin or darkness. He shares the strengths of God the Father and Jesus, such as omniscience, omnipotence, and eternality. Likewise, He is all-loving, forgiving, merciful, and just.

Throughout the Bible, we see the Holy Spirit pouring His power into followers of God. When we acting along with Joseph, Moses, David, Peter, and Paul, we may feel we have nothing in common with them, but the truth is that the Holy Spirit helped each of them change. He stands ready to help us change from the person we are today to the person we want to be, ever closer to the character of Christ.

A member of the Godhead, the Holy Spirit had no beginning and has no end. With the Father and Son, He existed before creation. The Spirit dwells in Heaven but also on Earth in the heart of every believer. The Holy Spirit serves as teacher, counselor, comforter, strengthener, inspiration, revealer of the Scriptures, convincer of sin, the caller of ministers, and intercessor in prayer.[90]

Characteristics of the Holy Spirit

- Psalms 139:7—The Holy Spirit is Omnipresent or can be everywhere at one time.
- 1 Corinthians 2:10–11—The Holy Spirit is omniscient or all-knowing.
- Judges 14—The Holy Spirit is sent by God for special services.
- Luke 1:35; Job 33:4—The Holy Spirit is omnipotent, all-powerful, and gives us life.
- Galatians 5:16–17—Holy Spirit fights for us (good versus evil or demonic forces unseen by you).
- Revelation 3:18—The Holy Spirit opens your eyes.
- Luke 1:35—The Holy Spirit does miracles.
- Hebrews 9:14—The Holy Spirit is eternal.
- John 15:26—The Holy Spirit is with us and helps us know the truth.
- John 16:13–15—The Holy Spirit tells you what is coming.
- John 14:16—The Holy Spirit is a comforter.
- Romans 1:28—God gave those who did not want to retain the knowledge of God (Holy Spirit) over to a depraved mind, which is considered evil.

90 Mary Fairchild, "Who Is the Holy Spirit? Third Person of the Trinity," Lear, 2019, https://www.learnreligions.com/who-is-the-holy-spirit-701504.

- Galatians 5:16–26 (NLT)— "So I say, let the Holy Spirit guide your lives. Then you won't be doing what your sinful nature craves. The sinful nature wants to do evil, which is just the opposite of what the Spirit wants. And the Spirit gives us desires that are the opposite of what the sinful nature desires..."
- Psalms 46:1–11—The Holy Spirit gives you courage.
- Psalms 91:1–16; 2 Corinthians 12:8–10—The Holy Spirit gives you relief.
- Acts 1:8—The Holy Spirit comes upon you.
- Romans 8:26—The Holy Spirit groans for you.
- Ephesians 5:18; 1 Kings 19:11; Romans 8:16; Revelation 2:7; Acts 13:2—The Holy Spirit speaks to you.
- Matthew 11:28–30—The Holy Spirit gives you rest.
- 1 Corinthians 3:16, 6:19—The Holy Spirit dwells within us.
- Ephesians 1:13, 4:30—The Holy Spirit puts His seal on us.
- Acts 16:6–11—The Holy Spirit closes doors.
- John 14:16, 15:26, 16:7—The Holy Spirit will come to us.
- John 14:26—The Holy Spirit teaches you.
- John 15:26—The Holy Spirit bears witness.
- John 16:13—The Holy Spirit guides you.
- John 16:7–8—The Holy Spirit convicts you.
- John 16:13—The Holy Spirit does what God says.
- Acts 10:19–21—The Holy Spirit can be trusted.
- 2 Corinthians 3:18—The Holy Spirit works within us.
- Acts 8:29—The Holy Spirit gives us commands.
- Romans 8:26—The Holy Spirit helps pray for us.

- John 16:8—The Holy Spirit convicts the world of sin, righteousness, and judgment.
- Romans 8:26—The Holy Spirit intercedes for you.
- Galatians 5:22—The Holy Spirit produces the fruit of the Spirit through you.
- Acts 1:8—The Holy Spirit empowers you for witnessing.
- Genesis 6:3—The Holy Spirit reaches for us.
- Acts 8:39—Holy Spirit performs miracles.
- 2 Thessalonians 2:13—The Holy Spirit gives believers of Jesus Christ a new holy nature.
- Acts 7:51—The Holy Spirit can be resisted.
- Ephesians 4:30—The Holy Spirit can be grieved.
- 1 Thessalonians 5:19—The Holy Spirit can be quenched.
- Hebrews 10:29—The Holy Spirit can be insulted.
- Matthew 12:31—Holy Spirit can be blasphemed (if you do this as a true Christian or non-Christian, or as part of a cult, you will **not go** to Heaven!)

References to the Holy Spirit in the Bible

- The Holy Spirit appears in nearly *every* book of the Bible.
- The Holy Spirit is a person.
- The Holy Spirit is included in the Trinity, which is made up of three distinct persons—The Father, the Son, and the Holy Spirit.

The following verses give us a beautiful picture of the Trinity in the Bible.

And Jesus, when he was baptized, went up straightway out of the water: and, lo, the heavens were opened unto him, and he saw the Spirit of God descending like a dove, and lighting upon him:
And lo a voice from heaven, saying, This is my beloved Son, in whom I am well pleased.

(Matthew 3:16–17 KJV)

Go ye therefore, and teach all nations, baptizing them in the name of the Father, and of the Son, and of the Holy Ghost:

(Matthew 28:19 KJV)

And I will pray the Father, and He will give you another Helper, that He may abide with you forever—

(John 14:16–17 KJV)

The grace of the Lord Jesus Christ, and the love of God, and the communion of the Holy Ghost, be with you all. Amen.

(2 Corinthians 13:14 KJV)

This Jesus hath God raised up, whereof we all are witnesses. Therefore being by the right hand of God exalted, and having received of the Father the promise of the Holy Ghost, he hath shed forth this, which ye now see and hear.

(Acts 2:32–33 KJV)

The Holy Spirit Has the Characteristics of Personality:

The Holy Spirit has a **Mind**:

Romans 8:27

And he who searches our hearts knows the mind of the Spirit, because the Spirit intercedes for the saints in accordance with God's will (NIV).

The Holy Spirit has a **Will**:

1 Corinthians 12:11

But one and the same Spirit works all these things, distributing to each one individually just as He wills (NASB).

The Holy Spirit has **Emotions**, he **Grieves**:

Isaiah 63:10

Yet they rebelled and grieved his Holy Spirit. So he turned and became their enemy and he himself fought against them (NIV).

The Holy Spirit gives **Joy**:

Luke 10:21

At that time Jesus, full of joy through the Holy Spirit, said, "I praise you, Father, Lord of heaven and earth, because you have hidden these things from the wise and learned, and revealed them to little children. Yes, Father, for this was your good pleasure" (NIV).

1 Thessalonians 1:6

You became imitators of us and of the Lord; in spite of severe suffering, you welcomed the message with the joy given by the Holy Spirit.

He **Teaches**:

John 14:26

But the Counselor, the Holy Spirit, whom the Father will send in my name, will teach you all things and will remind you of everything I have said to you (NIV).

He **Testifies** of Christ:

John 15:26

When the Counselor comes, whom I will send to you from the Father, the Spirit of truth who goes out from the Father, he will testify about me (NIV).

He **Convicts**:

John 16:8

When he comes, he will convict the world of guilt [Or will expose the guilt of the world] in regard to sin and righteousness and judgment: (NIV).

He **Leads**:

Romans 8:14

Because those who are led by the Spirit of God are sons of God (NIV).

He **Reveals** Truth:

John 16:13

But when he, the Spirit of truth, comes, he will guide you into all truth. He will not speak on his own; he will speak only what he hears, and he will tell you what is yet to come (NIV).

He **Strengthens** and **Encourages**:

Acts 9:31

Then the church throughout Judea, Galilee and Samaria enjoyed a time of peace. It was strengthened; and encouraged by the Holy Spirit, it grew in numbers, living in the fear of the Lord (NIV).

He **Comforts**:

John 14:16

And I will pray the Father, and he shall give you another Comforter, that he may abide with you for ever; (KJV)

He **Helps Us** in our Weakness:

Romans 8:26

In the same way, the Spirit helps us in our weakness. We do not know what we ought to pray for, but the Spirit himself intercedes for us with groans that words cannot express (NIV).

He **Intercedes**:

Romans 8:26

In the same way, the Spirit helps us in our weakness. We do not know what we ought to pray for, but the Spirit himself intercedes for us with groans that words cannot express (NIV).

He **Searches** the Deep Things of God:

1 Corinthians 2:11

The Spirit searches all things, even the deep things of God. For who among men knows the thoughts of a man except the man's spirit within him? In the same way no one knows the thoughts of God except the Spirit of God (NIV).

He **Sanctifies**:

Romans 15:16

To be a minister of Christ Jesus to the Gentiles with the priestly duty of proclaiming the gospel of God, so that the Gentiles might become an offering acceptable to God, sanctified by the Holy Spirit (NIV).

He **Bears Witness** or **Testifies**:

Romans 8:16

The Spirit itself beareth witness with our spirit, that we are the children of God: (KJV).

He **Forbids**:

Acts 16:6–7

Paul and his companions traveled throughout the region of Phrygia and Galatia, having been kept by the Holy Spirit from preaching the word in the province of Asia. When they came to the border of Mysia, they tried to enter Bithynia, but the Spirit of Jesus would not allow them to (NIV).

He Can be **Lied to**:

Acts 5:3

Then Peter said, "Ananias, how is it that Satan has so filled your heart that you have lied to the Holy Spirit and have kept for yourself some of the money you received for the land? (NIV).

He Can be **Resisted**:

Acts 7:51

"You stiff-necked people, with uncircumcised hearts and ears! You are just like your fathers: You always resist the Holy Spirit!" (NIV).

He Can be **Blasphemed**:

Matthew 12:31–32

And so I tell you, every sin and blasphemy will be forgiven men, but the blasphemy against the Spirit will not be forgiven. Anyone who speaks a word against the Son of Man will be forgiven, but anyone who speaks against the Holy Spirit will not be forgiven, either in this age or in the age to come (NIV).

He Can be **Quenched**:

1 Thessalonians 5:19

Quench not the Spirit (NKJV).[91]

The Holy Spirit Speaks in 2022 and into Eternity

Over the past months, the Holy Spirit has been giving me just a few pieces at a time so that I don't become overwhelmed by all the information I'm supposed to put in this book. This book actually started sixteen years ago, in 2005.

It is a morning in the New Year 2022. The Holy Spirit brought *prayer, being humble,* and *fasting* to my spirit (1 Kings 19:11–12). By the afternoon, I felt through the Holy Spirit that God was showing me that we needed to impart these things to you, the reader, in this book. God's Spirit put upon my heart that "you will take this book with you, and the people I will speak to around the world will need something to read that will guide them." This is sound advice that doesn't go against the Bible but instead tells people how to pray, fast, and be humble; how to seek the Lord God and Jesus to grow in faith right where they are—in whatever city, state, nation, or country.

God's correct chain of authority is apostle, prophet, evangelist, pastor, and teacher. It will be helpful to know this as you begin to encounter true Christian churches which mention and practice the Fivefold Ministry within their congregation.

As a Mormon, I would meet thousands of people, and I noticed that so many people had a religious spirit, but they were missing something. Once I became a Christian, I realized that what was missing was the guidance of the Holy Spirit. I put

91 Fairchild, 2019.

together a formula for recognizing the religious spirit vs. The Army of the Lord – 5 Distinct Roles, which you can read in Ephesians 4:11–12.

Religious Spirit vs. the Army of the Lord – 5 Distinct Roles

Religious Spirit—CODJL (An acronym developed by the author.)	**5-Fold Army of the Lord—APEPT** (Ephesians 4:11)
C—Criticize. People will criticize you, the church, the Bible, your family, your church, your work, affiliations, etc.	**A**—Apostles. Apostles lay the blueprint for God's design on earth, where the salvation of man is still being worked out through the nation of Israel. Apostles carry out what the Holy Spirit tells the Apostle to do.
O—Opinion. Others voice their opinions instead of following the Holy Spirit's guidance in the situation. Voicing strong opinions without researching content and context is usually because the person is operating in the natural world where opinions abound without facts to back them up (much like cable news stations today).	**P**—Prophets. Prophets Speak the Word of God through the Holy Spirit, which may include visions and dreams for the purpose of exhorting, counseling, and edifying Christ.

D—Debate. People love to debate from their sense of pride and ego. Debaters will try to undermine you and steal your joy, energy, and life. Debating things of God is meaningless because God is the author and finisher, the Alpha and the Omega, and His Word rings true forever and ever.	**E**—Evangelist. Evangelists preach the Word of God to people all over the world, usually not confined to a particular church. May also bring about healing, signs and wonders, and miracles through Christ Jesus.
J—Judgement. Others who do not agree with you pass judgment on everything, including expressing their strong opinions. These people who are judgmental tend to criticize everything and put a negative slant on it. These people tend to think they do not have any faults and forget to judge themselves before they speak or act.	**P**—Pastor. Pastors usually preside over a church congregation, the sheep, and they preach the Word of God and also bring about healing, signs and wonders, and miracles through Christ Jesus.

L—Legalism. People steeped in legalism seem to love the law for everyone else and try to find ways to bend it for their own benefit. Legalists often act holy (such as the Pharisees and Sadducees) but they are not actually pure in the Holy Spirit within their hearts.	**T**—Teacher. Teachers, throughout their life, study the Bible and know the Word of God; they teach others who do not know Christ and bring new Believers into the flock. Teachers teach one on one or to groups of people, as in a classroom setting.

WARNING—WARNING!

Satan (lucifer, devil, antichrist, false prophet) does not want you, your family, your church or business, or anyone to combine these three things: prayer, being humble, and fasting! Why? Because these three things are powerful in the Kingdom of God.

> For we wrestle not against flesh and blood (people) but against principalities, against powers, against the rulers of the darkness of this world, against spiritual wickedness in high places.
>
> (Ephesians 6:12 KJV)

Read John 10:10, Matthew 4:10, and 1 Peter 4:10.

Satan loves to attack you at your lowest point (i.e., while going through a divorce, a romantic breakup, loss of a job, financial difficulties, death of a loved one, loss of health, such as cancer, and many other things that can be considered low points in life).

The *fiery darts* or *attacks* from the enemy of our soul can lead to extreme frustration and even depression. During these attacks, satan wants you to doubt, deny and be disobedient to God, with the intention that you end up in Hell with him for eternity. Satan wants you to commit suicide, go to prison, destroy all your personal relationships, destroy business relationships, and do everything contrary to the eternity that God Himself has placed in your heart.

He Ecclesiastes 3:11 (NIV) says,

> has made everything beautiful in its time. He has also set eternity in the human heart...

God wants to bring you up if you learn to trust Him. Satan loves to attack you when your mind is resting or relaxed and your guard is down. Most of us rest or sleep between the hours of 11:00 p.m. till 5:00 a.m. —and this is when we need to be covered with prayer and ask the Holy Spirit to dwell with us. The enemy often will attack the human soul well after midnight and into the wee morning hours of 3:00 a.m.

Satan's ploy is to attack your mind, especially a mind that isn't on God twenty-four/seven. Your *mind* is the *battleground* where the enemy will try to deceive you. His talking points and strategy always involve deception and more deception. Satan sometimes adds a little truth with deception, but an apple is still an apple. Remember, there isn't a hybrid fruit called an *ornapple* or an *applerange*. If something looks like a half-truth and half-lie, then it's counted all as a lie. Don't fall for it!

Where there's darkness, there's danger. If there's just a tiny bit of light, this dispels complete darkness. In Africa, for example, lions love to attack under the cover of darkness when their prey is asleep or not on high alert.

While satan is trying to destroy you and everything about you, God will save you from the enemy's snare and always give you *100% truth* (Psalm 34:17). I am 100% certain that God is truth and that God is love. God loves us so much that He gave His only Begotten Son, Jesus Christ, to die on the cross for the sins of the world. And yet Jesus has risen, and He is coming back soon!

God created humans with free will. Be careful not to let the enemy gain control of your mind because you are partaking in evil and unholy things—such as gambling, prostitution, pimping, joining a cult, doing meditation outside of the Lord, playing ouija boards, being an atheist, trying to plot against and kill someone, etc.

When you partake in unholy activities and ungodly ways of thinking, you knowingly or unknowingly place your trust in satan. This is how crafty the concept of deception is. Ask the Lord always to give you wisdom and never allow you to be deceived. *James 1:5* (NIV) says,

> If any of you lack wisdom, let him ask of God, that giveth to all men liberally, and upbraideth not; and it shall be given him.

If you want to take control of your mind, which is part of your soul (remember, your soul, which is your will, mind, and emotions), you must (of your own free will) come to Jesus—repent of your wrongdoings, go to church weekly, attend a small church group weekly, pray, fast, and read your Bible. You will more and more each day have the mind of Christ when you do these things. The passage in 1 Corinthians 2:16 (KJV) says,

> For who hath known the mind of the Lord, that he may instruct him? But we have the mind of Christ.

I'm telling you these things because it's possible when you are seeking faith as a new Believer or a young Believer that you may get hurt or lose your trust in the process because of some of the hypocrisy which exists in society and the world—and yes, even in the Church.

Please understand that God is not a hypocrite, and the Church is not a hypocrite, but human beings can be hypocrites when they say they believe one thing and do another. Keeping your eyes focused on God and Jesus will help you avoid any dual-mindedness. James 4:8 (KJV) says,

> Draw nigh to God, and he will draw nigh to you. Cleanse your hands, ye sinners; and purify your hearts, ye double minded.

There may be things other Christian Church members do or maybe even wrongdoing by a priest, pastor, bishop, elder, reverend, etc., which may make you question the Christian faith. But remember that being a born-again Christian is based on a personal relationship with Jesus Christ. History shows that humans will fail miserably, especially on an eternal platform—without faith and belief in the one true God.

Always remember that God is our Almighty God, and humans with free will make mistakes. So, just pray for people who make mistakes because we all make mistakes. Ask the Holy Spirit to lead you to the true Christian Church, which you can consider your home church. With regular fellowship, Bible study, and being involved in Christian ministries, your faith and walk with God and Jesus will grow into a mature walk with the Lord.

Keep your eyes focused on God and look straight ahead—do not be drawn to the right or the left of the narrow path, or down—or you may get hurt (Ephesians 6:12). Without the full armor of God (Ephesians 6:13) through demonic powers, satan may be able to put thoughts into your mind, but satan can never read your mind or know and figure out everything about you if you give your life to Jesus and put on the full armor of God. When we walk hand in hand with God, we will hear our Lord, which will sound like a voice behind us, whether we look to the right or to the left (Isaiah 30:21).

The Full Armor of God

The armor of God, found in Ephesians 6:10–18, is made up of the following six items:

1. Belt of truth
2. Breastplate of righteousness
3. Shoes of the gospel
4. Shield of faith
5. Helmet of salvation

6. Sword of the spirit[92]

Without the full armor of God, satan will tempt you with drugs, alcohol, food or overeating, smoking, adultery, an affair, and many other things. Satan is the earthly lion, waiting for a lonely animal (you) to break away from the pack, i.e., your church, your small group, your youth group, etc. The enemy of our souls wants to separate you by yourself in the desert or a lonely highway or byway when you are the most vulnerable and weakest.

Your three enemies are some things seen and some things unseen:

1. The World

a. Our Lord said that the world would hate Him and hate Christians (John 15:18–21).

2. Our Flesh

a. "So then they that are in the flesh cannot please God" (Romans 8:8 KJV).

3. Satan

a. He is first mentioned in the Old Testament in Genesis 3:10 when the Serpent deceived Eve. In the New Testament, Jesus states that He saw satan fall like lightning from heaven (Luke 10:18).

92 "Armor of God: What Is It?" Bibleinfo.com., 2022, https://www.bibleinfo.com/en/questions/armor-of-god#shield.

Understanding the Power of Prayer, Being Humbled by Fasting and Fasting

It is so very critical to understand the power of prayer, be humbled by fasting, and allow God to move through your prayer and fast. Remember, not having something to eat is not fasting, *but having something to eat and drink and choosing not to partake of it for a spiritual outcome is fasting.*

- Matthew 17:21
- 2 Corinthians 6:4–5, 7:14
- Mark 8:29
- Acts 13:1–4, 14:21–22
- Isaiah 58
- Joel 2:12
- Philippians 1:6

The first question you might have is, can God talk to you today, *even if you're unsure whether you're a true Christian or not or if you feel you aren't special enough for God to notice?*

The answer is yes. God will talk to anyone that seeks Him.

- Jeremiah 29:11–13
- Psalms 66:19, 145:18–19
- 1 Peter 3:12
- 1 Kings 19:11–13
- Hebrew 4:12

God will answer you through His Holy Spirit as you read the Bible and earnestly seek His Word. God will also answer you when you attend church and small groups. God will also answer you through friends or circumstances. God can answer you in a small or soft, still voice in your spirit (1 Kings 19:11–13). God can use anything from a dream to a vision to a person, place, or thing. God can use anything He feels will capture your attention!

Let's lay the foundation before we build the house. I mentioned earlier in this book that God gave us or created us in three parts.

First, you have a *body* (blood, flesh, and bones, which equals a physical death). When you die, this is your *physical* death (Proverbs 2:18). When your body is dead, it decomposes or is cremated, but your spirit and soul are eternal.

Second, your *soul* (will, mind, and emotions, which equals a spiritual death) are the main characteristics or parts of who you are as an individual. Still, out of these three parts come arrogance, pride, selfishness, carnal ways, satan's ways, worldly ways, etc. (Romans 8:58).

Third, you have a *spirit* (conscience, communion, and wisdom equals an eternal death). As *heartfelt* Christians who accepted Jesus Christ as their Savior, they would immediately go to Heaven upon their last breath on earth. I believe that the Angels of the Lord are assigned to come and take your spirit and soul to Heaven.

If you haven't accepted Jesus Christ as your Lord and Savior before your physical death, your spirit and soul are claimed by the enemy of our souls, satan, and his unholy angels come to fetch you, and you will spend eternal life in Hell, from which there is no escape.

Here is a summary to explain the parts of your spirit (Revelation 20).

1. Conscience—we were created in God's image, which is why satan (antichrist, false prophet, satan's fallen angels) hates true Christians and wants to destroy us! Our conscience is in our DNA from God. At a young age and more so as an adult, we know when we lie, steal, and when we are doing something wrong.

   Three Parts of the Human Person—Summary

   This concept of the three parts of the human person is so critical to understand that your soul and spirit go on for eternity in Heaven or Hell. I am taking this time to reiterate and summarize what is an all-important, radical, life-changing principle.

   Again, each human being is comprised of three parts:

   a. Body—blood, bones, and flesh equals a physical death.
   b. Soul—will, mind, and emotions (pride, arrogance, vainness) equals a spiritual death.
   c. Spirit—conscience, communion, and wisdom equals an eternal death.

   The Human Conscience

   The *human conscience* can be thought of as an "inner voice" through which the Holy Spirit communicates (2 Kings 19:11). Satan copies the Holy Spirit in a counterfeit approach to Persuade people to listen to his voice in our conscience rather than the Holy Spirit's (God) voice.

   a. **Good Conscience** (2 Corinthians 6)—This is a person with a clean and healthy conscience of God. Their thoughts are honed by the fruit of the Spirit (Galatians 5:21–22), and human thoughts come from various things, such as emotion or experience. They feel at peace in their spirit and soul and experience the joy of God (Nehemiah 8:10), not wanting to harm anyone. They forgive and love everyone.

b. **The "Blinded" Conscience**—persons who commit sins worse than the other person, but they point out and admonish others for their sin. These people see the speck in the other person's eye but not the plank in their own eyes (Matthew 7:3–5).

   People with a "blinded conscience" will admonish other people for lying, adultery, stealing, gossiping, etc., but they continue to do some of these things themselves. They have no conviction of Christ, no grace for mankind, or understanding of God's mercy. People with a blinded conscience don't know how to keep their conversation right with the Holy Spirit. Instead, their opinion is always right.

c. **Defiled Conscience** (2 Corinthians 7:1)—They are vain, arrogant, prideful, and rebellious, it's all about them, and they really don't care about you.

d. **Evil Conscience**—They don't forgive others easily or at all, they have thoughts of evil, they want to kill or hurt someone, they don't trust anyone, they are very jealous, and they aren't afraid of taking someone's wife or husband. They have a hard time keeping their minds pure or holy and have difficulty speaking words of love, comfort, joy, exhortation, admiration, or praise.

What's the Remedy for Other than a Good Conscience?

The answer is simple. One must repent and take control of every thought going into their mind, soul, and conscience. For example, consider and take note of the way you may look at the opposite sex (lust), money (greed), pride (ego), and arrogance (self-importance; also egotism). With a pure conscience and spirit, you will be free from satan's demonic bondage and gain intimacy with God, Jesus Christ, and the Holy Spirit (our Triune God). You will no longer have "a wall up" or have a spirit or soul blocked from hearing God's voice. God has a plan for you in your earthly walk and for your life (Jeremiah 29:11). An example is like a glass of dirty water; you can't see through to the other side of the glass. However, if the water (which represents your mind and conscience through the Holy Spirit) is clear and clean, sin is eliminated through Christ. You will then be able to communicate more effectively with God, Christ, and the Holy Spirit. Then you will receive your spiritual inheritance in Heaven for all eternity. Also, out of your soul are your emotions which can bear fruit.

> But the fruit of the spirit is love, joy, peace, patience, kindness, goodness, faithfulness, gentleness, self-control.
>
> (Galatians 5:22–24 ESV)

2. Communion—we must have communion with Jesus every waking moment of the day. Not only taking un-

leavened bread and grape juice or wine when you take communion with the Church, but when we pray and talk with Jesus, fast, read the Bible (daily), go to church consistently, join a small group, and having the fruit of the spirit are all considered communion with God.

When you open your Bible on a daily basis and dig deeper into the Word of God, the Holy Spirit will draw you near and dear to Him, and you will begin to bear much fruit. You will desire to surround yourself with other Believers and fellowship with them, join or start a ministry, and in doing so, you may find that you are, in effect, dedicating your life to the Kingdom of God.

> But the fruit of the Spirit is love, joy, peace, longsuffering, gentleness, goodness, faith, Meekness, temperance: against such there is no law.
> (Galatians 5:22–23 KJV)

Jesus wants a personal relationship with you, much like you have a personal relationship with a family member, best friend, co-worker, etc. It's not about *just playing the game*. For instance, if your spouse, parents, or boyfriend or girlfriend are forcing you to attend church, your attendance may not be based on what's in your heart. Jesus wants a one-on-one relationship with you, and this relationship is authentic and comes from the heart and soul. Religion and church are important institutions, but a *personal relationship* with Jesus is the key to Heaven and what Jesus desires with you. Following what Jesus asks you to do out of obedience and love for Him is the free will response that Jesus recognizes when a person follows Him.

Remember, satan doesn't care about you at all. He wants you to *doubt* Jesus, *deny* the Bible and Jesus, and *disobey* God and the Word of God.

3. Wisdom—by humbling yourself through fasting, praying on your knees, reading the Bible daily (at least one or two pages), going to church, reading other true Christian books or magazines, attending a small weekly group, paying your 10% tithe, playing Christian music in your home, car, or workplace, and living according to how the Bible says to live and act. You will gain godly wisdom in the choices you make in your life.

   Always remember to do things out of love!

4. When we pray or talk to God, the Holy Spirit, or Jesus Christ, it doesn't matter which person of the Godhead you pray to—the trinity or Godhead acts as one. They see all, know all, and can be in many places at a time around the world. In contrast, satan can only be one place at a time.

   When you pray, you must bring the things you are praying for with a *humble* spirit. God is constantly searching the earth for the right heart, which is a *contrite and humble spirit* (Isaiah 57:15). To have a contrite spirit is to feel or express remorse or penitence. The Bible verse in 2 Chronicles 7:14 (KJV) says,

> If my people, which are called by my name, shall humble themselves, and pray, and seek my face, and turn from their wicked ways; then will I hear from heaven, and will forgive their sin, and will heal their land.

> Your old men shall dream dreams, your young men shall see visions.
>
> (Joel 2:28 KJV)

The prophet Joel, son of Pethuel, is the author of the *Book of Joel*. The book was written from Jerusalem between BC 835–796 to the people of Israel and *all later readers of the Bible*. Read Joel 2:14–28 to see how God speaks through the prophets who lived hundreds of years *before Christ* and even now in the 21st Century.

> Who knoweth if he will return and repent, and leave a blessing behind him; even a meat offering and a drink offering unto the LORD your God? Blow the trumpet in Zion, sanctify a fast, call a solemn assembly:
> Gather the people, sanctify the congregation, assemble the elders, gather the children, and those that suck the breasts: let the bridegroom go forth of his chamber, and the bride out of her closet.

Let the priests, the ministers of the LORD, weep between the porch and the altar, and let them say, Spare thy people, O LORD, and give not thine heritage to reproach, that the heathen should rule over them: wherefore should they say among the people, Where is their God?
Then will the LORD be jealous for his land, and pity his people.
Yea, the LORD will answer and say unto his people, Behold, I will send you corn, and wine, and oil, and ye shall be satisfied therewith: and I will no more make you a reproach among the heathen:
But I will remove far off from you the northern army, and will drive him into a land barren and desolate, with his face toward the east sea, and his hinder part toward the utmost sea, and his stink shall come up, and his ill savour shall come up, because he hath done great things.
Fear not, O land; be glad and rejoice: for the LORD will do great things.
Be not afraid, ye beasts of the field: for the pastures of the wilderness do spring, for the tree beareth her fruit, the fig tree and the vine do yield their strength.
Be glad then, ye children of Zion, and rejoice in the LORD your God: for he hath given you the former rain moderately, and he will cause to

> come down for you the rain, the former rain, and the latter rain in the first month.
>
> And the floors shall be full of wheat, and the vats shall overflow with wine and oil. And I will restore to you the years that the locust hath eaten, the cankerworm, and the caterpillar, and the palmerworm, my great army which I sent among you.
>
> And ye shall eat in plenty, and be satisfied, and praise the name of the LORD your God, that hath dealt wondrously with you: and my people shall never be ashamed.
>
> And ye shall know that I am in the midst of Israel, and that I am the LORD your God, and none else: and my people shall never be ashamed.
>
> And it shall come to pass afterward, that I will pour out my spirit upon all flesh; and your sons and your daughters shall prophesy, your old men shall dream dreams, your young men shall see visions:

Four Things to Include in Your Prayer and Fasting

If you do these four things, God promises He will also do something for you!

1. Humble yourself by fasting until you have a humble and contrite heart and spirit.
2. Pray with a humble and innocent heart and mind. No hidden agendas or get-rich schemes or anything going against the Bible.

3. Seek Jesus and show Him your love for Him as your Lord and Savior and for dying on the cross for you. Yes, You!
4. Repent or turn away from your sins. Sins may include things such as unforgiveness, hate, lust, adultery, lying, stealing, robbing, alcohol abuse, drug abuse (both legal and illegal drugs), crimes, etc.

Along with these four elements of being *humble, praying, seeking Jesus,* and *repentance*, God desires a relationship with you. Yes, a personal relationship—twenty-four/seven. Yes, I said—*God promises* that if you do these four things above, He will do at least three things for you which have eternal significance. These are the three things God promises to do for you if you do the four things above by prayer and fasting:

1. God will listen to you because of your true humbled heart and prayer and fasting for the right reasons. God will answer your prayers and fasting in His time, not yours.
2. God will forgive you of your sins. When you come before the Lord with a repentant heart, it doesn't matter if you went to prison or have done something really bad in the past.
3. God will heal the land, your house, and your family, and yes, He will heal you, too!

Fasting

As you pray, you must get rid of your *pride*—remember, pride comes from your soul. God says you have not because you ask not (1 Peter 3:15)! Ask God; He is waiting on you. God is a gentleman and will not force or push you to talk to Him in prayer or seek Him. You must want to do it (1 Peter 3:15).

Read these verses and discover or be reminded that God tells us how to pray and humble ourselves and that we will be persecuted for our faith in many ways.

> And when you pray, do not be like the hypocrites, for they love to pray standing in the synagogues and on the street corners to be seen by others. Truly I tell you, they have received their reward in full. But when you pray, go into your room, close the door and pray to your Father, who is unseen. Then your Father, who sees what is done in secret, will reward you.
>
> (Matthew 6:5–6 NIV)

> Humble yourselves, therefore, under God's mighty hand, that he may lift you up in due time.
>
> (1 Peter 5:6 NIV)

> Grieve, mourn and wail. Change your laughter to mourning and your joy to gloom. Humble yourselves before the Lord, and he will lift you up.
>
> (James 4:9–10 NIV)

> They mourned and wept and fasted till evening for Saul and his son Jonathan, and for the army of the LORD and for the nation of Israel, because they had fallen by the sword.
>
> (2 Samuel 1:12 NIV)

> Do not deprive each other except perhaps by mutual consent and for a time, so that you may devote yourselves to prayer. Then come together again so that Satan will not tempt you because of your lack of self-control.
>
> (1 Corinthians 7:5 NIV)

Why Fast?

Because by fasting and denying our body of food, water, TV, internet, or something else. We take away something that gives us pleasure or joy, and in the case of food or water, fasting humbles us. God is seeking a humbled heart in you.

You can decide to fast once a week, once a month, or whenever for however many days. What's important is what is in your heart and the reason why you are making a choice to fast.

As I travel around the world, I will fast for three days in each location or country for its people. For example, I will fast for the people of Japan, the Philippines, Canada, etc. (Leviticus 16:29–31).

The Lord expects us (you) to pray daily. Some people pray once a day, and some pray as needed, but daily. Some pray many times a day. For me, I pray daily, and if an issue or problem pops up, I pray on that! Here is a list of items for which I pray...

1. I pray for the second coming of Jesus Christ. We are in the "Church Age" right now. The next step is the "rapture" of God's Christian people that received Jesus Christ as their Lord and Savior. Sorry, not one single cult mem-

ber, leader, etc., will be in the *Book of Life*! You will not be allowed in Heaven but Hell for eternity!

2. I pray for all missionaries around the world. Originally there were no missionaries but apostles and elders that built the original Christian Churches. I pray for their safety and finances and that they will lead people to Christ.
3. I pray for my calling as an "End-Time Apostle" that the Lord will give me the wisdom and strength to do what He has called me to do in these last days around the world. The Lord has already shown me somewhere along my travels or missions that I will lose my life. I don't pray against that, I embrace it, and when the Lord is ready to take me, I am 100% ready to go.
4. I pray for Pastor Seiya in Japan that God will bless him and his team to plant thousands of home churches all over Japan and that he has the finances needed.
5. I pray for Israel and its people, its government, its military, and most importantly, the salvation of the Jews.
6. I pray for the Fivefold ministries around the world—The apostles, prophets, pastors, evangelists, and teachers of the gospel that they will touch people all over the world for Jesus.
7. I pray for the healing ministries that God will raise more people like Kathryn Kulman to bring healing to the world.
8. I pray for my repentance as a sinner so that I can stand on God's grace for my life.
9. I pray for my family members and friends.

10. I pray for my enemies.
11. I pray for the books I am working on and the people and companies associated.
12. I pray for the USA militarily and government.
13. I pray for other private things.

Please read the following verses which correlate to prayer and fasting:

- 1 Kings 21:9
- Acts 13:3, 27:9
- Isaiah 58:4–5
- Esther 4:16
- Mark 2:18

- 1 Kings 21:9
- Acts 13:3, 27:9
- Isaiah 58:4–5
- Esther 4:16
- Mark 2:18

You can also do corporate prayer and fasting as a group, as a family, as a husband and wife, as a church, as a ministry, as a business, etc. (Acts 13:1–4).

Prayer and Fasting

Prayer, praying, and prayerful fasting are akin to a foundation you pour before building a house (army). You and your team must be in alignment with the Holy Spirit and always be guided by the Holy Spirit, twenty-four-seven. We can also ask God for dreams in our sleep and visions (Acts. 2:17).

As I travel the world, I must humble myself by fasting and praying and seeking the Holy Spirit's direction for a particular group of people or nation—not my will be done, but yours, Lord! I will not move until I find out what God wants to do in that city, state, province, or country.

God's Grace Over My Calling

By God's grace, in March of 2018, I was in Israel on tour with Matt and Laurie Crouch (TBN Family), and 2,000 plus people gathered from Joseph Prince's Megachurch (josephprince.org) and Joel Osteen's Megachurch (joeosteem.com) as well. This was such an incredible blessing and miracle for a guy from Honolulu, Hawaii, to be there in Israel! God is good!

I learned while there that a Jewish male and female sign a contract when they want to get married. The bridegroom waits until they are close to the wedding date, and then he goes to the bride's home and blows the shofar at any time of the day or night. It could be at midnight or at any given time. The bride has little idea of when the bridegroom will blow his shofar and so you can imagine that she must have everything packed to leave at any given time. The Groom has already prepared a place for them to live in his parent's house, or the Groom has built, purchased, or rented a new home for their life as a married couple.

After the Groom picks up the Bride (without her knowing in advance the day or time), the couple celebrates for seven days and then has their wedding ceremony and celebration. Jesus gives us an example of this in a parable of Heaven, contained in Matthew 25 (NIV):

> At that time the kingdom of heaven will be like ten virgins who took their lamps and went out to meet the bridegroom. Five of them were foolish and five were wise. The foolish ones took their lamps but did not take any oil with them. The wise ones, however,

> took oil in jars along with their lamps. The bridegroom was a long time in coming, and they all became drowsy and fell asleep.
>
> At midnight the cry rang out: "Here's the bridegroom! Come out to meet him!"
>
> Then all the virgins woke up and trimmed their lamps. The foolish ones said to the wise, "Give us some of your oil; our lamps are going out."
>
> "No," they replied, "there may not be enough for both us and you. Instead, go to those who sell oil and buy some for yourselves."
>
> But while they were on their way to buy the oil, the bridegroom arrived. The virgins who were ready went in with him to the wedding banquet. And the door was shut.
>
> Later the others also came. "Lord, Lord," they said, "open the door for us!"
>
> But he replied, "Truly I tell you, I don't know you."
>
> Therefore keep watch, because you do not know the day or the hour.

Let me break this Matthew 25 parable down for you.

The number "10" means *judgment* or *completion* or *wholeness* in Biblical numerology (I mean, the number representing judgment, completion, or wholeness could have been 2, 4, 6, 9, etc. —but why 10?).

Jesus Christ is the "Bridegroom," and the true Christian Church is the "Bride". Therefore, the number "10" represents *all the true Christians* on earth today or in the world at any given time. We are in the "Church Age," and soon—any day now, Jesus (Groom) will rapture His true Christian Church (Bride) to reign with Him in Heaven (1 Thessalonians 4:17; 1 Corinthians 15:52).

The number "5" represents *grace*. Notice there are five virgins who are ready with their oil lamps and five virgins who leave to go get oil for their lamps. The oil in the lamps represents blessings and is used for anointing and blessing people. In Israel, olive oil is characterized by its sweet fragrance.

The five who are ready represent the Christians that are ready. The five virgins who left and came back only to find that the door was shut represent those who are Christians but were not ready at the time of the *rapture*.

We don't know why half of the Church or Christians on earth weren't ready. The parable doesn't say. Is it because they didn't read their Bible or lacked a relationship with Jesus Christ? Were they lazy, and did they forget or neglect to pay their tithing? Was there double-mindedness in their walk with the Lord? Did these Christians not share the gospel with others? We just don't know why they were left out or left behind—but this poses questions for all of us who might wonder whether we're ready to be raptured at any given time.

It is a sobering thought, indeed, that our loved ones could be left behind to face the "tribulation". I wonder how much more effort it would take to invite our neighbors, friends, relatives, and associates to church... That one invitation could be the road to salvation, and as one grows into a mature Christian, one should always strive to be ready for Jesus when He comes back to get us.

The Bible is like a life instruction manual. As Christians, we read the Word for inspiration, instructions on how to live, what we should stay away from, and repentance of our sins—but mostly about God's amazing love, grace, and provision for us. God has given us free will to choose to love and obey Him.

You may have noticed on the back cover of this book that there is a photo of me blowing a *shofar* (ram's horn) from Israel. As the End-Time Apostle to the World, the triune God (Father, Son, and Holy Spirit) is sending me to present to you and all who read my books a warning.

The warning is the same as that of the parable in Matthew 25. Jesus is coming back soon—any day now—and we need to be ready like the five virgins who had their oil lamps filled and the wicks trimmed, ready to light their lamps at the wedding banquet.

The Question Remains: Are You Ready?

Are you fulfilling God's calling in your life (Jeremiah 29:11)?

Are you part of a Fivefold Army at the present time?

If you are not part of a Fivefold Army operating in the gift of apostle, prophet, evangelist, pastor, or teacher—and you would like to become part of this army of the Lord, let me show you how.

Baptism of the Holy Spirit

When you are baptized by a true Christian Church disciple, pastor, bishop, reverend, apostle, evangelist, teacher, priest, etc., with the proper authority in a pool, ocean, under a shower, etc., you will become *born again*. Your *old self* died! Your *new* self just became clean by the *Holy Spirit*!

Baptism erases your past but not your future. Remember—before baptism, you must do the following:

1. **Confess that you are a sinner and in need of a Savior.** (Say in your heart, "I know I did this or thought that..."
2. **Repent**—put right what you are doing wrong (i.e., stop adultery, stealing, lying, drunkenness, etc.). Baptism is for the *dirty* and burial for the *dead*. When you come out of the water (*immersion*), you emerge *clean* and *born again*, and when you are baptized in the name of the Father, the Son, and the Holy Spirit, *you are a new creature in Christ* (2 Corinthians 5:17).

There are two types of baptisms:

1. **Water baptism** (repentance of sins)—Jesus was perfect and sinless, and yet He was baptized by John the Baptist to set an example for all of us who would decide to follow Him and accept Jesus as our Lord and Savior.
2. **Baptism of the Holy Spirit**—The Holy Spirit is the third person of the Godhead, which only manifested after Jesus was crucified, rose from the dead, and ascended to Heaven. Jesus said He would send His Comforter.

> And I will pray the Father, and he shall give you another Comforter, that he may abide with you for ever; Even the Spirit of truth; whom the world cannot receive, because it seeth him not, neither knoweth him: but ye know him; for he dwelleth with you, and shall be in you. I will not leave you comfortless: I will come to you.
>
> (John 14:16–18 KJV)

Speaking in tongues is the gift of the Holy Spirit, and if you ask God, He will give you this gift (Acts 2:1–4).

> And when the day of Pentecost was fully come, they were all with one accord in one place. And suddenly there came a sound from heaven as of a rushing mighty wind, and it filled all the house where they were sitting. And there appeared unto them cloven tongues like as of fire, and it sat upon each of them. And they were all filled with the Holy Ghost, and began to speak with other tongues, as the Spirit gave them utterance.
>
> (Acts 2:1–4 KJV)

A Simple Gospel Message

> The word *gospel* means "good news," which is the message of forgiveness for sin through the atoning work of Jesus Christ. It is essentially God's rescue plan of redemption for those who will trust in His divine Son to be reconciled to a just and holy God. The essential content of this saving message is clearly laid out for us in the Bible. In the apostle Paul's first letter to the Corinthians, he lays out the content of the gospel message.
>
> "Now, brothers and sisters, I want to remind you of the gospel I preached to you, which you received and on which you have taken your stand. By this gospel you are saved, if you hold firmly to the Word

I preached to you. Otherwise, you have believed in vain. For what I received I passed on to you as of first importance: that Christ died for our sins according to the Scriptures, that he was buried, that he was raised on the third day according to the Scriptures" (1 Corinthians 15:1–4 NIV).

In this passage, we see three essential elements of the gospel message. First, the phrase "died for our sins" is very important. As Romans 3:23 (NIV) tells us, "For all have sinned and fall short of the glory of God." The reality of sin needs to be acknowledged by all who approach the throne of God for salvation. A sinner must acknowledge the hopelessness of his guilt before God for forgiveness to take place, and he must understand that the "wages of sin is death" (Romans 6:23 NIV). Without this foundational truth, no gospel presentation is complete.

Second, the person and work of Christ are indispensable components of the gospel. Jesus is God (Colossians 2:9) and man (John 1:14). Jesus lived the sinless life that we could never live (1 Peter 2:22), and because of that, He is the only one who could die a substitutionary death for the sinner. Sin against an infinite God requires an infinite sacrifice. Therefore, either man, who is finite, must pay the penalty for an infinite length of time in Hell, or the infinite Christ must pay for it once. Jesus went to the cross to pay the debt we owe to God for our sin, and those who are covered by His sacrifice will inherit the kingdom of God as sons of the king (John 1:12).

Third, the resurrection of Christ is an essential element of the gospel. The resurrection is proof of the power of God. Only He who created life can resurrect it after death, only He can reverse the hideousness that is death itself, and only He can remove the sting that is death and the victory over the grave.

(1 Corinthians 15:54–55).

Further, unlike all other religions, Christianity alone possesses a founder who transcends death and promises that His followers will do the same. All other religions were founded by men and prophets whose end was the grave.

Finally, Christ offers His salvation as a free gift (Romans 5:15; 6:23) that can only be received by faith, apart from any works or merit on our part (Ephesians 2:8–9). As the Apostle Paul tells us, the gospel is "...the power of God that brings salvation to everyone who believes: first to the Jew, then to the Gentile" (Romans 1:16 NIV).

The same inspired author tells us,

"If you declare with your mouth, 'Jesus is Lord,' and believe in your heart that God raised him from the dead, you will be saved" (Romans 10:9 NIV).

These, then, are the essential elements of the gospel: the sin of all men, the death of Christ on the cross to pay for those sins, the resurrection of Christ to provide life everlasting for those who follow Him, and the offer of the free gift of salvation to all.[93]

---

93 "What Are the Essentials of the Gospel Message?" Got Questions Ministries, 2022, https://www.gotquestions.org/gospel-message.html..

~ Salvation Prayer ~

Dear Father God, Creator of all of Heaven and Earth.

I am praying this prayer right now, out loud, in Jesus' Holy Name to ask for forgiveness of my sins. When I say Jesus' Name out loud, the enemy of my soul, satan, must flee from me.

My life has not been perfect or easy, but I understand by accepting Jesus Christ as my Lord and Savior right NOW; that when I pass from this earth, I will open my eyes in eternity with You in the Heavenly Places which You have prepared for those who believe in You.

I ask that You pour out Your Holy Spirit upon me and within me so that I will have a heart that yearns to know and understand Your Word, Will, and Way; and by Your Spirit, I shall understand Your nature as well as my own to draw closer and closer to You each day.

Your great commission is that every knee shall bow and every tongue shall confess that Jesus Christ is Lord, to the glory of the Father.

I submit this heartfelt prayer to You,
In Jesus' Holy and Powerful Name,
Amen!

God moves in a village, tribe, community, location, city, state, province, wherever He needs to be on this planet Earth, wherever there are people. God will move His Spirit among the people with signs, wonders, and miracles! Man moves people with ceremonies, rituals, and traditions—which sometimes douses God's movement of the Holy Spirit, much like water from a firehose will douse a fire and put it out.

The Holy Spirit Fire of the Lord is the kind of fire you want under your feet and surrounding you as much as possible in these times. If you are following your ways and not God's ways, please read Isaiah 55:8 and Romans 8:28.

Characteristics of Angels: Whom Are They and What Are Their Roles?

Consider what Psalm 8 says (KJV):

> O Lord, our Lord, how excellent is thy name in all the earth! who hast set thy glory above the heavens.
> Out of the mouth of babes and sucklings hast thou ordained strength because of thine enemies, that thou mightest still the enemy and the avenger.
> When I consider thy heavens, the work of thy fingers, the moon and the stars, which thou hast ordained;
> What is man, that thou art mindful of him? and the son of man, that thou visitest him? For thou hast made him a little lower than the angels, and hast crowned him with glory and honour.
> Thou madest him to have dominion over the works of thy hands; thou hast put all things under his feet:

All sheep and oxen, yea, and the beasts of the field;
The fowl of the air, and the fish of the sea, and whatsoever passeth through the paths of the seas.
O Lord our Lord, how excellent is thy name in all the earth!

About Angels

Angels are referred to 100 times in the Old Testament and 165 times in New Testament.

- Job 38:4–7—Angels are created by God.
- Psalms 148:2—Angels praise Him, all His heavenly hosts.
- Isaiah 6:2; 1 Thessalonians 4:16—Angels have ranks like military
- Jude 1:9; 1 Thessalonians 4:16—There is an archangel named Michael.
- Matthew 24:36; 1 Peter 1:12—Angels are not all-knowing and are not omniscient.
- Revelation 7:11–12—Angels continuously praise God.
- Isaiah 6:3—When the angels are before God, they hide their faces and cry.
- Matthew 22:30—Angels do not marry; humans will be like Angels in Heaven in the Resurrection.
- Genesis 18:2–8—Angels can take human form.
- Luke 15:10—Angels rejoice when a human is baptized, born again, and saved.
- Hebrews 1:4–5—Jesus is above angels.
- Genesis 19:3—Angels do eat.
- Luke 16:22—Angels take you to Heaven when you die.

- 1 Thessalonians 4:16; Deuteronomy 19—Angels will participate in the second coming of Jesus Christ.
- 1 Corinthians 11:9–10—Man was not created for woman, but woman for man. It is for this reason that a woman ought to have authority over her own head because of the angels.
- 2 Peter 2:11—Angels are greater in might and power.
- Revelation 8:1—Angels will be silenced for thirty minutes when the seventh seal is opened.
- 1 Corinthians 6:3—Angels will one day be judged by true Christians in Heaven. On earth, Angels are of a higher rank than humans.
- Matthew 26:53; Mark 5:9—How many Angels are there? A *legion* is 6,000 divided by ten *cohorts* divided by six *centuria*, which equals 72,000 (60 centurions/a centurion commands 100 men).
- Mark 12:25; Luke 20:36; Matthew 22:30—Angels do not marry.
- Psalms 34:7, 91:11–12—Angels guard you.
- Matthew 2:13—Angels can guide human believers to decisions and circumstances.
- 1 Corinthians 4:9; Ephesians 3:10—Angels only know what God reveals to them.
- Ezekiel 1:14; Daniel 9:21; Job 37:3—Angels travel 186,000 miles per second or at the *speed of light*.
- Hebrews 1:14—Angels can be sent by God to encourage you and answer your prayers.
- Jude 6; 2 Peter 2:4—Angels are capable of committing sin.

- Hebrews 1:13–14—Angels are ministering spirits to God's servants.
- Job 38:7—Angels sing for joy.
- Genesis 6:1–4—Angels can rebel against God.
- Exodus 25:18–22; Ezekiel 1:5–28—Cherubim is an Angel with a particular form.
- Isaiah 37:16—God is above Cherubim Angels.
- Isaiah 6:3—Seraphin has six wings and can take on human form.
- Nehemiah 9:6; Revelation 7:11Angels minister to God.
- Luke 2:13–14—Angels rejoice in God's work.
- Psalms 103:20; Daniel 6:23—Angels serve God.
- Luke 1:26—Angels deliver messages.
- Daniel 6:22–23—Angels protect people.
- Zechariah 1:9–11—Angels patrol the earth.
- 2 Kings 6:16—Angels fight evil.
- Hebrews 1:14—Angels are not all ministering Angels to help those humans in the inheritance of salvation.
- Acts 5:17–23—Angels go through doors or even prison doors!
- Mark 8:38; Revelation 14:10—Angels are called God's "holy angels," who do His bidding, not ours.
- Genesis 3:4; Revelation 12:4, 7–9, 9:11—Angels follow and work for satan.
- Matthew 18:10; Hebrews 1:13–14—Angels help Christians during their lifetime on earth.
- Hebrews 1:14, 2:7; 2 Samuel 4:17; 2 Peter 2:11; Psalms 103:20; 2 Thessalonians 1:7—Angels have superior intelligence, superior power.

Other Angels Scriptures

- Psalms 91:9–16, 104:4
- Hebrews 1:7, 13:2
- John 1:51
- Ephesians 3:10
- Revelation 7:1–2, 7:11, 9:15, 12:7
- Matthew 18:10, 26:53, 24:31
- Luke 20:35
- Exodus 33:1–2
- 2 Samuel 24:15
- 2 Kings 19:3
- Daniel 6:21

What an amazing journey to read about the characteristics of God the Father, Jesus the Son, and the Holy Spirit. Angels are mentioned throughout the Bible, and because angels are of a supernatural origin, humans on earth are fascinated about how they might engage with angels in God's plan for us.

As we go forward towards the end of the Church Age, we must keep in mind that the next ages to come are the Rapture of the true Christian Church, the Tribulation, the Great White Throne of Judgment, and the Millennial Reign. God will send more Angels to stand guard over His people and the countries He wishes to protect, and there are places on the globe which He may not choose to protect because the people have given themselves over to other gods. For example, Islam, Buddhism, Hinduism, and other cults. And soon, God will also use Angels to pour out judgments on the earth (Revelation 8:1).

In the next chapter, we will look at interesting historical and current themes emerging from the European Union, NATO, United Nations, and related organizations on the world stage;

and how these current events are playing into the prophecies of Ezekiel 38 and 39.

It is my hope that after you've read this book, you will realize that Jesus is the only ***way***, ***truth***, and ***light*** and that you will make a decision to receive Christ as your Lord and Savior.

CHAPTER 11

What's Up with Russia and the EU?

It is amazing to study the characteristics of God, Jesus, the Holy Spirit, and angels. However, what about today? What is going on today, and how do we see God working and using His personality to prepare us and the world for the final end game? What events are happing right now that affect our future as Christians and non-believers? Over the next few chapters, you will find the answers to these questions and more.

As I am writing this chapter in 2022, I would like to pose another question to you. "Why is the invasion of Ukraine by Russia so very significant?"

The answer: If Russia successfully takes control of Ukraine, this will divide the Orthodox Churches as the Ukrainian Orthodox Church claims to be the true church for the Ukrainian people. Baptists in Western Ukraine are preparing to shelter fellow believers in the event of a Russian invasion at the easter border. "Prayer is our spiritual weapon, said Igor Bandura, Vice President of the Baptist Union of Ukraine. "God can undo what the politicians are planning."[94]

94 "On Ukraine-Russia Border, Baptists and Pentecostals Endure as Invasion Looms," BCNN1 WP, 2022, https://bcnn1wp.wordpress.com/2022/01/05/on-ukraine-russia-border-baptists-and-pentecostals-endure-as-invasion-looms/.

Companies all over the world will be sanctioning Russia from sports events, banking, supplies, etc. The headline news for February 27, 2022, in Hawaii, read:

The world is reacting to Russian President Vladimir Putin's new invasion of eastern Ukraine as Western nations try to forestall a winder invasion.[95]

Putin has made it very clear that his reason for the war on Ukraine goes far beyond the NATO issue. He opposes Ukraine's efforts to draw closer to Western Europe in any fashion. The United Nations confirmed at least 240 civilian casualties from the fighting, including thousands of people having been wounded and thirty-three children.[96]

Ukraine is the largest land mass or country next to Russia—603,550 square kilometers, including 44 million people, with a GDP of $195 billion.[97] Russia's invasion and warfare of Ukraine give Russia more of the Eastern Europe territories. What countries will Putin go after next?

Russia has 100,000 to 200,000 military boots on the ground, compared to Ukraine's military troops of 30,000–40,000.[98] As of March 2022, the United States and other nations are sending Ukraine weapons, food, and other supplies—but to date, no

---

95 Emily Cristobal, "With Loved Ones Stuck in Ukraine, Maui Residents Call for an End to the War,." HawaiiNewsNow, 2022, https://www.hawaiinewsnow.com/2022/02/27/with-loved-ones-stuck-ukraine-maui-residents-call-an-end-war/.

96 Michael Shields, "U.N. Reports at Least 240 Civilian Casualties, 64 Deaths in Ukraine," Reuters, 2022, https://www.reuters.com/world/europe/un-reports-least-240-civilian-casualties-64-deaths-ukraine-2022-02-27/.

97 Lexi Lonas, "10 Things to Know about Ukraine," The Hill, 2022, https://thehill.com/policy/international/596722-10-things-to-know-about-ukraine/.

98 "More than 100,000 Russian Troops Placed on Ukraine's Borders, YouTube: Voice of America, 2022, https://www.youtube.com/watch?v=qjyCjxSIcuM.

human troops are being sent. Fifty-five years have passed since Russia had planned to attack Israel in June of 1967. If it were not for U.S. President Johnson putting a stop to Putin's plans, there might have been a war on Israel as recently as 1967. Why did Johnson put a stop to Putin's plans? Because President Johnson was a godly man. However, if the current president of the United States of America is not a godly man of virtue, Russia will see this weakness and be free to attack and destroy Israel.

We know from Bible prophecy that God Himself will defend Israel, and Israel will prevail, with the entire world watching and witnessing this end-game event. All glory and honor will belong to God alone, and at this time, millions will come to Christ. The end-time Christians will finally come to Christ, not because of an enduring faith but because they have seen with their very own eyes the miracles and power of God Himself.

During the end-time events, Revelation 13:3–4 states the antichrist will be shot in the head, but he will not die because of demonic powers, and he will obtain healing from the false prophet. The antichrist will tell everyone that he is actually God or Jesus, or the Savior (2 Corinthians 11:14). The antichrist wants to control all humans while Jesus gives you the freewill to follow Him. The antichrist will attempt to kill everyone who doesn't follow him with the *mark of 666* (*the mark of the beast*) and kill or cut off their heads (Daniel 8:24; 2; Revelation 20:4). The antichrist will set up an office in the third temple to be built in Jerusalem.

The Bronze Statue in Daniel 2:32–42

Who were the countries mentioned in the bronze statue in Daniel's vision? Babylon (fell to the Medes and Persians), Persia, Greece (successor to the Medo-Persian Empire), and Rome ("iron" empire").

Who is the clay/iron empire yet to come? Europe. The ten toes in Daniel's vision (Daniel 2:41–44) are described as partly iron/partly brittle (clay). The feet (ten toes) may represent the full number of nations in the end times. Iron represents civil power, and clay represents religious powers who claim God's authority. Iron and clay do not mix well, symbolic of the conflict between the government (antichrist spirit) and the Church and the persecution of the Church by the antichrist spirit in the end times.

It's critical to remember that the antichrist is a *counterfeit* of God and Christ. Many people will be deceived into thinking that he is the savior because they may have ignored the warning signs and the calling that the one true God has extended to them.

Alphabetical List of Countries of the European Union (EU) with Accession Dates

Country	EU Accession Date	Schengen Area Member	Eurozone Member
Austria	1/1/1995	Yes	Yes
Belgium	1/25/1957	Yes	Yes
Bulgaria	1/1/2007	No	No
Croatia	7/1/2013	No	No
Cyprus	5/1/2004	No	Yes
Czechia	5/1/2004	Yes	No
Denmark	1/1/1973	Yes	No

Estonia	1/1/1973	Yes	Yes
Finland	1/1/1995	Yes	Yes
France	3/25/1957	Yes	Yes
Germany	3/25/1957	Yes	Yes
Greece	1/1/1981	Yes	Yes
Hungary	5/1/2004	Yes	No
Ireland	1/1/1973	No	Yes
Italy	3/25/1957	Yes	Yes
Latvia	5/1/2004	Yes	Yes
Lithuania	5/1/2004	Yes	Yes
Luxembourg	3/25/1957	Yes	Yes
Malta	5/1/2004	Yes	Yes
Netherlands	3/25/1957	Yes	Yes
Poland	5/1/2004	Yes	No
Portugal	1/1/1986	Yes	Yes
Romania	1/1/2007	No	No
Slovakia	5/1/2004	Yes	Yes
Slovenia	5/1/2004	Yes	Yes
Spain	1/1/1986	Yes	Yes
Sweden	1/1/1995	Yes	No

List of Countries of the European Union (EU) with Accession Dates[99]

99 "List of 27 European Union Member Countries," Countries of the World.,2022, https://www.countries-ofthe-world.com/european-union-countries.html.

European Union Flag

European Union Flag[100]

The circle of stars in the European Union (EU) Flag represents the Queen of Heaven, a counterfeit to both the true queen and Heaven, mentioned in the chapter on Nimrod. The European Union flag comprises twelve golden stars on a blue background. Officially it is claimed that the circle of twelve stars represents *solidarity and harmony between the peoples of Europe*, the number twelve *denoting perfection, completeness, and unity* (in the Bible, twelve denotes *governmental perfection*).

> An alternative explanation is that the flag was inspired by the halo of 12 stars around the Catholic pictures of the Madonna and is an interpretation of Revelation 12:1. The Catholic Church claims that the woman in Revelation represents the Virgin Mary or "Mother of

100 © [Ricochet64] — adobestock.com

> God". In reality, Revelation 12:1 actually refers to the woman "Israel" and the 12 tribes of Israel.
> The European Union flag could therefore have strong Roman Catholic significance, and *ecclesiastical Babylon* could be Vatican-centered. The Bible supports this idea. For example, Revelation 17:9 says that the woman sits on seven mountains (ancient Rome was built on seven hills) and is clothed in purple and scarlet (Cardinals' dress in scarlet or red and Bishops' dress in purple).[101]

Consider that many individuals do not feel safe in their own country. When this happens, those people may seek asylum in another country in search of safety and protection. "In 2020, Germany had the highest number of accepted asylum seekers in Europe at over 128 thousand people, followed by Spain and France at 124 thousand and 86 thousand, respectively."[102]

CERN, which stands for European Council for Nuclear Research (translated from French) and is located on the Franco-Swiss border near Geneva, says in its mission statement that its "work helps to uncover what the universe is made of and how it works."[103] They do this by providing a unique range of particle accelerators to facilitate research to advance the boundaries of human knowledge.

---

101 "The European Union in Prophecy | Is the EU the Revived Roman Empire?" Seeking Truth, 2022, https://seekingtruth.co.uk/the-european-union-in-prophecy/.
102 "Asylum Grants in Europe 2020," Statista, 2022, https://www.statista.com/statistics/293350/asylum-grants-in-europe/.
103 "Our Mission | CERN," CERN, 2022, https://home.cern/about/who-we-are/our-mission.

In one sense, their work is discovering the mind of God because science often leads to the discovery of how things are things are created. However, the work of these scientists does not give credence to our Creator or God. In fact, just outside of its headquarters building sits an ancient statue of *Apollyon*, the goddess of destruction. According to Merriam-Webster, the definition of Apollyon is "*the angel of the bottomless pit in the Book of Revelation*."[104]

Is this just an interesting Greek name for a piece of artwork in front of the CERN building—or, again, is this a sign of the times? How many of us have actually looked up the definition of Apollyon and questioned why a statue of the same name would be placed in front of the building? One question leads to another.

Satan, in his craftiness, always tries to lie, deceive, and hide. Here the enemy's spirit is at work, disguised as an art form and in the name of science—scary stuff.

United Nations

There are currently 196 member countries of the United Nations. Of the world's 196 countries, there remain only two permanent non-member observer states: the Holy See (Vatican City) and Palestine.[105] Every member has equal representation in the UN General Assembly. The United Nations was created in 1945 following World War II. Its mission is to maintain international peace and security by preventing conflict mediating for nations in conflict and creating the condition to hold peace.

104 "Apollyon," Merriam-Webster Online Dictionary, Merriam-Webster, Incorporated, 2022, https://www.merriam-webster.com/dictionary/Apollyon.
105 Matt Rosenburg, "Non-Member Countries of the United Nations," ThoughtCo, 2020, https://www.thoughtco.com/non-members-of-the-united-nations-1435429.

The United Nations voted in 2021 to move forward against Israel in an "unprecedented' open-ended biased probe against Israel concerning the Gaza conflict, saying that the Israeli forces committed war crimes. This is completely demonic! Satan is moving to destroy Israel and the Jewish (Hebrew) people, and America (Christians). Since we (you) are heading to the *end game* or *end times* one can readily see that we are living out Ezekiel 38 and 39, Jeremiah 16:14–15, Luke 21:24, and Revelations 13:1–2.

Today through China's "Belt and Road Way" or "Belt Road Initiative" alliances, Russian alliances, and Islamic nations alliances, these demonic countries or nations are moving against God! Get Ready! You are in the end game—the end times are now, and there are certain things you can do to affect the eternal destiny of yourself and your family.

125 Countries Voting Against Israel

Afghanistan	Albania	Algeria
Andorra	Angola	Armenia
Austria	Azerbaijan	Bahrain
Bangladesh	Barbados	Belarus
Belgium	Belize	Bolivia - Plurinat
Botswana	Brazil	Brunei Darussalam
Bulgaria	Burkina Faso	Burundi
Cambodia	Cameroon	Central AFR Rep
Chad	Chile	China
Comoros	Congo	Costa Rica
Cote D'Ivoire	Cuba	Cyprus

Dem pr of Korea	Dem rep of Congo	Denmark
Djibouti	Dominica	Ecuador
Egypt	El Salvador	Eritrea
Estonia	Ethiopia	Finland
France	Gabon	Gambia
Germany	Ghana	Greece
Grenada	Guinea	Guinea - Bissau
Guyana	Iceland	India
Indonesia (currently has the highest Islamic population in the world. Soon, India will be number one)	Iran—Islamic VREP	Iraq
Ireland	Italy	Japan
Jordan	Kazakhstan	Kiribati
Kyrgyzstan	Lao PDR	Lebanon
Liberia	Libya	Liechtenstein
Lithuania	Luxembourg	Madagascar
Malaysia	Maldives	Mali
Malta	Mauritania	Mauritius
Monaco	Montenegro	Morocco
Mozambique	Namibia	Netherlands
New Zealand	Nicaragua	Niger
Nigeria	Norway	Oman

Pakistan	Papua New Guinea	Paraguay
Peru	Portugal	Qatar
Rep of Korea	Rep of Moldova	Russian Federation
Saint Vincent Gr.	Saudi Arabia	Serbia
Seychelles	Singapore	Slovenia
Somalia	South Africa	Spain
Sri Lanka	Sudan	Suriname
Sweden	Switzerland	Syrian Arab Republic
Tajikistan	Thailand	The FYR Macedonia
Tunisia	Turkey	Tuvalu
Uganda	United Arab Emirates	United Kingdom (England, Scotland, Wales and Northern Ireland) Notice in the End Game or End Times England won't stop Russia, Iran, and other countries from attacking Israel, and many ask why?
United Rep Tanza	Uruguay	Venezuela
Viet Nam	Zimbabwe	
	Abstention	

Antigua - Barbuda	Argentina	Australia (strong alliance with the USA, but Australia is becoming weak with China funding and politics)
Bahamas	Benin	Bhutan
Bosnia-Herzegovina	Canada (notice above USA is Canada and below USA is Mexico, of which both are voting to abstain? They both will follow the antichrist and false prophet in the "One World Government" coming soon to you!)	Croatia
Czech Republic	Dominican Rep	Equatorial Guinea
Fiji	Haiti	Hungary
Jamaica	Kiribati	Latvia
Lesotho	Mexico (see note Canada)	Panama

Paraguay	Philippines (notice Philippines is a very strong catholic country, yet they are NOT backing Israel, where Jesus Christ is from?)	Poland
Romania	Rwanda	Solomon Islands
South Sudan	Trinidad-Tobago	Tuvalu
Uganda	Vanuatu	
Opposed—9 countries:		Guatemala
Honduras	**ISRAEL (Apple of God's Eye! Any country or nation coming against Israel will be destroyed (Genesis 12:3)	Marshall Islands
Micronesia	Nauru	Palau

Togo	** UNITED STATES OF AMERICA (the land of the free and brave. The most giving nation on earth, now the USA has grown weak and will experience a financial collapse)	Cabo Verde
Cameroon	Central AFR Rep	Colombia
Dem Rep of Congo	El Salvador	Georgia
Guinea-Bissau	Kenya	Lithuania
Malawi	Mongolia	Myanmar
Rep of Moldova	Saint Kitts-Nevis	Saint Lucia
Samoa	San Marino	Sao Tome-Principe
Sierra Leone	Swaziland	The FYR Macedonia
Timor-Leste	Tonga	Zambia

The UN has a prayer room that is currently under lock and key. In the prayer room are dozens of prayer mats and a medium-sized black box, just like in Mecca, Saudi Arabia. According to the UN, the black box represents all the gods of the earth. Imagine praying to a black box when you can just pray to God.

Kaaba In Mecca, Saudi Arabia[106]

Photo of Kaaba, House of God, located in Mecca, Saudi Arabia. As a Muslim, you are to make a pilgrimage to this site at least once in your lifetime to visit the Kaabal and offer up your prayers.

More about the Kaaba and the Black Stone

"The Kaaba is a small stone building in the court of the Mosque at Mecca that contains a sacred black stone and is the goal of the Islamic pilgrimage and the point toward which Muslims turn in praying."[107]

"During a pilgrim's ritual, many tend to seek the black stone situated in the eastern corner of the Kaaba. While the black stone is thought to be whole, which can be seen placed in a sil-

106 © [Aviator70] — adobestock.com.
107 Allan Basuga, "Lesson 6 Islam," SlideShare, 2019, https://www.slideshare.net/AllanBasuga/lesson-6-islam-168855759.

ver encasement,"[108] it is comprised of eight small rocks but is molded together using Arabic frankincense.

Sketch of the Black Stone for Kaaba[109]

"Its significance is that it is the only surviving stone from the original structure built by Abraham and Ishmael. Muslims believe that Abraham (known as Ibrahim in the Islamic tradition) and his son, Ismail, constructed the Kaaba."[110]

The original city was called Becca, which eventually became Mecca. Today the Kaaba is considered the number one sacred place (besides the Dome of the Rock in Israel). Read about Tefillin in the Appendices section. Interestingly, the Kaaba resembles a large Tefillin. We can view this as another of satan's ploys throughout history to create a counterfeit of the real thing.

According to popular Islamic legend, the stone was given to Adam on his fall from paradise and was originally white but

108 "Describe the Kaaba What Is the Black Stone," Precious Link, 2022, https://www.precious-l.com/btvhtd/describe-the-kaaba-what-is-the-black-stone.
109 © [theblackrhino] — adobestock.com.
110 "Describe the Kaaba What Is the Black Stone," 2022.

has become black by absorbing the sins of the thousands of pilgrims who have kissed and touched it. The black stone is a rock set into the eastern corner of the Kaaba. When Abd al-Malik began construction on the Dome of the Rock (currently in Jerusalem), he did not have control of the Kaaba, the holiest shrine in Islam, which is located in Mecca.

Other Kingdoms

Libya became independent as a kingdom in 1951.[111] A bloodless military coup in 1969, initiated by a coalition led by Colonel Muammar Gaddafi, overthrew King Idris I and created a republic.[112] Among the fifteen most thriving economies in Africa, alongside South Africa, Nigeria, Algeria, Egypt, and Cameroon, Libya is home to the largest proven oil reserves in Africa.[113]

The current OPEC (Organization of the Petroleum Exporting Countries) members are Algeria, Angola, Equatorial Guinea, Gabo, Iran, Iraq, Kuwait, Libya, Nigeria, the Republic of the Congo, Saudi Arabia, the UAE (United Arab Emirates), and Venezuela.

Sudan has a population of 44.77 million, with 91% of Muslims practicing the Sunni tradition: 5.4% Christian and 2.8% folk religions.[114] Despite a government-led national dialogue

111 Wikipedia Contributors, "Libya." Wikipedia, The Free Encyclopedia, 2022, https://en.wikipedia.org/wiki/Libya#Independence,_Kingdom_and_Libya_under_Gaddafi_(1951–2011).

112 Ibid.

113 Jedrzej George Frynas and Manuel Paulo, "A New Scramble for African Oil? Historical, Political, and Business Perspectives," *African Affairs* 106 (423): 229–51, https://doi.org/10.1093/afraf/adl042.

114 "2019 Report on International Religious Freedom: Sudan," U.S. Department of State, 2020, https://www.state.gov/reports/2019-report-on-international-religious-freedom/sudan/.

in 2016, violence persists in Darfur and eastern Sudan despite peace-keeping missions via United Nations/African Union Darfur (UNAMID).[115]

The most significant narrative in terms of where we are today on the world map is that Libya, together with Sudan, *does not recognize Israel as a state*. This is essentially *denial* of what modern society recognizes and gives credence to their unfriendly and hateful views toward Israel.

In the *end game*, many Islamic Muslim groups such as FTO's Afghan Taliban, Abu Sayyaf Group (ASG) Itamas, Boko Haran, Al-Shabaab, and the Lord's Resistance Army (LRA) will come against Israel in an alliance to destroy God's people. These allied forces will not prevail against the "Apple of God's Eye," and God Himself will destroy any country or nation that comes against Israel.

115 Abdi Latif Dahir, "Fresh Violence in Darfur Adds to Sudan's Crises," The New York Times, 2021,https://www.nytimes.com/2021/11/26/world/africa/sudan-darfur-violence-protests.html.

CHAPTER 12

NATO and Its Significance

I have included this chapter because Israel has enjoyed a special relationship with NATO for over three decades and was the third country to gain non-NATO alliance status as early as 1989.[116]

Israel realizes that the Russian invasion of Ukraine has created an imbalance in the security order in Europe and that the European Union is facing a new dawn of minimizing conflict on the continent. Europe and NATO are now looking to the east to strengthen alliances.[117]

I believe that the antichrist and the false prophet will lead the world as a one-world government, one-world religion, and a one-world financial currency. Any nation or people who refuse to come under their leadership will be martyred for their Christian faith or receive the mark of the beast to suffer later the consequences of their soul and spirit not being able to enter the gates of Heaven.

---

116 Rina Bassist, "Israel Draws Closer to NATO," Al-Monitor: Independent, Trusted Coverage of the Middle East, 2022, https://www.al-monitor.com/originals/2022/06/israel-draws-closer-nato.

117 Ibid.

NATO—North Atlantic Treaty Organization

> The NATO headquarters are located in Brussels, Belgium, while the headquarters of Allied Command Operations is near Mons, Belgium. Since its founding, the admission of new member states has increased the alliance from the original twelve countries to twenty-nine.[118]

It is in the current events...

> Where we find fulfillment in Deuteronomy 33:17. God is surely referring to Israel's ambition to build and rule a global village, a world government, and pushing all the nations of the world together. Today, America works with other nations to build "permanent alliances" —military (e.g., NATO), economic (e.g., the IMF and the WTO), financial, cultural, educational, scientific, and technological (i.e., via the UN). America today aspires to lead a global village.[119]

Please refer to the following table to see the current members of NATO and its partner countries.

118 Gordon Skene, "Contemplating NATO - Worries Over Cold War - 1949 - Past Daily Reference Room – Past Daily: News, History, Music And An Enormous Sound Archive," Past Daily, 2019, https://pastdaily.com/2019/09/24/contemplating-nato-worries-over-cold-war-1949-past-daily-reference-room/.

119 "What the Bible Says about IMF," Bible Tools, 2022, https://www.bibletools.org/index.cfm/fuseaction/Topical.show/RTD/CGG/ID/9769/IMF.htm.

Member Countries of NATO		
Year	Country	Spending
1949	Belgium	
1949	Canada	$212.77 Billion
1949	Denmark	
1949	France	$477.05 Billion
1949	Iceland	
1949	Italy	$232.81 Billion
1949	Luxembourg	
1949	Netherlands	$113.76 Billion
1949	Norway	
1949	Portugal	
1949	United Kingdom	$655.27 Billion
1949	United States	$6.85 Trillion
1952	Greece	
1952	Turkey	$180 Billion
1955	Germany	$491.32 Billion
1982	Spain	$123.36 Billion
1999	Czech Republic	
1999	Hungary	
1999	Poland	$113.76 Billion
2004	Bulgaria	
2004	Estonia	
2004	Lativa	
2004	Lithuania	

2004	Romania	
2004	Slovakia	
2004	Slovenia	
2009	Albania	
2009	Croatia	
2017	Montenegro	
2020	North Macedonia	

Member Countries of NATO[120]

NATO's Global partners include Afghanistan, Australia, Colombia, Iraq, Japan, the Republic of Korea, Mongolia, New Zealand, and Pakistan. The antichrist and false prophet will be leading NATO in the end times, and those who refuse to follow the antichrist will be persecuted and destroyed.

> In 2014, in response to its aggressive actions in Ukraine, NATO suspended all practical cooperation with Russia. (...) This cooperation included projects that did deliver results over time, but their suspension has not undermined the security of the Alliance or our ability to counter challenges such as terrorism. (...) Since Russia began its aggressive actions against Ukraine, Russian officials have accused NATO of a series of threats and hostile actions.[121]

120 "NATO - Topic: NATO-Russia Relations: The Facts," NATO, 2022, https://www.nato.int/cps/sn/natohq/topics_111767.htm.
121 "NATO - Topic: NATO-Russia Relations: The Facts," 2022.

Remember, if Russia takes over Ukraine and no other countries come to Ukraine's aid, including the United States. Russia will feel more empowered to attack Israel for its many resources. Putin's outstanding tactics include lying and deception. Lies and deception come from the enemy of our souls—satan. Lying and deception also stem from human arrogance and pride. The major religion in Russia is Russian Orthodox, to which Putin is supposed to belong. However, over 21 million Muslims live in Russia.[122] One out of every ten Russians is Muslim. In the early 1990s, Russia had around 800 mosques, and today, Russia has over 7,000 mosques—which shows the tremendous growth of Muslims and the connection to the Middle East.[123]

Muslim populations in European countries in 2016 were comprised of 5.72 million Muslims in France, approximately 95 million Muslims in Germany, and 4.13 million Muslims in the United Kingdom.[124]

Collective Security Treaty Organization (CSTO) or Tashkent Pact or Tashkent Treaty

This organization is made up of Russia, Armenia, Belarus, Kazakhstan, Tajikistan, land Kyrgyzstan. Non-members are Ukraine, Uzbekistan, Turkmenistan, Georgia, and Azerbaijan. The CSTO was set up by Russia like a NATO group. However,

122 Himani Pant, "Russia's Demographic Trajectory: Dimensions and Implications," Observer Research Foundation (ORF), 2022, https://www.orfonline.org/research/russias-demographic-trajectory-dimensions-and-implications/.
123 "Russia Builds More than 8,000 Mosques, Islamic Schools in 20 Years," 2015, TASS, 2015. https://tass.com/society/821145.
124 D. Clark, "Muslim Populations in European Countries Statistic," Statista, 2020, https://www.statista.com/statistics/868409/muslim-populations-in-european-countries/.

these three Baltic States, Estonia, Latvia, and Lithuania, belong to NATO.

Financial Debt Crisis Soon

We are warned through reliable resources financial crisis is coming soon, which will lead to the antichrist (satan's apostle) and the false prophet (satan s prophet).[125] These end-time events will create a one-world government and one-world religion because it will be necessary for the end-time rulers to try to control what's left of humanity and one way to control people is to have one system of government and one religion.

We are hearing about forums and entities coming together in an effort to solve world economics. One such agency, "The World Economic Forum (WEF), is an international organization for public-private cooperation. The Forum engages the foremost political, business, cultural and other leaders of society to shape global, regional and industry agendas."[126] Recently, the WEF has been collaborating with the Chinese Communist Party (CCP) for a one-world government.

Unfortunately for those who do not believe in God and have not accepted Jesus Christ as their Lord and Savior, religion in the last days will also take on a one-world form. The last day's one religion will be to bow to the antichrist. This is truly the end of humanity left on earth when it comes to that.

Over seventy countries are collapsing, and 170 countries or over a billion people are currently close to financial collapse.

125 "The World Bank Warns of a Global Recession, so Is It Inevitable? | Counting the Cost," YouTube: Al Jazeerza, 2022, https://www.youtube.com/watch?v=VbQEMsioXxM.
126 CLEARIAS Team, "World Economic Forum (WEF)," ClearIAS, 2022, https://www.clearias.com/world-economic-forum/.

Issues such as the Covid 19 Pandemic with Delta, Omicron, and other variants, Monkeypox, and the Russia-Ukraine War all contributing to the end time events in the last two years (2020–2022). Not to mention exorbitant gas and oil prices, high-interest rates, troubled nations borrowing money, food shortages which have caused the inflation in food costs, and other factors.

These countries and others are now facing a "debt crisis":

Sri-Lanka
Egypt
Tunisia
Lebanon
Argentina
El Salvador
Deni
Ghana
Ethiopia
Kenya
South Africa
Turkey[127]

We need to ask ourselves, among all these end-time facts—what's next for America, the free world, and the rest of the world?

127 CLEARIAS Team, 2022.

How Do Genesis 16:12 and 17:20 Play into Modern Times? Consider this Bible verse in the very first Book of the Bible:

> And as for Ishmael, I have heard you: I will surely bless him; I will make him fruitful and will greatly increase his numbers. He will be the father of twelve rulers, and I will make him into a great nation.
>
> (Genesis 17:20 NIV)

This Bible verse has come to pass with the wealth of the OPEC countries in the Middle East and the influential Arab nations that exist today at the forefront. Contrast Genesis 17:20 with Genesis 16:12 (NLT?):

> This son of yours will be a wild man, as untamed as a wild donkey! He will raise his fist against everyone, and everyone will be against him. Yes, he will live in open hostility against all his relatives."

God gave a blessing to Ishmael as a father of twelve rulers or nations, just as He blessed Abraham with a promised son, Isaac, who continued his father's line through his son, Jacob (1506 BCE), and Jacob's sons became the twelve tribes of Israel. On the other hand, we can see through history the results of how generations of leaders on either side have exercised their free will within and outside of the biblical context—we see the consequences of free will in terms of the social, political, economic affairs of its people—which is a continuum that brings us to 21st Century in the year 2022. Israel is essentially a Bible prophecy. Any nation with any relationship with Israel is significant since God is working out man's salvation through the nation of Israel.

Being apprised of what is happening with the UN, NATO, and other alliances will allow us to keep up with socio-political events as these relate to biblical prophecy and where humankind is at the current time.

These ancient prophecies or blessings which God made upon Abraham, Isaac, Ishmael, and Jacob can also be viewed as 3,528 years of biblical prophecy in the making.

Speaking of biblical prophecies, we will take a look at major end-time prophetic verses in Revelation in the next chapter. The word "revelation" is described in the Oxford dictionary as:

1. a surprising and previously unknown fact, especially one that is made known in a dramatic way; i.e., "revelations about his person life."
2. The divine or supernatural disclosure t humans of something relating to human existence or the world, i.e., "an attempt to reconcile Darwinian theories with biblical revelation."[128]

128 "What Does Revelation Mean," Oxford Online Dictionary, Lexico.com, 2022, https://www.google.com/search?q=what+does.revelation.mean&ie=UTF-8&oe=UTF-8&hl=en-us&client=safari#crs=q:revelation characters,stick:H4sIAAAA-AAAAAONgfcRYwC3w8sc9YanoSWtOXmNM5OLozCtJLSpOTS4RUuJi9y9ILUrMSxESFxLlEnbLTC7JzM9LzHHOSCxKTAYpEzJAqFEVUubiDErNSSx.

CHAPTER 13

Revelation 6 Explained

If we view the Bible as a book of scripture verses to teach us how to live the way God intended for humans to live, worship God, and attain all the good things (including eternal life in Heaven), one could say that the Bible is really a life manual to each of us, not the Quran or Hadiths, or some other man-made doctrine or set of beliefs.

I submit to you, then, that the Bible is the most fascinating piece of literature on the face of this earth in all of the histories of literature.

Because we are living at the end of the Church Age, we will hear a continuing stream about what I call "End Game prophecies" coming to pass or at least discussions of such among people who really care about what the truth is—*because the Truth will set you free* (John 8:32).

Revelation 6 verses 1–8 Explained

The Four Horseman of the Apocalypse

Because these colorful and immensely apocalyptic passages are in the Bible, God is symbolically showing us what is getting ready to happen to the world in the end game soon!

Are you and your family, best friends, friends, neighbors, co-workers, bank teller, dentist, doctor, etc., ready?

The "White Horse" is the antichrist (meaning against God, Christ and the Holy Spirit, and all that God stands for); or the antichrist can be thought of as satan's apostle (always remember satan copies God because he can't create, only God can), not Jesus Christ. See Revelation 16, Daniel 7:21, and Revelation 13:7.

Soon the antichrist will conquer the world, not only your country but the whole earth as we know it today. This will be the first time that a ruler will be able to conquer the earth.

Hitler (an example of antichrist and Heinrich Himmler would be Hitler's false prophet), Genghis Khan, Alexander the Great, Augustus Caesar, Napoleon, Cyrus the Great, and Tamerlane are examples of leaders throughout history who tried to conquer the world.

Drawing parallels to the days of Hitler, which took ten years before he became chancellor or President of Germany. German was in financial collapse and was looking for a leader to pull them out of it. Similarly, there will be a worldwide financial, social, and economic collapse, and the world will be looking for a leader to pull them out of this catastrophic worldwide mess.

The antichrist will pose as the savior to save the world, again copying Christ. Pay attention to this. What I am telling you now involves you, me, and all of humankind who are on earth right now. You are now in the *end times* or the *end game*, the beginning of the apocalypse described in the Bible.

The "Red Horse" is War. A quarter of the world's population will perish or die through war. We are currently in a spiritual war between Russia and Ukraine, and thousands of innocent people are dying. We are on the verge of China trying to take over Taiwan. China has already taken over Hong Kong as of July 1, 2022.

According to the United Nations, the current population of the world is projected to be 8 billion people by November 15, 2022. "The United Nations suggests that the global population could grow to around 8.5 billion in 2030, 9.7 billion in 2050, and 10.4 billion in 2100."[129] See Revelation 6:3, 12:3, and John 10:10.

We are living at the end of the Church Age, where we will begin to see the antichrist and false prophet will rise in power in the world and make themselves known. The antichrist will destroy three prime ministers, presidents, or kings from three nations during this period because these leaders will go against the evil desires and schemes of the antichrist. Seven nations will submit to the evilness of the antichrist and do his bidding (Revelation 13:1–4).

The "Black Horse" represents a great famine on the earth that will take place like never before! Did I say never before? These four horsemen are symbolic of unprecedented events which will soon be occurring. Prices have skyrocketed for food, gas, oil, water, fruits, vegetables, wheat, and barley—everything will continue to go up in price, and this is already happening today. Thousands of poor people around the world will not be able to afford milk for their babies, food for their children, and even their animals. Vegetables, fruits, barley, and wheat will continue to be scarce.

The "Pale Horse" represents death, which translates to thousands to millions of people will die around the world. Globally

129 "World Population to Reach 8 Billion on 15 November 2022," United Nations, Accessed September 29, 2022, https://www.un.org/en/desa/world-population-reach-8-billion-15-november-2022.

people are still experiencing famine, water shortages, war, etc. Still, now the tempo increases as the fourth horseman brings everything to a climax that is apocalyptic in nature—bringing death to the un-repentant and to those who refuse to know Christ as their Lord and Savior.

Do not be asleep at the wheel or be lulled into a false sense of security, thinking the antichrist spirit will not attack you during this period. If we are left on earth during the Great Tribulation to suffer famine, disease, torture, etc., some of us might wish that we were dead.

The symbolic future is also represented in Revelation 5 with the four seals. Jesus is giving you the warning to come to Him (Jesus Christ) and repent, repent, repent before it's too late!

The four horsemen are nearly upon us. Some of us can almost hear the hoof beats coming from a not-too-far distance. Get Ready!

Locust Swarm[130]

130 © [Alexey Protasov] — adobestock.com.

Swarms of locusts invaded the Middle East, including Saudi Arabia, Iraq, Jordan, Israel, Lebanon, and Syria, and may reach Turkey next if the country doesn't take action. This was reported on world news on April 30, 2021.[131]

Examining once again the black horse symbolizes *death* in the apocalypse, we can see a precursor to some of these end-time events. For example, even as you read this, Iran (ISIS, JHAD), and others want to implement worldwide sharia law, a code for all living Muslims (Daniel 7:25). Its president already openly proclaimed to wipe Israel off the face of the earth. They also want to take over the world from the infidels (all others besides Muslims), especially Jews and Christians.

Right now, there are over 800 million radical Muslims, Muslims who feel it's ok to lie to infidels.[132] When death takes its toll on the existing human population, it will take seven months to bury millions of dead bodies (Ezekiel 38:22; Revelation 16:10).

I've already mentioned the attacks on Israel by Arab nations since Israel became a modern state in 1948. I believe these attacks are leading up to the end time, the final attack on Israel, which is described in Ezekiel 38.

Take a look at these dates involving Arab countries attacking Israel. It will be very telling as the world watches who or what country will lay back and which countries will attack Israel again for booty (gold, silver, gas, oil, etc.).

---

131 "Swarm Of Locusts Threaten Livelihood Of Millions In African, Asian And Middle Eastern Countries," YouTube: NBC News, 2020, https://www.youtube.com/watch?v=2PVkVv7XRVk.

132 Patrick Worrall, "FactCheck: How Many of the World's Muslims Are Radicalised?" Channel 4 News, 2015, https://www.channel4.com/news/factcheck/factcheck-worlds-muslims-radicalised.

1948—Egypt, Iraq, Jordan, Lebanon, and Syria
1967—Egypt, Syria, and Arab states
1973—Egypt, Syria, and Arab states

Currently, the Arab nations include Twenty-two states (Arab league): Algeria, Bahrain, Comoros, Djibouti, Egypt, Iraq, Jordan, Kuwait, Lebanon, Libya, Mauritania, Morocco, Oman, Palestine, Qatar, Saudi Arabia, Somalia, Sudan, Syria, Tunisia, the United Arab Emirates, and Yemen.

The Arab Maghreb Union

The Arab Maghreb Union is a trade group of Arabs aiming for political and economic alliances in the future. The major players are the Maghreb in Africa, Algeria, Libya, Mauritania, Morocco, and Tunisia. The Palestine Liberation Army (PLA) is the military wing of the Palestinian Liberation Organization (PLO), set up in 1964 with the Arab League. The Arab nations that want Israel destroyed are Palestine, Lebanon, Syria, Iraq, and Egypt, and they will be developing alliances with Iran in the end game.

Jesus is now reversing everything! Loss of souls means every human on earth who, through free will, receives Christ as their Lord and Savior. The loss of land (earth) since Adam and Eve were banished from the Garden of Eden shall be turned into a new heaven on earth!

I pray daily for Jesus' rapture of His Church and the second coming; and the return of His church to heaven (Revelation 5:8). I encourage you to begin praying daily as well for Jesus to come and get you! Your prayers are recorded and stored in heaven.

Every Believer should take Revelation 5:9 to heart because this verse applies to every person on this earth. This is part of the great commission (Matthew 28:16–20) to tell others about Christ so that a decision can be made which will affect one's eternal destiny.

> And when he had taken it, the four living creatures and the twenty-four elders fell down before the Lamb. Each one had a harp and they were holding golden bowls full of incense, which are the prayers of God's people. And they sang a new song, saying:
> "You are worthy to take the scroll
> and to open its seals,
> because you were slain,
> and with your blood you purchased for God
> persons from every tribe and language and people and nation.
>
> (Revelation 5:8–9 NIV)

"Persons from every tribe and language and people and nation" means every modern city, state, nation, and province—every person in prison, on the mountain, at sea—everyone! Everyone will hear the Gospel of Jesus Christ! (Matthew 24:24).

The Bible talks about witnesses during the end time tribulation. During the seven years of tribulation, the two witnesses could be Enoch and Elijah (Elias) or Moses and Elijah (Matthew 17:1–12). Also, during the tribulation, there will be 144,000 Jewish witnesses who will be testifying to the people left on the earth about Jesus Christ (2 Thessalonians 2:7–8; 2 Peter 3:9; Acts 17:31).

Noah and his family were chosen to survive when the earth was destroyed by water. "One catastrophic flood occurred in Mesopotamia around 3000 BC, and another occurred between the Mediterranean and the Black Sea around 5500 BC. Depending on where and when Noah lived, either flood would have **destroyed** all the civilizations at that time."[133]

God did set His rainbow in the sky as a promise to never again destroy the earth by flood (Genesis 9:13). However, He did not say that He won't allow the earth to be destroyed by other means—after He removes the true Christian Church in what we call "The Rapture".

One of the areas in which satan is extremely active in the world today is the area of human sexuality. Our collective enemy is doing everything he can to not only deceive us but to destroy us (whom God created humanity to be—in His image). The enemy of our souls takes human sexuality—what is a sacred act meant for marriage and propagation or multiplying to fill the earth, and he has made it something *divergent and deviant*.

The following section on homosexuality is included here so that we might all be aware of the profound impact this concept and practice has on society and what many views as social norms in every religion, cult, or country.

Homosexuality

Here is a link, if you would like to look this up, to the countries where same-sex marriage is legal:

133 "The Harmony of Faith and Science. Real Science. Stronger Faith," True Creation, 2016, https://truecreation.org/#chapter5.

https://www.goodmorningamerica.com/culture/story/29-countries-sexmarriage-officially-legal-56041136

Homosexuality really stems from a tainting of what truth stands for in terms of a moral absolute, which is designed by God. Today it is a constant struggle with those searching for truth in human sexuality, and it becomes truth vs. political truth. Also, the premodern view is that truth is objective and people are equally valued. The post-modern view is that truth is "my truth," based on lived experiences. Currently, 7.1% of adults in the U.S. identify as lesbian, gay, bisexual, or transgender (LGBT).[134] About 10% of LGBTs identify as transgender.

The Bible clearly and consistently declares that homosexual activity is a sin (Genesis 19:1–13; Leviticus 18:22, 20:13; Romans 1:26–27; 1 Corinthians 6:9; 1 Timothy 1:10). "Gomorrah was a biblical place always associated with Sodom. They are found on the Biblical Timeline between **2000 BC and 1900 BC**."[135] The Bible tells us that these cities were destroyed with fire and brimstone raining down from the heavens because of sexual immorality (Genesis 19:24). Two hundred forty years passed between the flood during Noah's time and Sodom and Gomorrah. It took Noah one hundred years to build the Ark, and the people at that time had a hundred years to repent—but the Bible tells us that no one except the eight individuals on Noah's Ark was saved.

God, in His Sovereignty, is unchanging. If in the time of Sodom and Gomorrah He was against homosexuality, God is

---

134 Jeffrey M. Jones, "LGBT Identification in U.S. Ticks Up to 7.1%," Gallup, Inc., 2022, https://news.gallup.com/poll/389792/lgbt-identification-ticks-up.aspx.
135 "Sodom and Gomorrah," Amazing Bible Timeline with World History, 2022, https://amazingbibletimeline.com/blog/sodom-and-gomorrah/.

surely against homosexuality today (1Timothy 1:10). Homosexuality is unhealthy for humans. The U.S. Federal Government spends $28 billion yearly for studying HIV Aids with 650,000 deaths, compared to $514.7 million for breast cancer and 43,250 deaths.[136] Additionally, anal sex is not meant for humans as the anus is very sensitive and not meant to be stretched in this manner; and there are myriad bacteria which is inside the rectum which is transferred to another human being.

Since the beginning of time, satan has been tempting humans to fall, and one of the prominent themes he has used is to pervert human sexuality. We are indeed living in end times with respect to the perversion of human sexuality. In the coming tribulation period, the antichrist spirit will be more prevalent in terms of sexual immorality, drug use, alcohol use, greed, pride, and everything ungodly associated with the antichrist and false prophet.

An interesting thing, I believe, is that in the tribulation, the converted Jews from Judaism to Christ will flee to Petra in Jordan, and God will provide food, water, and safety like He did for Moses and the 1.3 million Jews fleeing Egypt. Another interesting note is that for thousands of years, Muslims have been praying at this same site—thinking they are praying toward mecca or Islam's holiest site. Mecca is a desert valley in western Saudi Arabia, the birthplace of the Prophet Muhammad and

136 "Federal HIV Budget," HIV.Gov., 2022, https://www.hiv.gov/federal-response/funding/budget; "Global HIV & AIDS Statistics — Fact Sheet," UNAIDS, 2021, https://www.unaids.org/en/resources/fact-sheet; "Breast Cancer Statistics | How Common Is Breast Cancer?" American Cancer Society, 2022, https://www.cancer.org/cancer/breast-cancer/about/how-common-is-breast-cancer.html; "2021 NCI Budget Fact Book - Research Funding," National Cancer Institute [NIH], 2022, https://www.cancer.gov/about-nci/budget/fact-book/data/research-funding.

the Muslim faith. The fourth horseman, or the horse of death, includes all who will die from annihilation and wars or have died because of man's (and woman's) sinful nature. Consider the information provided here on innocent lives taken before they even have their first breath of air.

Genesis 9 details a covenant between God and mankind that good will never again flood the earth (like in the days of Noah), but satan loves to copy God and uses the rainbow now as a logo and symbol for LGBT rights, etc. The rainbow is actually God's promise never again to flood the earth.

Widespread Abortion Is Growing Worldwide

Roe vs. Wade in the United States made headline news when this was overturned by the U.S. Supreme Court on June 24, 2022.[137] Interestingly, this landmark decision was the basis of establishing a constitutional right to abortion which would end its fifty-year-anniversary in January 2023.

> Abortion is the termination of a pregnancy by the removal or expulsion of an embryo or fetus. Abortions can be performed surgically or by medication. Abortion is a controversial subject, with many people believing that it is a woman's right to choose. At the same time, others have religious, political, and personal reasons to believe that abortions are wrong or a sin. Currently, *abortion is illegal in twenty-six countries,* but not in the United States.

137 Nina Totenberg and Sarah Mccammon, "Supreme Court Overturns Roe v. Wade, Ending Right to Abortion Upheld for Decades," NPR, 2022, https://www.npr.org/2022/06/24/1102305878/supreme-court-abortion-roe-v-wade-decision-overturn.

The Supreme Court decision of Roe vs. Wade states that governments cannot regulate a woman's decision to have an abortion before the fetus's viability. After viability, no government can impose a regulation that favors a fetus's life over the mother's. Even with this decision, abortion has caused nationwide controversy and has divided people into pro-life or pro-choice camps.

Abortion laws vary by state. Recently, some states have been proposing legislation to further restrict abortions earlier than fetus viability. States have introduced the "heartbeat" bill, which prohibits abortions have six weeks of pregnancy or when a fetal heartbeat can be detected.

The abortion rate is calculated as the number of abortions per 1,000 women ages 15–44 years old. The ten states with the highest abortion rates were:

1. District of Columbia (32.7)
2. New York (29.6)
3. New Jersey (25.8)
4. Maryland (23.4)
5. Florida (20.6)
6. California (19.5)
7. Nevada (19.4)
8. Connecticut (19.2)
9. Rhode Island (17)
10. Delaware (16.7)[138]

138 "Abortion Rates by State 2022," World Population Review, 2022, https://worldpopulationreview.com/state-rankings/abortion-rates-by-state.

"According to the World Health Organization WHO, more than 1.2 million abortions have been performed worldwide in the first ten days of 2021."[139] This data is according to a report by *Worldometer*, formerly *Worldometers*, a reference website that provides counters and real-time statistics for diverse topics. It accounts for facts for everything from health to food production, economics and death rates.

What does the Bible say about abortion?

> The Bible never specifically addresses the issue of abortion. However, there are numerous teachings in Scripture that make it abundantly clear what God's view of abortion is. Jeremiah 1:5 tells us that God knows us before He forms us in the womb. Psalm 139:13–16 speaks of God's active role in our creation and formation in the womb. Exodus 21:22–25 prescribes the same penalty—death—for someone who causes the death of a baby in the womb as for someone who commits murder. This law and its punishment clearly indicate that God considers a baby in the womb to be just as much a human being as a full-grown adult. For the Christian, abortion is not a matter of a woman's right to choose to have a baby. The baby is already present and living. Abortion is a matter of life or death of a human being made in God's image (Genesis 1:26–27, 9:6). *So what does the Bible say about abortion?* Simply put, *abortion is murder*. It is

139 "World Health Organization: More Than 1.2M Abortions Have Been Performed World Wide In First 10 Days Of 2021," Ventura Broadcasting Company, 2021, http://www.venturabroadcasting.com/world-health-organization-more-than-1-2m-abortions-have-been-performed-world-wide-in-first-10-days-of-2021.

the killing of a human being created in the image of God.[140]

As a born-again Christian, your eyes are opened to the things in the world which seem to prevail, which are not of God, Jesus, or the Holy Spirit. Remember that the Holy Spirit will always be there to guide you, help you, and comfort you.

I believe that we are living in the end times. As explained in another chapter, it was prophesized over me in 2005 that I would be writing books. I did not believe it then because I don't even like to write, much less write a book. I believe God had me write twelve books explaining the world's major religions and cults because we are living in a time like no other, and God will use the voice of many to reach the lost before He sends Jesus to return to earth.

The Holy Spirit will help those that need help—today, tomorrow, in the end times, and during the *tribulation*. God is doing everything He can to help the proud and arrogant people who are fighting to accept Jesus into their hearts. Again, these proud or stubborn people will still be on earth, even when the true Christian Church has been raptured or taken up to heaven.

Please take time to reference these Bible verses:

- Daniel 7:7–8
- Revelation 13:4, 14:9–13
- 1 Thessalonians 4:15–18
- 2 Thessalonians 2:5–7
- Matthew 24:2–3, 32–36, 44
- Mark 8
- 2 Peter 3:14–15
- Psalms 9:5–20
- Luke 16:1–3, 21:25
- John 16:33
- 2 Corinthians 12:9

140 "What Does the Bible Say about Abortion?" GotQuestions.Org, 2022, https://www.gotquestions.org/abortion-Bible.html.

The number of *men* is six. The number 666 represents satan (*imperfection*) because it is less than 777, the triple number for perfection), and is a number that marks the beginning of the end times where false prophets and prophetesses will arise, and government deception, disputes among nations, global devastation, false churches, false believers, and pestilence will be prevalent and the recurring theme.

But have faith! You have been given all the tools and Bible verses to come to a full knowledge of Christ Jesus. Have faith no matter what we are going through in this world—because the Bible tells us clearly that the Gospel of Jesus Christ shall be preached to all the world!

So then, if one is, in fact, reading the Bible and understands what God intended for humanity and that Jesus asked us to fulfill the great commission of telling others about Him, what do we do in the everyday meantime?

In the next chapters, we will look at what could be described as the extraordinary design God has specifically for you today: free will and two places that are eternal—Heaven and Hell.

If one compares the vast difference between Heaven and Hell, I would think this may be a pivoting point from believing in things of this world to believing in the things of God. What is interesting is the transforming power of Psalm 37:4 (NIV), "Take delight in the Lord, and He will give you the desires of your heart." You will no longer want to follow Muhammed, Allah, or a false god or false prophet. You will, in fact, be on a quest to find the one true, Triune God.

When one delights in the Lord, slowly or suddenly, the desires of your heart become what God is calling you to do. The

Lord knows everything about us, every thought, and every hair on our heads. Imagine for a moment that He inspired the Psalmist to write this verse and that He knew by drawing close to Him that one's desires would then be God's desires. What are the desires of our hearts? The answer to this question is one way that reveals a person's *delight* or love for our Lord.

Do we love God to the extent that the desires of our hearts are really His desires?

CHAPTER 14

Heaven or Hell?

Consider this question: If you were to die today, do you think you would go to Heaven or Hell? Do you even believe in Heaven or Hell? If you believe that good exists in the world, you should also believe that Heaven exists. If you believe that evil exists in the world, you should also believe that Hell is real and exists.

God created us as eternal beings. He also created us with free will. Therefore, bondage or works, as in the Mormon Church and other cults, are the result of free will. As Christians, we are saved by *grace* and *Christ* alone. Not works! The angels in Heaven were also created as eternal beings with free wills. One particular angel in Heaven became so proud and arrogant that he soon fell from grace thinking he was greater than God—and was cast from Heaven as lucifer—and when satan fell to earth, it is told that he took a third of the angels with him (Revelation 12:4).

The world we live in today is, unfortunately, ruled by satan. All one has to do is glance around at our broken world—wars and rumors of wars, death and destruction, disease and famine, suffering, mass murders and heinous crimes, the abomination of the traditions of society and the sanctity of marriage, the rampant practice of satan worship, cults, pornography (shown on television during prime time), alcoholism and drug addiction, mistrust of our government and the media, and so on.

Can any of the above be considered godly things that resemble love, peace, forgiveness, salvation, or faith? No, *absolutely not!* This is because it is all about man's free will, the choices that one has made, and the consequences of those choices throughout history to this very day, propelling us into our future destiny.

A simple exercise to illustrate the forces of good and evil at work in your life would be to take one day or the hours of your wakeful experience and become acutely aware of the thoughts that enter your mind and the feelings and desires of your heart. If you are honest with yourself, you will find that your thoughts may vacillate between good and evil. Even something seemingly "innocent" as constant overeating (lust of the flesh) or occasionally getting drunk at dinner parties is not godly—everything should be in moderation when it comes to our desires for earthly things.

If you feel that you have no evil thoughts, desires, or lusts of the flesh whatsoever, then you are a saint, and God should recognize you as such. If you have just one thought that is not godly, for instance, judging someone based on their looks or status in society, coveting something that someone else has, cursing under your breath at the "other driver," listening to rock music that is decidedly on the dark side (including the way the music sounds, the lyrics, the title, the album cover), taking "recreational drugs," or perhaps being dishonest with a hidden agenda and justifying it as a harmless "need to know basis" or a "little white lie"—any of these kinds of thoughts or desires are part of spiritual warfare to attract your attention off God and goodness and holiness, and be in and of the world.

The Bible gives us hope and inspiration for everyday living despite our fallen world. Sometimes the human tendency is to take what is good in our lives for granted. Until we are faced with an obstacle, dilemma, or life-changing event, we often are living in the status quo and are perhaps just glad that we have peace and security.

However, in terms of our Spirit (conscience, communion, and wisdom), God has first chosen us to be with Him and follow Him, but we must employ our free will and respond. God has given us the instruction book of all times for healthy, vibrant, joyful, and mindful living—the Holy Bible—and in it are passages and verses which, when taken to heart, are amazingly profound and prophetic for everyday life.

Let's take a look at how God created humans: with three distinct parts to our existence.

> You, dear children, are from God and have overcome them, because the one who is in you is greater than the one who is in the world.
>
> (1 John 4:4 NIV)

Communion with a God We Cannot See

As a human being, you are created with three parts to your existence, and each of those three parts has three parts:

- ***Body***—blood, flesh, and bones, which equals a physical death.
- ***Soul***—will, mind, and emotions (out of this comes pride, arrogance, etc., towards God and people) which equals a spiritual death.
- ***Spirit***—communion (daily with God, not just on Saturdays or at church on Sundays), conscience (in your birth, you know many things from your DNA—how to lie, steal, mislead, etc.), and wisdom (gained by praying daily, reading the Bible, attending church, attending small group, paying tithes, etc.), which equals an *eternal death*.

Your Spirit can have the wrong kind of communion, not the fellowship God intended. For example, communion with satan equals evil, wisdom with satan equals evil, and conscience with satan equals evil. This wrong kind of communion is a pathway to Hell or is Hell.

One day Jesus Christ will "restore" all three parts of the human being made in the image of God:

- Body (physical)—Ezekiel 36, 37.
- Soul (Spirit)—Isaiah 43.
- Spirit (Eternal) when we are in Heaven.

When God speaks to us, and His Spirit is evident in our lives, He actually bypasses the "body" and "soul" and operates in the "spirit" together with your spirit. You can pray and or talk to God or Jesus as soon as you awaken to consciousness in the morning when you're driving to work, and while you're preparing dinner, even when you are conducting business with clients, at your son's cross-country race, at a theatre, in the shower, and as you lie in bed right before you close your eyes and go to sleep; anywhere, anytime.

In order for anyone to have a meaningful relationship with another person, one would need to seek out that person, get to know him, talk with him, and commune with them. On earth, we establish relationships with other people because we are able to see each other face to face. It does take faith to establish a relationship with God and His son, Jesus, when we cannot see God or Jesus in person. It does take faith to talk with God and Jesus when we don't necessarily hear a voice speaking back. This is where the Word of God, the Bible, comes into play. It is the Word of God that will speak to anyone who begins seeking the Bible for the answers to the mysteries of life. I assure you that your questions will be answered if you seek to find the answer within the Bible. It would also be a good idea to fellowship with others to study what the Bible says. Bible studies help us to apply God's Word to our everyday life.

When we hear pastors and Christians saying over and over, "God wants to have a personal relationship with you," or when judgment day comes, and we are all standing before the Lord, and we witness God saying to someone, "I do not know you" because that person never sought to know, understand, or recognize God—it may be too late when we all stand before God on Judgment Day.

As we grow in the Word of God and begin to understand more and more the true meaning of life, it is as if we are suddenly speaking a strange new language of truth. The reason why it will be somewhat strange is that the rest of the "world" —outside of the Church, our circle of believers, our family, and our friends—are not speaking the same truth. When you tune in to an evangelist on television, and you can hear beyond their passionate sermons, the words of truth will usually ring clear. I've come to believe that some of these evangelists are so passionate because they know what they are saying is based on the Bible, and the Bible is true. These seemingly fanatical evangelists are the way they are because they feel a sense of urgency to share with the world the truth. We are probably witnessing the power of the Holy Spirit as these evangelists are impassioned to speak about Christ from the pulpit.

I am not saying that I am endorsing every other evangelist on the block. Like anything of value and substance that a person invests their time into, the thing or person must be evaluated for its worth. You are going to have to conduct your research. Whatever you doubt or question, you must test the item in question for yourself. Because each of us has inevitable mortality and none of us will live forever, people often plan for their retirement years to be relaxing and pleasant. However—what about after retirement, in old age, when we are perhaps in the sunset of our lives?

By writing this book, I tend to consider such things as life and death. For a minute, contemplate Heaven with me. In John 14:1–3 (TLB), Jesus is speaking to the apostles about leaving them soon. He says,

> "Let not your heart be troubled. You are trusting God, now trust in me. There are many homes up there

> where my Father lives, and I am going to prepare them for your coming. When everything is ready, then I will come and get you, so that you can always be with me where I am. If this weren't so, I would tell you plainly."

Because God originally created man to have a relationship with Him, and thus with all of mankind, it would make sense that these relationships are so important that He would want to continue similar relationships with us in heaven. I believe we retain our identities as who we were on earth; only we are now identified with Christ for all of eternity, and we retain our free will.

It seems reasonable that we would also retain our likeness (we look pretty much the same but with a different heavenly body) and our outward appearance. Otherwise, we would not be the unique individuals God had created on earth, and fellow brothers and sisters in Christ wouldn't recognize each other. I have had time to rethink this recognition aspect since the original thought, and I've decided that fellow Believers would probably recognize each other's *spirit* as much or more than each other's actual appearance. The one huge difference is that our bodies will never get sick, old, or perish.

Revelation 21–22 is chocked full of imagery of Heaven on the new earth. The new earth is described as having no oceans with a new sky. The Holy City, the new Jerusalem, comes down from God, out of Heaven. It is a glorious sight, beautiful as a bride at her wedding. These verses go on to say that "the home of God is now among men" (Revelation 21:3 TLB). God is sitting on the throne as He says, "...I will give to the thirsty the springs of the

Water of Life—as a gift! Everyone who conquers will inherit all these blessings, and I will be his God and he will be my son" (Revelation 21:6–7 TLB).

In a vision, John is taken to a towering mountain peak, and from there, he watches a wondrous city, the holy Jerusalem, descending out of the skies from God. John goes on to describe what he saw:

> It was filled with the glory of God, and flashed and glowed like a precious gem, crystal clear like jasper. Its walls were broad and high, with twelve gates guarded by twelve angels. And the names of the twelve tribes of Israel were written on the gates. There were three gates on each side—north, south, east, and west. The walls had twelve foundation stones, and on them were written the names of the twelve apostles of the Lamb.
>
> (Revelation 21:11–14 TLB)

John tells of the angel with a golden measuring stick to measure the city and its gates and walls.

> When he measured it, he found it was a square as wide as it was long; in fact, it was in the form of a cube, for its height was exactly the same as its other dimensions—1,500 miles each way. Then he measured the thickness of the walls and found them to be 216 feet across...
>
> (Revelation 21:16–17 TLB)

The city itself is described as pure, transparent, gold-like glass. The wall is made of jasper and was built on twelve layers of foundation stones inlaid with gems. The first layer with jasper; the second with sapphire; the third with chalcedony; the fourth with emerald; "the fifth with sardonyx; the sixth layer with sardus; the seventh with chrysolite; the eighth with beryl; the ninth with topaz; the tenth with chrysoprase; the eleventh with jacinth; the twelfth with amethyst" (Revelation 21:20 KJV).

According to John's vision, the twelve gates were made of pearls—each gate from a single pearl, and the main street was pure, transparent gold, like glass. John even addresses the lighting. In Revelation 21:23–25 (TLB), it says:

> And the city has no need of sun or moon to light it, for the glory of God and of the Lamb illuminate it. Its light will light the nations of the earth, and the rulers of the world will come and bring their glory to it. Its gates never close; they stay open all day long—and there is no night!

Then we are given a description of "...a river of pure Water of Life, clear as crystal, flowing from the throne of God and the Lamb, coursing down the center of the main street. On each side of the river grows Trees of Life, bearing twelve crops of fruit, with a fresh crop each month; the leaves are used for medicine to heal the nations" (Revelation 22:1–2 TLB). John's vision gives us more than a casual observation of heaven on earth. He describes in detail the twelve foundational layers of stone and gems.

For instance, why would God let His angels bother showing John in such painstaking detail the exact measurements of the buildings and the city if the city were not actually a physical place and the different layers of gemstones if the foundation were to be poured of just concrete or cement? I believe God has given us just a tiny little taste of the glory of Heaven, just enough to whet our appetites and give us some kind of anticipation, something to behold for now in our mind's eyes and hearts.

A pastor once said he believed that God or Jesus has not told us exactly what Heaven would be like because mere humans would know that their earthly surroundings—no matter how grand—would pale in comparison to the glory of Heaven. Many people would even contemplate taking a shortcut out of their lives on earth just to get to Heaven earlier. People would be in such a great hurry to get to Heaven if they only knew what Heaven was really like! However, as Christians, we know that there is no shortcut to Heaven, nor is there a stairway to Heaven—for everything works out in God's timing.

Pastor Wayne Cordeiro of New Hope International once said in his sermon to over ten thousand people, "Whatever you want to grow in, whether it be faith, love, or finances—that area will be stretched because God knows what's going to happen around the corner. Many things are won or lost in the stretch. Life happens in the stretch."[141] Too often, we want to control things in our life that are better left to God. One such all-important matter is the exact day and time that each of us who believe in Je-

141 "Sermons by Pastor Wayne Cordeiro| New Hope West," New Hope West, 2022, https://newhopewest.com/sermon/seeing-things-up/.

sus Christ will arrive at the pearly gates. No one knows exactly when Jesus will return—so we need to be ready!

The reason why God sent His only son, Jesus, into the world was to save it, not condemn it. God gave men in the Old Testament the prophecies of the future so that when these events occurred in the future, even 2,000 years later, all will believe in the Word of God by having read about historical events and witnessing the events that have come to pass and comparing it with the hundreds of prophecies in the Bible.

Our Lord God and Creator of all of Heaven and Earth, gives each of us a warning in Revelation 3:1–6. We need to be ready. Having our names written in the Book of Life is critical to our souls since we are created as eternal beings. Then again, there are those that believe in faith alone without researching what the Bible says. This is not to say that research is not important, for it is the Bible scholars themselves who help to validate the Bible further. The power of God's Word is absolutely supernatural. One can experience supernatural power in the realization of truths by reading the Bible for oneself. But a word of caution... expect to be changed by the Holy Spirit. One cannot remain the same if one is truly experiencing the Word of God. We can only grow from our rich experiences and share them, not shrink back into obscurity.

How many Bible scholars have set out to research the Bible intending to dispute its findings, only to become believers themselves? Read *Who Moved the Stone* (Morrison) for further intrigue on that subject.

A Deeper Conversation about Heaven and Hell

What will Heaven be like?

God's intention for all mankind (yes, you included!) from the very beginning is to be with Him in Heaven (2 Peter 3:9; Ezekiel 18:32, 33:11). By you receiving Jesus Christ on earth, you have actually received Heaven because Jesus is Heaven (Psalms 103:9; 2 Corinthians 5:6–8; 1 Kings 8:30; Revelation 21:27). Your name will be written in the *Book of Life* in Heaven. Like a hotel reservation, if your name is not written in the book, you will not be able to enter Heaven.

Where is Heaven? It is beyond outer space. That is why no astronaut, satellite, or super telescope has ever had a glimpse of Heaven until the Hubble Telescope was pointed at the right place in the middle of the Whirlpool (Milky Way) galaxy about thirty million light-years away and discovered an X shape—could this be the cross of Jesus? You can verify this X shape as being an astronomical find recorded by NASA and the Hubble Telescope websites.

The Bible tells us that Heaven is past earth's atmosphere and outermost space (2 Corinthians 12:1–2; Psalms 14:2). The Bible says that earth and Heaven will be destroyed, and a Heaven will come down to be on a new earth created specifically for that purpose. This may be beyond our wildest imagination, our most amazing dream. However, this is what God wants us to know beforehand right now, wherever we may be.

The light in Heaven will come from God's presence and His Glory (Revelation 21:23). In Heaven, there is no death, sickness, disease, *no COVID-19 or Omnicron variant*, no mourning, crying, pain, depression, disability, etc. (Revelation 21:4). In Heaven, you will meet family members, best friends, neighbors, co-workers, loved ones—everyone who has a relationship with Jesus Christ, just like you have (Matthew 8:11, 17:3–4; 1 Thessalonians 4:17). You will recognize all relationships in heaven, but these relationships will be different from earth (Luke 20:24–36). Time has no meaning in Heaven. Eternity is outside the time clock we know on earth. You will look like you do now, but with a glorified body. (I'm certain a lot of us will be very happy about that since we are used to seeing the exterior of our existence on earth!) With our new bodies, we still will be able to eat and enjoy food and fellowship with one another.

When you die and go to Heaven because you received Jesus as your Lord and Savior, you will not be judged or go before God to be judged. You received Christ, repented of your sins, you forgave, and you realized that Jesus paid the price for you! Hallelujah! (Romans 8:1).

The Heavenly Environment

- There is joy, peace, and happiness.
- Once you are in Heaven, you can never, never leave. You are there for eternity.
- There is Hope.
- There is an abundance of light, which comes directly from God.
- Heaven has a beautiful smell.
- There is water to drink and the water of eternal life.
- There is food to eat.
- All the earth things you did, like tithing, fasting, prayer, etc., are all bound in Heaven.

- There will be fellowship with family, friends, best friends, neighbors, coworkers, and others if they have accepted the true Christ as their Lord and Savior.
- You will feel loved and at home.

Some Questions to Consider:

- Can I earn my way into Heaven? Answer: No.
- Do I deserve to go to Heaven? Answer: No.
- Can I pay my way into Heaven? Answer: No.
- May I do work to get to Heaven? Answer: No.
- Without receiving Jesus, can I go to Heaven? Answer: No.
- If I'm the president of a company, can I go to Heaven? Answer: No.
- If I'm the president of a country, can I go to Heaven? Answer: No.
- If a Christian person dies on earth, do they become your guiding angel? Answer: No.
- Is there a second chance once you die to receive Jesus and go to Heaven? The answer is **No**. You will go straight to Hell upon death.

Humans are created differently from angels, so angels do not become humans, and vice versa. Whoever the human race believed in the Old Testament and God, such as Abraham, Isaac, and Moses, those people immediately went to "paradise" upon their death. Paradise was the other side of Hell, but not experiencing or receiving the things of Hell. When Jesus died on the cross, He was gone for three days. It is said that Jesus claimed the keys to death and Hades for Himself through His death and resurrection (Revelation 1:17–18). Jesus essentially went to paradise to set free these saints before Jesus' death. Now paradise is empty, and only Hell exists there. After Jesus' death and resurrection, any human that received Jesus Christ as their Lord and Savior will go to Heaven upon death. A person can be dying in a hospital, nursing home, car accident, heart attack, or cancer. Whatever or whenever you die, your next breath will be with Jesus as your Lord and Savior.

We are in the "Church Age" right now (*see Chapter 12, End-Time Apostle*). The "rapture" of the Church comes next. It can be anytime now! Are you ready? Did you read Romans 10:9 (KJV)?

> That if thou shalt confess with thy mouth the Lord Jesus, and shalt believe in thine heart that God hath raised him from the dead, thou shalt be saved.

Did You Get Baptized in Water By the Right Authority?

If yes to all of these queries, then praise God!

If no, then *why not*? Contact one of the true Christian churches in your city or area. Christians living during Christ's return will meet Christ in Heaven (Luke 26; Ephesians 4).

Adult Christians wonder if their children, who are not yet able to make profound decisions for themselves, or who can understand the salvation concept of Jesus Christ, whether their child will be in Heaven with them. For example, if your child died young by an accident or incident, was eliminated by abortion, or if your child had a mental illness or disability and they didn't have the chance to know and understand Christ—the answer is yes, they too will be waiting for you in Heaven. Your children are sanctified by your decision to receive Christ. And the radical thing is that God chose You—you ultimately did not choose Him.

Will my dog, cat, horse, rabbit, parrot, etc. be in Heaven with me? God created all animals with bodies (blood, flesh, bones) and souls (will, mind, emotions), but animals do not have a *spirit* (conscience, wisdom, communion) like humans. Humans have all three elements: body, soul, and spirit. Jesus is riding a horse on his second coming from Heaven.

How Old Will I Be in Heaven?

The Bible doesn't say, but some Bible scholars think that we will appear as if we're in our thirties. I will just be glad I'll be in Heaven and not Hell at any age that God decides to have me be!

Satan can only be in one place at one time. Not like the Godhead of God, Jesus, and the Holy Spirit. The Godhead is all-knowing and all-seeing, and they can be everywhere!

You cannot go to heaven by Joseph Smith, Muhammed, Allah, Buddha, Hinduism, nothing but Jesus, and through one of the Christian Churches mentioned in this book! I implore you to think about your *eternal existence* and not have any no's, if's, and's, or but's! Jesus is the *only* way. Nothing but Jesus can get you to Heaven!

In closing, God is perfect and a just and loving God. Like in court, if someone robbed your house or stole your car, would you want the judge to let them go? No! You would want some kind of justice.

God applies the same principles to the laws of Heaven. Your sins of lying, cheating, stealing, or whatever were placed on a perfect and innocent person instead—Jesus—so that by accepting Jesus as your Lord and Savior, you have exchanged your sins for eternal life with Him! Because of this, we can have a personal relationship with Christ and Heaven—and *not* Hell… Unless Hell is your choice.

The Lord spoke to me in the middle of the night about Hell! He put upon my heart that many people do not understand Hell, believe in it, or don't think it is a possibility that they would ever go there. Well, the Lord is not slow in coming back, even though humanity has waited for Him for nearly 2,000 years. The Lord God does not desire that *not even one soul* perishes outside of the Heaven He designed for us (2 Peter 3:9).

I've carefully and thoroughly discussed the bliss of Heaven above, and I wouldn't do anyone justice if I did not also discuss the torments and anguish of Hell. ***The torments and anguish of Hell—an eternal regret you MUST avoid!***

Hell is for satan and his angels. Hell is not meant for humans, but with our free agency and not receiving Jesus as our Lord and Savior, you will go to Hell immediately upon death.

Hell is located in the center of the earth. Scientists say that the temperature is 5,200 to 9,392 degrees Fahrenheit.[142] To put this in perspective, "the temperature of the inner core is far above the melting point of iron" (Ephesians 4:9; Matthew 12:40; Luke 23:43).[143] Heaven has fire, 24/7 (Matthew 25:41; Mark 9:48). When people go to Hell, they are in pain, tormented, abused, feel lost, depressed, hopeless, weeping, grinding their teeth,

142 "Core," National Geographic Society, 2022, https://education.nationalgeographic.org/resource/core?_gl=1*1vblqcu*_ga*NjI5NDQxMzIuMTY2NTAwNDg1NA..*_ga_JRRKGYJRKE*MTY2NTAwNDg1NC4xLjEuMTY2NTAwNDk2Ni4wLjAuMA..
143 Ibid.

miserable, lonely, unloved, etc., (Matthew 13:42). In Hell, there are worms and darkness (Matthew 8:12).

Your soul (will, mind, emotions) and your spirit (conscience) realize that you made a mistake and that you could have accepted Jesus as your Savior, but your soul (pride, disobedience) realizes it is too late and you will not be able to go to Heaven for all of eternity. Wow!

You realize you have no freedom in Hell and that you are separated from Jesus, God, and the Holy Spirit (2 Thessalonians 1:8–9).

What Will Hell Be Like?

Once you go to Hell, you can never leave! You can never leave—you are there for eternity. May this be a sobering wake-up call to those who do not know Jesus.

Hell was created or meant for satan (devil, lucifer) and his fallen angels, never meant for human beings. However, because of our free will and choice, we have consequences for our choices or decisions.

- There will be no life of your choosing.
- There will be no happiness.
- There will be no water.
- There will be no food.
- There will be brimstone—sulfur smell, burning bodies, the smell of flesh and hair burnt, stink, and you might be burnt too.
- There will be no furniture, no beds, no pictures to look at, nothing.

- There will be fire.
- There will be constant turmoil with hardly any sleep.
- You will be confined to a cell.
- There will be a lot of darkness.
- You will feel unloved and lost.
- You cannot take a rest, vacation, or break.

The devil brings himself and darkness (no light, smell, fear, hopelessness), no water, and no food because only Jesus is the bread of life, Jesus is the water of life, etc. Jesus takes all these things or quantities to Heaven, while satan takes the opposite things to Hell.

The devil is in control of our ideas, philosophies, standards of living, and opinions. Humans (you and I) have sometimes made money and material things a god, especially if we placed more importance on these things than relationships, people, or God Himself. If we place too much importance on money and material things, we, in essence, allow pride and arrogance to control us—and the enemy of our souls, the devil, would like nothing more.

You are continually tormented by evil spirits. Why? Because you are made in God's likeness and these evil spirits hate, hate, hate God! We are an extension of God, and the enemy of our souls hates those who love God. All the relationships and things you had on earth will be lost. You will not be remembered for *anything*! You will wish that you could cease to exist, be nothing, non-existent—because, in your cognizant soul, you imagine that if you're nothing, then perhaps you wouldn't need to suffer the torments of hell. But unfortunately, the torments will go on forever and ever. Your choice—receive Jesus as your Lord and Savior (Romans 10:9) and go to Heaven or fail to receive Christ as your savior and go to Hell for eternity.

Characteristics of Satan, Devil, Lucifer, Dragon

Let me say that because of COVID-19 (HB-house bill 6666), satan is using this virus to destroy and stop godly Christians from going to church. For example, during 2021–2022, *one-third* of Christians stopped going to church, and as a by-product of this, regular tithing is not being paid, and Bibles are not being read.[144] Because of the social distancing, either mandated or self-imposed due to fear that is real or imagined, many Christians made decisions to opt-out of their small groups (cell group or mini church), canceled dentist and doctor appointments, ceased going to the gym for healthy work-outs and exercise—and the list goes on.

Satan wants you and your family to be weak so that he (satan) can attack you with fiery darts of fear and try to isolate you from your cell Christian group or church pack. Like a pack of wolves hunting a moose, once the wolf pack identifies the weakness in their prey, they attack, just like satan makes his plan of attack on me and you!

Now that we are in the "End times," I feel in my spirit that we have perhaps six years left before Jesus' second coming. I explain this in other chapters of this book.

In 2022 the signs of the times have made its presence clear. Many powerful and anointed men and women of God have

144 "Evangelist Nathan Morris, Guest Speaker at King's Chapel in Honolulu, HI," 2022.

passed on from this earth. There is a spiritual shift on earth and in Heaven. The guard is *changing*! Paul and Jan Crouch, Billy Graham, Prophet Morris Cerilio, Kathryn Kulman, Egheart Bunke, and others who have passed on. It's up to the next in line of anointed men and women of God to become as powerful or more as those that have gone before them and take their rightful place at the Gate—just like the sentry guards over Jerusalem.

The spirit of the antichrist is more prevalent than ever on earth in this end-time era. Satan is ready to take over the nations and the world with his antichrist spirit and a false prophet. Satan is ready to run his *one-world order* government and *one-world* religion, create a totally *cashless society* and implement *the mark of the beast 666* and complete control.

Today, right now—a forerunner to the 666 mark of the beast has emerged in the name of technology and medicine. Tags are inserted into the skin the size of a rice grain via vaccine needles. The pattern of these tags is just under the skin, and they become similar to a bar-code tattoo. Instead of ink, this highly specific medical record consists of copper-based quantum dots. "The quantum dots are composed of nanocrystals, which emit near-infrared (NIR) light that can be detected by a specially equipped smartphone."[145]

Satan is bad, bad, bad news—like Hitler, Stalin, every murderer, child abuser, every killer who walked the earth—all combined x 1,000, and not only that, but the enemy of our souls is also on steroids!

145 "Quantum Dots Deliver Vaccines and Invisibly Encode Vaccination History in Skin., Genetic Engineering & Biotechnology News, 2019. https://www.genengnews.com/topics/drug-discovery/quantum-dots-deliver-vaccines-and-invisibly-encode-vaccination-history-in-skin/.

I've been studying Hitler because he is like the antichrist. Hitler took ten years before he became president.[146] December 2022 will mark the halfway mark before the antichrist takes charge, and 2028–29 (Shemitah) will mark ten years for the antichrist. Also, the Lord showed me now, just as Auschwitz and Hitler did, the antichrist will have his own Auschwitz for the world, and all mankind that doesn't receive the mark of the Beast, 666, will die. There will be billions who will die, not millions.

God is saying to us, "*wake up, people!* Wake up! Wake up, my true Christian sons and daughters!"

On a largely secular online television channel, natgeotv.com, the Roman Emperor *Neron Kaisar's* (Nero's) name was translated into the Hebrew alphabet and assigned numerical values.[147] His name added up to 666. In Revelation 13:18 (KJV), we read,

> Here is wisdom. Let him that hath understanding count the number of the beast: for it is the number of a man; and his number is Six hundred threescore and six.

Bible Verses to Take to Heart with a Wake-up Call:

- John 10:10—satan wants to kill, steal and destroy you!
- Ezekiel 28:13–15; Isaiah 14:12—God made satan.

---

146 "The Hidden Side of World War II: Last Secrets of Nazis," YouTube: Best Documentary, 2022, https://www.youtube.com/watch?v=unN7e---Mbg.
147 "Nero as the Antichrist," U Chicago Education, Accessed October 5, 2022, https://penelope.uchicago.edu/g̃rout/encyclopaedia_romana/gladiators/nero.html.

- Luke 22:31—satan needs permission from God to do anything 1 Peter 5:8—satan will be your adversary throughout your life.
- Revelation 9:11—satan will abandon you in prison, when you're on drugs or overdosed, when you have no money, when you have a gambling debt, when your dying, when you need help, when you're indisposed and suffering as an alcoholic.
- Psalms 109:6; Revelation 12:10—satan will accuse you of any sin you committed so that you can go to hell for eternity with him.
- Revelation 12:9—satan will deceive you with money, fame, a bigger house, a nicer car, or work.
- Ezekiel 28:13–15; Isaiah 14:12–14—satan is filled with pride.
- 2 Corinthians 11:14—satan has servants and a chain of command like the military.
- Matthew 12:22–29—satan is known as a strong man.

The True Christian Church and the Cult

The following are some examples (not a complete list) of true foundational Christian Churches which God has set up on the earth.

- Pentecostal—originated in Los Angeles in the 20th Century.
- Presbyterian—originated in Scotland in the 16th Century.
- Baptist—originated in Europe in the 17th Century.

- Methodist—originated in Britain by John Wesley in the 18th Century.
- The Protestant Reformation began in Wittenberg, Germany, on October 31, 1517.
- Lutheran—originated in Germany in the 16th Century by Martin Luther.
- Nazarene—was founded in October 1895 in Los Angeles, CA.
- Charismatic Church—began on April 3, 1960, when Dennis J. Bennett, rector of St. Mark's Episcopal Church in Van Nuys, CA, recounted his pentecostal experience.
- Seventh Day Adventist—began in the 1830s–1840s during the period of the Second Great Awakening, the Millerite movement.
- Calvary Chapel–Chuck Smith, founder in Costa Mesa, CA, in 1965.[148]

Once you become a Christian, it would greatly benefit you and your walk with Christ if you follow your pastor, bishop, reverend, priest, Christian doctor, apostle, prophet, prophetess, teacher, evangelist, etc. Be certain that what you hear in terms of guidance and advice doesn't contradict the Word of God, the Bible. After all, we are only human and ask God for wisdom and a spirit of discernment. Learn to *let go* of any negative words, spiritually empty things, worldly, or hedonistic ideas presented

148 "Date and Founders of Christian Faith Groups," Religious Tolerance, 2019, http://www.religioustolerance.org/chr_den1.htm; Wikipedia Contributors, "History of the Church of the Nazarene," Wikipedia, The Free Encyclopedia, 2022, https://en.wikipedia.org/wiki/History_of_the_Church_of_the_Nazarene; "1960 Charismatic Movement - BEAUTIFUL FEETBEAUTIFUL FEET," Beautiful Feet: Reviving Believers & Churches, 2022, https://romans1015.com/charismatic-movement/.

intentionally or unintentionally by another person. Leave the bad stuff behind and take the good stuff to go! Ultimately, only trust God 100% of the time.

The Implications of Many Practices Which Are All Considered the Cult:

- Mormons
- Jehovah Witnesses
- Community Church
- Islam (Muslims)
- Hinduism
- Buddhism
- Unification Church
- Christian Science
- Unity School of Christianity
- Unitarian
- Scientology
- Wicca
- New Age
- Nation of Islam
- Bahai' Faith
- Hare Krishna
- Transcendental Meditation
- Satanism
- Spiritualism
- Santeria
- Voodoo
- Theosophy
- Anthroposophy
- Eckankar
- Meditation
- Astrology
- Horoscopes
- Shinto
- Taoism
- Confucianism
- Marxism
- Communism
- Socialism
- Taoism

- Soka Gakkai
- International Free Mason
- Rosicrucianism (AMORC)
- Kabbalah Centre
- The Church of Satan
- Daoism
- Sikhism
- Muslim Brotherhood Metaverse network 3D (social connection)
- Fortunetellers, soothsayers, witchcraft, sorcerer, sorcery (Deuteronomy 18:10–13)

Sadly, the above list of *cults* is not exhaustive but indicative of man in his arrogance and pride who would not only like to question the authority of God and the Holy Bible but create a customized religion to suit their needs. The cult leaders do this for political power and to create a platform for demonic activity or practices, which is clearly forbidden in Deuteronomy 12:32 and 18:10–13, and the last thing imparted to the Apostle John from God in Revelation 22:18–19.

Other practices that border, dabble in, or are directly related to cults are:

- Palm readings
- Crystal ball gazing
- Numerology other than biblical
- Hypnotism
- Transcendental Meditation ™
- Far Eastern meditation

- Seeing psychics
- Tarot cards
- Ouija boards
- Seeing mediums
- Seeing spiritists
- Horoscopes
- Astrology
- I Ching
- Crystals
- Channeling
- Reincarnation
- Astral projection
- ESP
- Dungeons & Dragons
- New Age Movement Activities
- Necromancy

The word *cult* is derived from the Latin word cultus, meaning mysterious, hidden, and very secretive demonic forces.[149] Demonic spirits or forces can come through the phone (i.e., psychic readings, reading the horoscopes in the paper, TV, radio, laptop, iPhone, etc. You must guard your spirit. If you follow these evil spirits, you will not be raptured with Jesus' church or be part of the second coming of Jesus Christ.

Warning: Stop engaging with the enemy of our souls.

Satan wants to kill, steal and destroy you, your family, and all of humanity (John 10:10). You must fight back with the armor of God every day (Ephesians 6:14–17) with the belt of truth, the breastplate of righteousness, the shoes of readiness and peace, the shield of faith, the helmet of salvation, and the sword of the spirit! This is the daily price you must pay and the daily price of dying to yourself of pride, greed, and arrogance!

149 "Cult," WordHippo Thesaurus, 2022, https://www.wordhippo.com/what-is/another-word-for/cult.html.

Satan will attack your mind with thoughts and ideas. Your mind is the battleground for satan. You need to play Christian music in your home and car. Satan can't stand Christian music or anything of God. You must also read the Bible daily to gain wisdom.

Comparison of Christianity and the Cult

Christianity	Cult
Christians are led by God, Jesus Christ, Holy Spirit.	Cults are led by satan, devil, and lucifer.
The Holy Bible is the absolute Word of God.	The cults believe the Bible is not the Word of God, and they add their ideas to the Bible in other books, such as the Quran.
There are no hidden secrets in Christianity.	There are many hidden secrets in cults (i.e., the Mormon Temple rituals are copied from Masons).
Romans 10:9 and John	
3:16 says everyone who chooses God will go to Heav-en for all eternity.	100% you will go to Hell, for all eternity
Christians believe there is healing from God.	Cults do not believe in healing.
In Christianity, there are blessings.	Cults have no blessings.

Christians live in the light of Jesus Christ.	Cults live in darkness.
Christians feel whole.	Cults feel a void.
Christians are free in Jesus' grace.	Cults feel as if they are in bondage.
Christians are not God but are His disciples.	Cults believe they are god or that you are god.
Christians may commit sins but can be forgiven with repentance.	In cults, there is no repentance.
Christians fast and Pray.	In cults, there is no fasting.
Christians listen to Christian music.	Cults listen to demonic music.
There is no demonic activity in a true Christian Church.	There are demonic spirits within the cult.
Christians receive divine instruction from living apostles, prophets, pastors, teachers, and Evangelists.	Cults have no current guidance from God, Jesus, or Holy Spirit but are led by demonic forces from satan.
Christians see and receive current-day miracles.	In the cults, there are no miracles.
Christians have the Holy Spirit living within them.	The cult members do not have the Holy Spirit living inside them.

Body—blood, flesh and bones. **Spirit**—wisdom, conscience, and communion. **Soul**—will, mind, and emotions	**Soul**—will, mind and emotions **Body**—blood, flesh and bones. **Spirit**—lost spirit equals eternal death
Christians believe in God, Jesus, and the Holy Spirit.	Cults believe in satan, the antichrist, and the false prophet.
Jesus' Resurrection with 500-plus witnesses	No resurrection, no witnesses

Considering the rampant number of cult practices around the world, one can see that spiritual warfare is on the rise. Here are a number of other statistics showing how technology and socio-economic factors can be distractions from God and our faith.

Recent Statistics Show Spiritual Warfare Is On the Rise

Youth are using TikTok to commit suicide. TikTok is known in China as Douyin, a video-focused social networking service owned by the Chinese company ByteDance Ltd.[150] Who can deny that when young people commit suicide, whether by accident or on purpose, something has gone horribly wrong and is beyond human comprehension and control?

150 Salvador Rodriguez, "TikTok Insiders Say Chinese Parent ByteDance Is in Control," CNBC, 2021, https://www.cnbc.com/2021/06/25/tiktok-insiders-say-chinese-parent-bytedance-in-control.html.

Are there implications if, in six years, as some studies show, 40% of world scientists will be from China? Does the world have any trust left after Covid 19? The controversy of the virus originating from the Wuhan laboratories?

Satan has been instrumental in breaking up marriages in the U.S. Consider the following statistics:

- Christians have a 54% divorce rate.
- Non-Christians have a 52% divorce rate.
- Second marriages account for 60% of divorces.
- Third marriages have an 87% divorce rate.
- Workplace affairs account for 55% of all affairs.[151]

One of the main desires for females in the U.S. is to attain financial security to pay off all credit cards and have a zero balance, and for men, they wish to attain financial security to purchase a house. There are many reasons for divorce in the U.S., including disagreements over finances, religion, how to raise children, and a lack of effective communication to resolve these issues.[152]

It is important first to understand that satan does have a chain of command over every city, state, country, province, nation, and continent! How is this so, you ask? Because in Ephesians 6:11–15, God is telling us (yes, you and me) that satan and his demonic workers can be anyone disguised as a nice, decent citizen in your neighborhood, city, state, etc.

---

151 Gary Smalley, *The DNA of Relationships*, Tyndale House Publishers, 2004.
152 Ibid.

The nice person next door who is practicing a false religion could be a warlock, a witch, an evil-minded person who is against God, or just someone who is lost. The enemy of our soul wishes ultimately to mean us harm, kill, and destroy our families and us (John 10:10).

We have learned from the COVID-19 pandemic that we cannot just trust anyone to influence us in a way that is unholy or goes against God's Word. Just because that person may be a doctor, dentist, family member, friend, neighbor, co-worker, realtor, etc., doesn't mean that we can trust this person with things affecting the destiny of our spirit and soul.

In John 10:10 and 1 Peter 5:8, God's Word shows the wiles of the enemy. Even though you might think to yourself that you live in a peaceful neighborhood and do not see satan at work in your neighborhood, this is said not to cause undue fear or paranoia about your neighbor—but to ask you to be sure of whom you include in your close circle of family and friends that you trust.

If God calls you to witness to others about Jesus Christ, then you are going into neighborhoods, cities, states, countries, etc., where you may come up against many demonic forces. God will equip you with a team and with the armor of God if you are a missionary. I talk about this in another book, *The Five-fold Army—5 Distinct Roles.*

Let's break this down a bit. Do you see homelessness, drugs, gangs, prostitution, human trafficking, abortion, graffiti, or signs such as shoes hanging from telephone wires? If so, these are all the result of satan working in the demonic to destroy human beings, especially those who love God.

In relationships, do you know anyone who has had an affair outside of marriage, arguing, strife, competition, etc., among anyone you affiliate with? These negative conditions for human beings are caused by satan's workers among us.

Satan is 100% real, and he wants to take as many people as possible to Hell with him. For all eternity. Once citizens end up in that other worldly, fiery furnace, they can never bargain their way out. Thus the sense of urgency I have been given to let others know the truth about some of these false religions and cults which exist in the world and have managed, with satan's help to attain a surprising number of followers. Satan's chain of command: witches, warlocks, strong men, false prophet, and the antichrist.

> For we wrestle not against flesh and blood, but against principalities, against powers, against the rulers of the darkness of this world, against spiritual wickedness in high places.
>
> (Ephesians 6:12 KJV)

- Heaven—Accepting Jesus Christ as Lord and Savior of one's life, asking for forgiveness of sins, and repenting of sins makes heaven no longer a sinful nature.
- Hell—When one rejects Jesus Christ as Lord and Savior and continues to operate in a sinful nature, then Hell is their reality.
- Satan wants to bring you into disunity, and God wants to bring you into unity.

- Revelation 12:10—Satan condemns humanity on Earth. He accuses everyone, and yes, that means you and me! Revelation 12:10 explains that satan is our accuser.

Revelation 13:1 (NIV)

> The dragon stood on the shore of the sea, and I saw a beast coming out of the sea. It had ten horns and seven heads with ten crowns on its horns, and on each head a blasphemous name.

Revelation 13:1 Explained

- The Dragon—satan's antichrist. He will be evil to the core, bad in all respects, violent, prideful, vain, arrogant, and he doesn't care about human life. He essentially acts in a savage manner, is lawless and wild, and he hates God, Christ, and the Holy Spirit. He (satan) will even appoint him as an apostle (Daniel 7:8; Revelation 13:1–4).

  Satan always copies God and forms the unholy trinity, which is comprised of satan, the antichrist or satan's apostle, and the false prophet in a continuum against Christians, humanity in general, and our Triune God (God the Father, Jesus Christ, and the Holy Spirit).
- The Sea (Mediterranean)—a gentile worldly man who is coming quietly from Europe.
- The Ten Horns—represent ten nations, ten prime ministers, ten presidents, ten countries' oligarchs (Daniel

2:41; Revelation 17:12), and satan, the antichrist, and the false prophet will dominate them.

- The Seven Heads —mean seven consecutive leaders out of the ten will be destroyed, at which point satan, the antichrist (satan's apostle), and the false prophet will create "one nation" and implement a *one-world government, one-world religion, one-world finance*, etc.

Author's Note:

The Bible does not give a name for the antichrist or false prophet because people will try to kill that person and take him out. The antichrist's name and false prophet's name will come out into the open and be known to the general public once the "Rapture of the true Christian Church" occurs (which marks the end of the Church Age) and the next stage, the "Tribulation" begins.

I also feel the Bible has the antichrist, false prophet, and the time and day of the rapture of the Christian Church and Tribulation coded in it. This insight will entail many years of Bible study, attending prophetic conferences and Bible Study courses, and drawing close to Jesus so that the Holy Spirit may impart knowledge.

The following chapters defend and explain the Christian faith (apologetics) and provide Bible Study tools for personal growth as a Christian in the modern world. Included are interesting facts and figures, personal accounts, and testimonies—all a testament of faith in Jesus Christ, our Lord and Savior.

It is my sincere hope and prayer that you come away blessed and super-charged that the end game is really the beginning of things to come where God Himself and all those who believe upon Him shall prevail in Heaven on earth and the ages to come.

Get ready!

CHAPTER 15

A Contrast Between Heaven and Hell

The inspiration for presenting a chapter about Heaven or Hell comes from scripture, but most importantly, it's God's plan for humanity—including You. If it were not for Bible verses that back up what is being presented here in terms of Heaven or Hell, what I might write about these two eternal destinies would rather come from my own imagination—and not God's plan.

I felt that a comparison chart of Heaven vs. Hell in terms of where you might find biblical references would be helpful and that when you, in turn, share these verses, one may see at a glance where the verses are located.

It is my hope and prayer that you will have 100% certainty about accepting Jesus Christ as your Lord and Savior so that you may inherit the Kingdom of God (Heaven).

Jesus, in His own words, summed it up in John 14:6 (NIV), "Jesus answered, 'I am the way and the truth and the life. No one comes to the Father except through me."

Bible Verses that Mention Heaven vs. Hell

Exodus10:21	Matthew 7:12, 10:15, 10:28, 12:37, 13:30,13:49, 18:24, 22:13, 23:14–15, 24:51, 25:41 (refers to the devil), 25:46
Leviticus 17:11	Mark 9:47
Numbers 32:33	Luke 12:24, 13:3, 16, 19:27, 19:27, 24:16, 28:18
Deuteronomy 6, 11:41, 17, 32:22	John 1:17, 3:17–18, 3:36, 5:29, 10:10, 14:2, 14:6, 14:22, 15:18
Job 7:9, 10:22, 15:16, 17:16, 24:20	Acts 17:28
Psalms 1:2, 11:6, 18:32, 32:10, 36:5, 50:22, 73:18–19, 74:20 (*refers to modern-day Hamas*), 78:49, 88:4, 88:12, 103:17, 116:3, 127:2, 139:2, 140:10, 141:7	Romans 10:9
Proverbs 7:27, 16:6	1 Corinthians 2:19
Ecclesiastes 6:4, 9:10	2 Corinthians 5:10–11
Isaiah 9:6, 14:9–11, 24:22, 32:18, 38:18, 45:5, 57:20–21	Galatians 3:26
Jeremiah 20:11	Ephesians 3:19
Lamentations 3:6	Hebrews 10:28
Ezekiel 26:20	James 1:17, 2:7, 2:16
Ezekiel 26:20,	1 John 4:16, 5
Amos 5:18–19	Jude 13
Zechariah 9:11	Revelation 1:16, 13:6, 14:10–11, 20:15, 21:8

Please take a moment to compare and contrast what Heaven will be like vs. Hell.

Heaven	**Hell**
Heaven is an eternal place.	Hell is an eternal place.
Heaven is filled with light.	Hell is filled with darkness.
Heaven is a place of complete Peace.	Hell is filled with torments, turmoil, and gnashing of teeth.
There are no more tears or pain in Heaven.	Anguish and emotional and physical pain are in Hell.
There will be food to eat, water to drink, and Bread of Life in Heaven.	There is no food or water in Hell.
Heaven is filled with hope and love.	Hell is filled with fear and despair.
Heaven is filled with happiness and joy.	Hell is a place of sadness and suffering.
There is fellowship with loved ones in Heaven.	There is no fellowship in Hell and you are alone.
Heaven is comfortable and relaxed.	In Hell, one is confined to a cell with no comforts.
In Heaven, one is loved by God, angels, and those who have accepted Christ as their Savior will be at home in a heavenly abode forever.	Hell is a place meant for the enemies of God.

Heave has pleasant and beautiful smells/aromas.	Hell has the smell of sulfur and burning flesh.
In Heaven, one will have work and a purpose for God, which one will love.	There is no purpose in Hell except to suffer and rot in a place that one cannot imagine.
In Heaven, there will be singing praises to God almighty.	In Hell, there will be crying out in anguish and terror.

God created us with a free will from which to choose to believe or not to believe. It is of one's free will that we decide to believe or not. If God created all of us to believe automatically, we would be like created robots. What pleasure would God derive from His little robots that automatically praise Him or believe in Him? Not much. This would be silly for such an all-seeing, all-powerful God to do.

God created us to have a personal relationship with Him. He created us with free will, and it is out of this free will that we commune with Him, seek Him and His Word, believe in Him, and act accordingly. This gives God much pleasure seeing that people recognize Him and love Him out of their own free will!

I've been listening to several televised evangelist pastors just about every night for the past several months. Not because I have suddenly turned into a fanatical religious person, but because I feel God has called me and stirred up within me a quest to be more aware than ever before of the times we live in and how this relates to Bible prophecy.

The interesting thing is this... How is it that pastors from Hawaii, California, Georgia, Tennessee, and Florida are all addressing the end times that we are living in today? These pastors are speaking to their churches and congregations the way Paul spoke to the Corinthians, Galatians, or Ephesians. They evangelize from the west to the east, stretching out to the Pacific and Atlantic oceans. It is also highly unlikely that these pastors stay at home and watch television, much less watch other pastors' televised sermons to compare notes. How is it that these pastors in different states and timelines are basically saying the same thing?

It is because they are referencing the Bible—the Word of God. It is because God has called them to speak on His behalf. It is because they are caught up in the language of truth and that they are walking in the power of the Holy Spirit.

There are over forty-one references in the Holy Bible regarding the Holy Spirit. For instance, in Romans 5:13 (NIV),

> May the God of hope fill you with all joy and peace as you trust in him, so that you may overflow with hope by the power of the Holy Spirit.

In 1 Corinthians 6:19–20 (NIV),

> Do you not know that your bodies are temples of the Holy Spirit, who is in you, whom you have received from God? You are not your own; you were bought at a price. Therefore, honor God with your bodies.

I believe God has called His people, especially ordained men and women of God, to be aware of and speak of the signs and seasons of the times in which we are living in today. Here are a few online articles for further reading on the signs and seasons of our times:

- Ray C. Stedman, Signs and Seasons: Foundations for Living, 1967. https://www.raystedman.org/old-testament/genesis/signs-and-seasons
- The John Ankerberg Show, What Nations Will Be Involved in the Military Attack Against Israel Predicted in Ezekiel 38? 2020. https://jashow.org/articles/what-nations-will-be-involved-in-the-military-attack-against-israel-predicted-in-ezekiel-38/
- Lorimer Wilson, IMF Plans to Force a Cashless Society on World Unfolding—Here's How, 2020. https://munknee.com/imf-plan-to-force-a-cashless-society-on-world-unfolding-heres-how/

We can no longer shrug off the socio-political or economic events of the day as politics as usual in our society, state, country, or world. What we are experiencing and witnessing today are the end-time Bible prophecies being fulfilled right before our very eyes more than ever before. The commonality is that we are all contemporaries of the current time. Most of the things we witness are not pleasant, and our human nature is not to speak of them as much as possible. We most likely do not speak of them because it is too much to bear. For instance, one only needs to do a quick internet search to note major earthquakes, tsunamis, hurricanes, and floods around the world that have caused such severe human disasters and loss of life in just the last five years alone to realize that these events mean something far beyond random acts of God.

Acts of God. This is what insurance companies call these natural disasters. Is it because the insurance companies believe that a higher power exists in the form of a living God, or is it because of a lack of anything else to call it? I believe the person or group who first drafted the insurance declaration outline was actually someone who believed in God and that God Himself is in control of these natural disasters.

On January 12, 2010, a 7.0 earthquake struck Haiti with a loss of life of over 100 thousand.[153] I'll never forget witnessing split-second news footage of an earth-moving tractor that had scooped up bodies and proceeded to dump the bodies into a mass grave. That news clip forever changed the way I viewed the devastation in densely populated areas. It has been over twelve years since the 7.0 earthquake occurred in Haiti.

As heart-wrenching as this catastrophic event is, it was my personal hope that the people of Haiti, especially its government, had seen God in the compassion of the United States armed forces and rescue units—many of them Christian organizations—as these soldiers brought relief and aid to the injured, sick and dying. It is my prayer that God will continue to use this event to help further the Word of God and bring about more believers by the millions in Jesus Christ.

In other parts of the globe, consider the very real prospect and implications of radical Islamic organizations and govern-

153 Andrew Cawthorne, and Catherine Bremer, "U.S. Pours Aid into Haiti, Survivors Fight for Food," Reuters, 2010, https://www.reuters.com/article/us-quake-haiti/u-s-pours-aid-into-haiti-survivors-fight-for-food-idUSTRE60B5IZ20100116.

ments having nuclear weapons. Or what about the epidemics and pandemics of new viruses and infections, widespread pollution of drinking water, ongoing wars, and rumors of wars? In my awareness of the times we live in, this is why I choose to imagine Heaven. I think Heaven's door is very close, and our current generation will continue to experience many of the end-time prophecies in the Bible—which means that Heaven must also be just around the corner. On the other hand, "soon" can be a long time in the spectrum of eternity.

Before Jesus returns, we can be sure that there will be a reawakening of the Church, revitalization in Christian groups and with Christians in general, and a major outpouring of God's Word to the world that so very needs it. When this outpouring of God's Word occurs, it will be unmistakable. At this time, Christians will begin to be persecuted—even in the U.S.—beyond the somewhat "mild" verbal persecution—the onslaught will be as with the persecution of the early churches.

Believers will welcome the resurgence of God's Word upon our nation and the world, and unbelievers will despise it. Ultimately, the apocalyptic events which the Bible describes in Ezekiel, Daniel, Revelation, and the harmony of the gospels Matthew, Mark, Luke, and John will be made manifest while the world continues around us with us in it, and many more will come to believe while others will come to despise and persecute those who believe.

What Is Hell like?

To obtain a glimpse of what Hell would be like for some, consider this parable:

"There was a certain rich man who was clothed in purple and fine linen and fared sumptuously every day. But there was a certain beggar named Lazarus, full of sores, who was laid at his gate, desiring to be fed with the crumbs which fell from the rich man's table. Moreover the dogs came and licked his sores. "So it was that the beggar died, and was carried by the angels to Abraham's bosom. The rich man also died and was buried. And being in torments in Hades, he lifted up his eyes and saw Abraham afar off, and Lazarus in his bosom. Then he cried and said, 'Father Abraham, have mercy on me, and send Lazarus that he may dip the tip of his finger in water and cool my tongue; for I am tormented in this flame.' But Abraham said, 'Son, remember that in your lifetime you received your good things, and likewise Lazarus evil things; but now he is comforted, and you are tormented. And besides all this, between us and you there is a great gulf fixed, so that those who want to pass from here to you cannot, nor can those from there pass to us.' Then he said, 'I beg you therefore, father, that you would send him to my father's house,' for I have five brothers, that he may testify to them, lest they also come to this place of torment." "Abraham said to him, 'They have Moses and the prophets; let them hear them.' "And he said, 'No, Father Abraham; but if one goes to them from the dead, they will repent.' 'But he said to him,' If they do not hear Moses and the prophets, neither will they be persuaded though one rise from the dead.'"

(Luke 16:19–31 NKJV)

The idea behind the parable of the rich man and Lazarus suggests but does not necessarily reveal, what life may be like after death. The purpose is to help listeners realize something of the bliss of Heaven and something of the torment of Hell. If this parable of a rich man who died and went to Hell and a poor beggar who died and went to Heaven is not a wake-up call to those of us living in our "splendid comfort zones," then, short of witnessing Jesus emerge in the sky, I'm not sure what is.

Why did the rich man in the parable above end up in torment? Did his eternal destiny have to do with the stewardship (or lack thereof) of his wealth on earth? The Bible does not say but instead contrasts the rich man with a poor beggar who ends up in Abraham's bosom.

Today, millionaires (rich men) are said to give 9% to charity.

> The question of "how much giving is enough?" has always dogged the wealthy. John D. Rockefeller, one of the fathers of American philanthropy, tithed 10 percent of his income to his church ever since his first paycheck. Warren Buffett and Bill Gates took the 10 percent even higher, arguing through their Giving Pledge organization that the rich should give away at least half their wealth.[154]

God, on the other hand, in His Sovereign Authority, asks us to bring in a full tithe of 10%. The scripture verse in Malachi 3:10 is the only place in the Bible where God actually invites humans to *test* him on this tithing principle.

154 Robert Frank, "Millionaires Give Nine Percent of Income to Charity," CBNC, 2013, https://www.cnbc.com/amp/id/49596515.

> Bring ye all the tithes into the storehouse, that there may be meat in mine house, and prove me now herewith, saith the LORD of hosts, if I will not open you the windows of heaven, and pour you out a blessing, that there shall not be room enough to receive it.
>
> (Malachi 3:10 KJV)

Consider also that in Luke 18:22, Jesus asked the rich man to sell all that he had and distribute to the poor and that he would have treasure in heaven, and he beckoned the man to "come follow" Him. Jesus is very clear when He said that the Scriptures had warned us again and again about the great chasm which will separate those who believe in and live and act accordingly from those who do not. When Abraham said in the parable above, "If they [unbelievers] 'do not listen to Moses and the Prophets,' neither will they be persuaded if someone rises from the dead" (Luke 16:31 NASB). Abraham's sentiment still rings true today—thousands of years and generations upon generations later.

I just want to clarify at this point that Jesus is the only person who rose from the dead and who can save all of mankind if we will only recognize Him for who He is—the Son of God and live and act accordingly. We shouldn't have to live through more tribulations or the actual, end-time tribulations just to believe that Jesus Christ is the Son of God and therefore recognize Him as our Lord and Savior of our own free will.[155]

155 Eckhardt, 2021.

Given a last-minute chance to decide, is it probable that a person would like to exist for all eternity in Heaven or in Hell? And here you have the ultimate, no-brainer answer to the ultimate question: Heaven, of course! Perhaps imagining what the opposite of Heaven might be like for even a moment would be the motivating turning point for many.

Consider for a moment what a terrible experience would be like—the saddest moment, the most excruciating physical pain, the greatest shame, and the harshest word. The ugliest, scariest, dirtiest scenario that one can possibly experience. Imagine a person having to relive these awful experiences *over and over again* for all eternity. The environment in Hell will be one with a continuing sulfur (fire, smoke, and brimstone) smell, and there is fiery heat all around everyone who does not accept Jesus as their savior. One's lungs will be smoke-filled, hot, dry, and burning sensation. There is a Lake of Fire with unbearable pain within one's will, mind, and emotions. One's spirit is committed to torment for all eternity (Psalm 11:16; Revelation 19:3, 20, 20:18, 21:8; Isaiah 30:33, 34:9–10; Luke 16:24; Ezekiel 38:22).

Imagine a person is feeling so much physical pain, like a toothache that begins in the mouth, swelling the cheeks and face until it pounds in one's head like a hammer, until their entire body is writhing in pain so that they finally collapse on the ground from sheer exhaustion... only to awaken in darkness with the toothache starting all over again.

Imagine a person who is drunk. I am not referring to a glass of wine at a wedding feast or out to dinner. I am talking about sheer drunkenness, partying, and carousing for no reason. Or imagine a person high on drugs and partying until they are sick and tired of the scene they are in, but it won't stop. They can't just leave the party and go home to a nice, comforting bed and sleep it off. No, instead, the beat of a sinister sound will drone on and on, and the anguished laughter, screams, or wailing continues as they and others in the scene finally collapse on the floor only to awaken to another haunting scenario in which they had invested much of their time while alive on earth.

The choice is clear for me. I choose to imagine heaven on earth right now, today, tomorrow, and the next day. I don't want to take any chances in jeopardizing my faith and what I've invested in for most of my life. My assets and everyone and thing I value will be stored up as investments toward my future in Heaven. God, Jesus, and Heaven are my secure investments that won't crash with the economy or deplete in value. For example, I am giving my home, truck, assets—everything to be used for God's Kingdom here on earth once I depart from this earth, and that is a moment in time that only the Lord knows.

Imagining Heaven is something anyone can do at any time. When one realizes that their imagination begins to focus on an eternal life scenario that can manifest itself—at any moment—and then they will begin to imagine Heaven in very realistic terms. This, in turn, creates great anticipation of this promised eternal life to come.

Imagine a place where we become like the angels, with new bodies that never become sick, old, or perish—a place where we will live in glory with our Father in Heaven and His Son, Jesus. Unimaginable visuals and imagery abound, and perceptions are absolutely fantastic to our senses!

Imagine being with your parents and siblings in perfect bliss within a grand mansion or palace, with beautifully endless landscapes and the entire world in perfect harmony where there are no more tears, pain, or wars. *It only gets better than our wildest imaginations!*

"When we get to heaven, I believe there are going to be a lot of wonderful surprises," said Pastor Chuck Smith, "I think that angels will take us on universal tours, and we'll be able to tour other galaxies."[156] Pastor Smith used this idea to bring home the point that "God so loved the world that he gave His only begotten Son, that whoever shall believeth in Him, shall not perish but have everlasting life" (John 3:16 KJV).

God moves in a village, tribe, community, location, city, state, province, wherever He needs to be on this planet Earth, wherever there are people.

God will move His Spirit among the people with signs, wonders, and miracles! Man moves people with ceremonies, rituals, and traditions, which sometimes douses God's movement of the Holy Spirit, much like water from a firehose that douses a fire and puts it out. The Holy Spirit fire of the Lord is the kind of fire you want under your feet and surrounding you as much as possible in these times.

I'd like to end this chapter with great advice which comes straight from the Word of God. If you are following your ways and not God's ways, please read the following verses from the Bible:

> "For my thoughts are not your thoughts, neither are your ways my ways," declares the LORD."
>
> (Isaiah 55:8 NIV)

156 Chuck Smith, 2009, "Excerpts Taken from Sermons of Pastor Chuck Smith: Sermons T4261 and T4262," *The Word for Today.*

And we know that in all things God works for the good of those who love him, who have been called according to his purpose.

(Romans 8:28 NIV)

CHAPTER 16

End-Time Apostle

The End-Times Apostle from Hawaii

Looking back at my life of sixty-three years, I see how the Lord has pulled me from the mountaintop of the Hawaiian Islands to use me on the front lines as His vessel and bondservant. As with any nation, an ambassador represents that nation in another country. For example, the U.S. has ambassadors all over the world. I see now that I am an *Ambassador for Christ,* and I represent Christ wherever I go around the world.

Often in a cult (such as the time growing up as a Mormon), the person or family does not see the falsehoods of a cult or the truth of a true religion of God—especially if indoctrinated into the false religion as a child. You are trusting your parents, and your parents trusted their parents. Many do not question the world in which they are indoctrinated. But I did. The Lord raised me up to question the Mormon faith, and the first book I wrote is about a wake-up call from Mormonism to Christianity.

When the FBI studies fake U.S. currency, they don't study the fake U.S. currency. The FBI studies the correct and 100% true U.S. currency, i.e., $20, $50, $100 bills, etc. so that they immediately know it is fake when they see a fake currency. This example is very much what it is like being in a cult, seeing and living in a cult such as Mormonism, and studying how cult leaders use tactics and indoctrination, which affects thousands of people from all religions, nations, cults, etc.

Studying the true religion of Christianity and the Word of God, the Bible, has given me a wide perspective to address the fake cults in the same way that the FBI can recognize the fake dollar bill.

Knowing what I know now, the Lord has used me to write this book in a human effort to influence you toward the truth and away from deception—especially if you are in bondage with a cult such as Islam, Hinduism, Buddhism, Mormonism, Jehovah Witness, and many others. However, it will be you asking God, Jesus, and His Holy Spirit for salvation. The Holy Spirit at work will bring you from one religious practice to the truth.

Do not be afraid (Isaiah 41:13; Joshua 1:9; Psalms 118:6; Philippians 4:6–7). God is in control. Just seek Him with an open, honest heart in prayer. Ask Him to show you three times in a vision or dream that what you are reading in this book is true or false.

What Is the Role of an Apostle?

God had sent the Apostle Paul to Ephesus to preach the Gospel. For three years, Apostle Paul set up *home churches* with thirty to forty people or disciples, who usually met in well-to-do family homes, and they were taught the Gospel of Jesus Christ. Paul traveled some 1,800 miles mostly by foot, withstood and endured persecution, imprisonment, house arrest, and beatings, and almost died twice for preaching the Gospel.

While in Rome under house arrest, Paul wrote four books: Ephesians, Philippians, Colossians, and Philemon. The Greek translation for apostle is "one who is sent off," or an ambassador for Christ.[157] As a modern-day End-Times Apostle, the Lord has prepared me for this ministry even while serving in the Mormon Church. I questioned their doctrines and tenets. This allowed me to see what was false and find the truth and become a born-again Christian in December 1999.

While in the Mormon Church, I lived in various states, such as Utah, Idaho, Wyoming, and Oregon. While in the U. S. Navy, I lived in California. Later, I lived in Massachusetts, New York, and Arizona, and presently I reside in Hawaii, where I was born. During my time in the Navy on the USS Gridley CG21 at dry dock, I signed up for the Bob Barker Show, *The Price Is Right*. Against some pretty big odds, I needed to impress a number of producers while standing in line for the show. I ran from one line to another to answer questions from various producers. I guess I impressed the producers, but not only that, but this local boy from Honolulu also ended up winning the Showcase Prize! This prize could completely furnish a house and included items from the carpet to the stove to the furnishings. Winning on this show is a combination of luck and skill and a very big deal for a guy from Honolulu.

Memorabilia shows just the carpet prize portion of the Showcase prize, which was everything needed to furnish a home! At the time of this big prize win, I still went by my given name, Dece Paul Milles. I was named the firstborn son of my parents in December. People had difficulty pronouncing my name, and quite frankly, it was kind of unsettling to have

157 Wikipedia Contributors, "Apostle." Wikipedia, The Free Encyclopedia, 2022, https://en.wikipedia.org/wiki/Apostle.

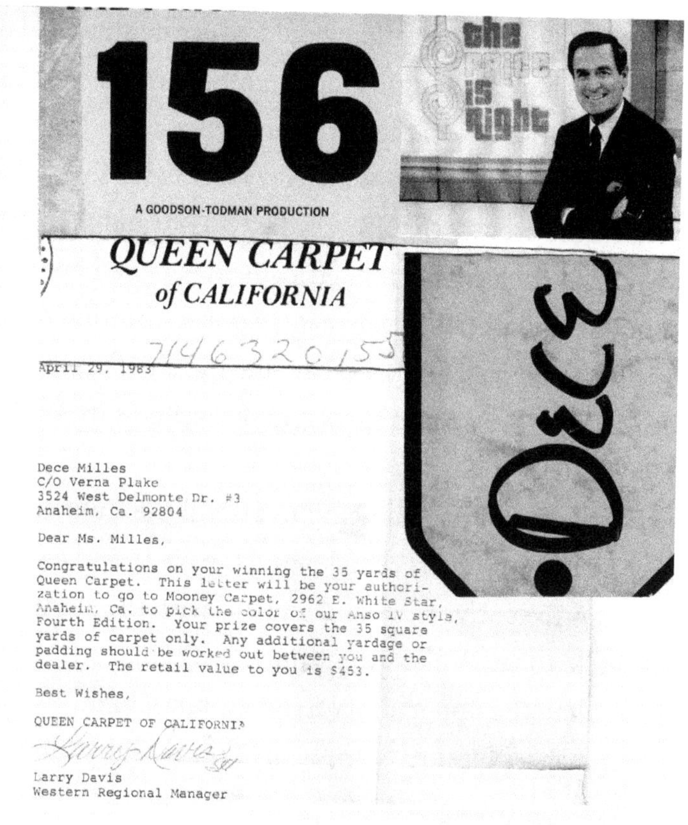

QUEEN CARPET
of CALIFORNIA

7146320155

April 29, 1983

Dece Milles
C/O Verna Plake
3524 West Delmonte Dr. #3
Anaheim, Ca. 92804

Dear Ms. Milles,

Congratulations on your winning the 35 yards of Queen Carpet. This letter will be your authorization to go to Mooney Carpet, 2962 E. White Star, Anaheim, Ca. to pick the color of our Anso IV style, Fourth Edition. Your prize covers the 35 square yards of carpet only. Any additional yardage or padding should be worked out between you and the dealer. The retail value to you is $453.

Best Wishes,

QUEEN CARPET OF CALIFORNIA

Larry Davis

Larry Davis
Western Regional Manager

Price is Right Winning Prize Package

a name that people couldn't say and that I wasn't particularly fond of.

Intending no disrespect for my parents, I thought to change my name, and on October 4, 1984, at the age of twenty-six, my given name was changed to *Constantine Ikaika Nightingdale* and notarized by then Lieutenant Governor of Hawaii, John Waihee. The Lord God had changed Paul the Apostle's name from Saul, and I feel that the Lord changed my name from Dece to

Constantine. When I knew that would be my new name, I could not explain where this came from, except that the Holy Spirit was speaking to me even then, at age twenty-six.

My experience as a cook in the Navy was extensive. I started cooking for the crew of the USS Gridley (CG21) and then worked my way up to cooking for the Officer's Mess, then became the Captain's personal chef. After that, I cooked for nine Admirals as their personal chef and then became the chief instructor for the USA Navy—Mess Specialists A and C schools in San Diego, CA (RTC/NTC).

I was able to obtain financing to attend the Culinary Institute of America in New York following the Navy, and as a result, I became an Executive Chef and worked with the University of Hawaii at Manoa. While attending the Culinary Institute of America, I had the opportunity to meet Julia Child.

It was such a pleasure to meet the famous Julia Child while attending the Culinary Institute of America in New York.

Living in or traveling through forty-nine states allowed me to meet many different people of different cultures, including sampling various cuisine, which was a priority for me as a chef. I was able to see how different people of different cultures live, work, and play. The one last state that I will travel to in the near future is Alaska.

I want to see and experience Alaska because I've been back and forth across the U.S. map to forty-nine states, except Alaska. I have enjoyed salmon fishing in Idaho and Wyoming, but I would like to experience salmon fishing in Alaska. Fishing has been a way of life for me since I was a small child. I also want to be there in person to taste Alaskan cuisine and the culture as

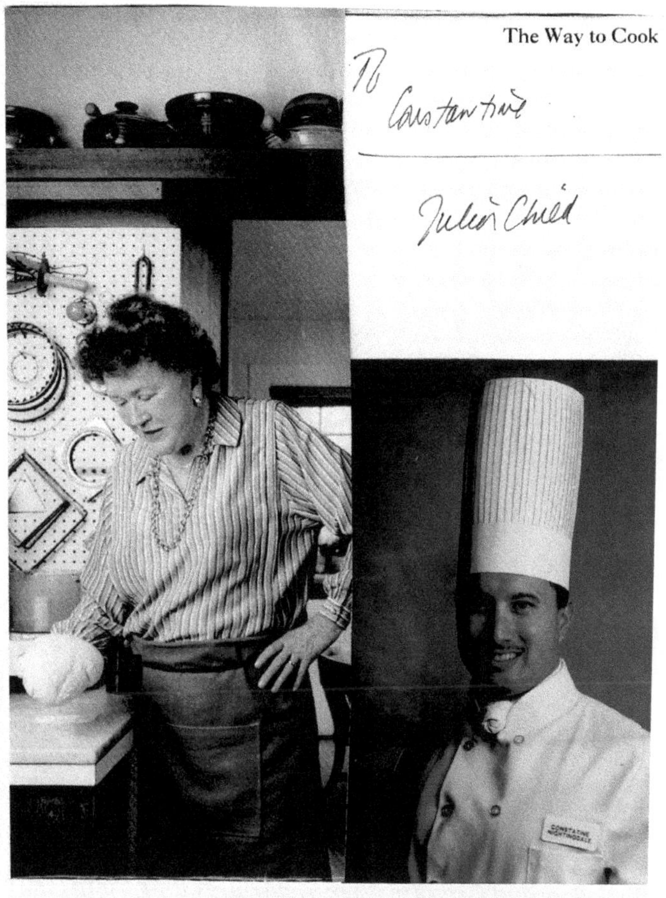

Julia Child and Culinary Art Student, Constantine Nightingdale

I travel to remote places and develop friendships all over the world.

Growing up in Hawaii with an ethnic background of Hawaiian, Hungarian, Chinese, and Portuguese allowed me to experience growing up with different cultures and enjoy various ethnic cuisine. My maternal grandmother (on the right in the photo below), who was Portuguese, would love to cook and prepare five to eight dishes for dinner on a regular basis. As a small child, I enjoyed her cooking, and the various tasty dishes certainly influenced me to want to cook on a professional level.

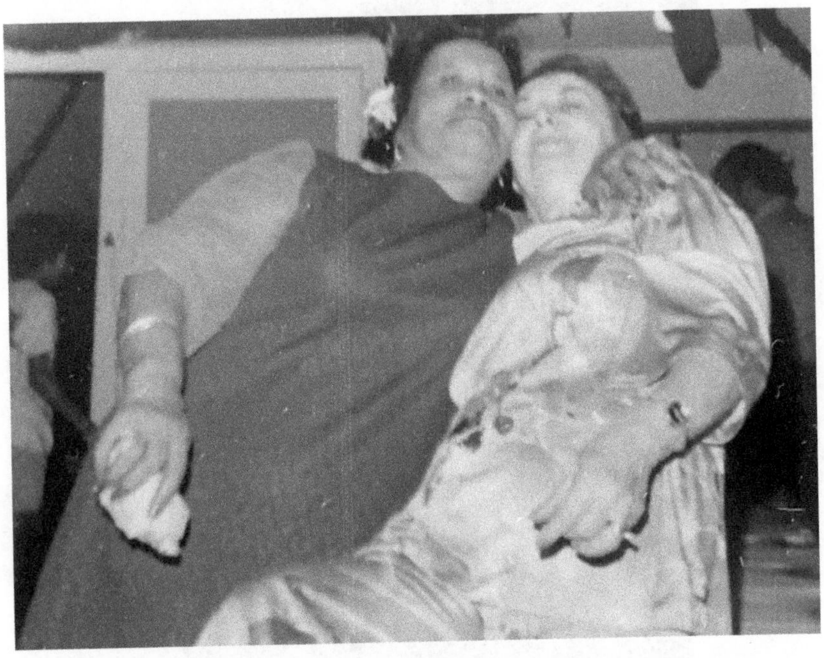

Two Grandmothers: (left) Ida Kanekoa Milles, Hawaiian Paternal Grandmother, and (right) Rose Viera Chang, Portuguese Maternal Grandmother, who influenced me to become a Culinary Chef.

DNA of End-Times Apostle

When I am on the mission field traveling to various countries around the world, it helps to relate to the local cultures by having a multi-racial ethnicity. Growing up in Hawaii is almost a given that you will embrace and respect the different ethnic groups and customs.

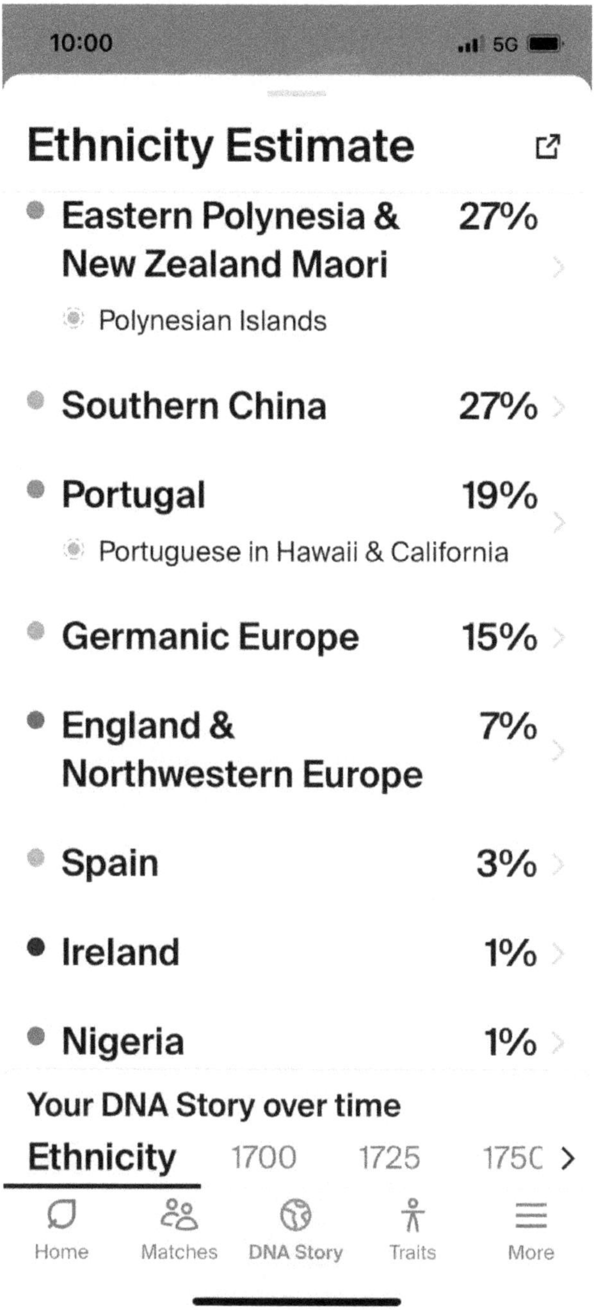

10:00 5G

Ethnicity Estimate

Eastern Polynesia & New Zealand Maori	27%
Polynesian Islands	
Southern China	27%
Portugal	19%
Portuguese in Hawaii & California	
Germanic Europe	15%
England & Northwestern Europe	7%
Spain	3%
Ireland	1%
Nigeria	1%

Your DNA Story over time

Ethnicity 1700 1725 175C >

Home Matches DNA Story Traits More

Ethnicity Chart Ancestry.com

Interestingly when I did my DNA study from Ancestry.com, the results came back with at least eight different ethnicities. There is a tradition that the saliva of a firstborn son has healing and blessing properties. Being declared a first-born son myself, I understand. Being the firstborn son of a Hebrew was a big deal in ancient Israel, for the eldest son would inherit many blessings (Mark 7:31–37, 8:22).

When I decided to take the ethnicity test from Ancestry.com, I received a simple saliva test kit. You are to collect about a tablespoon of saliva into a test tube filled with a certain solution and return it to Ancestry. This made me think about the saliva of a firstborn and its significance and how Jesus also used his saliva (spit) to heal a blind man. The question here is, was it really Jesus' saliva that activated healing, or was Jesus showing something to us in the Jewish tradition? Why did Jesus spit into the mud and put the mudpack on the blind man's eyes (John 9:6)? He could have just said, "Be healed." The reason is that He wanted to show the Jewish people and the Gentiles of that day that the Jewish tradition of being the eldest son, whose saliva is blessed with healing properties, applied to Him as well.

Healing

> "...I am the Lord, who heals you."
>
> (Exodus 15:26 NIV)

Jesus Christ equals Jehovah Rapha.

Any person on this earth can be healed by Jehovah Rapha. This means you, your family member, friend, best friend, spouse, co-worker, neighbor, your doctor, dentist, bank teller, etc.

A. Because a person is made up of three parts, I am reiterating it here to explain the healing principle:
   i. Body—flesh, blood, and bones equal a physical death.
   ii. Soul—will, mind, and emotions equal a spiritual death.
   iii. Spirit—conscience (see chapter on human conscience), wisdom, and communion equal an eternal death.

   There is no other religion on earth today that shows Jesus Christ's death on the cross for mankind's sins and Christ's resurrection (Psalms 107:20; Acts 16:31; Matthew 1:21; 1 Peter 2:24; Mark 6:56; Matthew 9:21–22; John 19:30).

B. Jesus is the only way to eternal life. John 14:6 (KJV) says, "Jesus saith unto him, I am the way, and the truth, and the life. No one comes to the Father, except through me." Also, please take a look at Mark 9:23, 1 John 3:8, Hebrews 1:3, Colossians 1:15, John 10:10, and 1 Peter 5:8.

   Many cults perform fake healings, but the healings never last. When Jesus Christ heals you, it is for your lifetime and eternity. Christ will give you life eternal, and satan will give you death eternal.

C. After three days, Jesus Christ was resurrected from the tomb. Today He sits on the right hand of God. The Holy Spirit is on the left side of God. Read John 20:21, John 14:12, and Hebrews 13:8. Christ is ready to heal you right now. Do you have faith that He can? Do you put your faith in Christ? If your answer is yes—let Christ heal you today.

D. When you seek Jesus Christ in prayer, praise and worship, and fasting, He will start the work in your life. Read 2 Corinthians 5:17 and Lamentations 3:21–24.

E. It's possible that every single family member, best friend, friend, spouse, child, co-worker, neighbor, doctor, dentist, bank teller, etc., who comes to Jesus Christ to be healed, they can be healed immediately. Read Matthew 8:16, Matthew 12:15, John 14:26, Romans 8:28, and John 16:13–15.

F. Have faith that the same Christ who died for your sins is the God of healing, restoration, freedom from bondage, disease, cancer, etc. Christ will clear it! Read Ephesians 2:8–9, Mark 1:40–42, John 1:14, Mark 9:17–27, John 11:1–44, Acts 9:36–42, Hebrews 12:2, and Matthew 6:10.

G. Because you were created in God's image and because you are a child of God, you can have 100% health. For example, Christ is 100% healthy; he is not sick, and neither should you be sick. Read Revelation 1:13–18 and Galatians 2:20. Now be healed in the mighty name of Jesus Christ. Go out and pray for other friends and family members to be healed too.

Christ can heal anyone—no matter who you are, where you are, or your circumstances.

Community and Outreach Experience

Here are a few of my outreach experiences. From 2000 to 2001, I was the Hawaiian Islands Coordinator for Chuck Colson's Ministry—Angel Tree for Hawaii kids of incarcerated parents. Then 2001 to 2003—United States Veterans Initiative Inc., I assisted in developing programs for the homeless veterans in Kapolei. Next, from 2004 to 2010 worked to develop the Hawaii Dream Service Center, Hawaii Christian Community Land Trust, and Hawaii Christian Community Foundation (all 501 C3 Non-Profits).

In March 2018, I took a trip to Israel and opened ministries in Texas and Mexico. Before this, I assisted in opening up churches in Hawaii and the Philippines. Also, in January 2008, I participated in "Statewide Prayer Watches" at Aloha Stadium and planned and managed events at various Waikiki hotels to bring nonprofits, government agencies, and churches to work together to reduce homeless, drugs, prostitution, gangs, crime, etc., in Hawaii.

Ongoing Mission Field

As I travel throughout the world planting home churches, I have established a personal Covenant with the Lord to do the following:

- *Pray!*
- Seek the guidance of the Holy Spirit.
- Tithing
- Connect New Hope International (NHI) locations to new locations from online campuses (19–20,000 people in 200 countries on seven continents)
- Set up online locations for gifting tests.
- Three-day fasting in each location.
- Cover locations to NHI campus pastors.
- Seed planting and harvest.

- Small group or cell group teaching, pastoring, and mentoring.
- Last days teaching.
- Sharing meals and fellowship.
- Speaking in tongues, witness miracles, signs, healing, wonders, and much more as the Holy Spirit leads!

Here is a list of the first thirteen countries I will be visiting to help plant home churches in 189 plus locations over the next several years:

1. Japan
2. Philippines (Laoag, Quezon, Iloilo)
3. Australia
4. Canada
5. Taiwan
6. United Kingdom
7. Germany
8. New Zealand
9. Fiji
10. India
11. South Korea
12. Italy
13. Russia

In each of the countries, I will visit three major cities to assist in planting, God willing, thousands of home churches in over 189 locations, where it has been determined that 19–20,000 plus people are already watching online at enewhope.org.

The Lord also reminded me that I must share this scripture verse from Revelation 3:1–6 (KJV):

> And unto the angel of the church in Sardis write; These things saith he that hath the seven Spirits of God, and the seven stars; I know thy works, that thou hast a name that thou livest, and art dead. Be watchful, and strengthen the things which remain, that are ready to die: for I have not found thy works perfect before God. Remember therefore how thou hast received and heard, and hold fast, and repent. If therefore thou shalt not watch, I will come on thee as a thief, and thou shalt not know what hour I will come upon thee. Thou hast a few names even in Sardis which have not defiled their garments; and they shall walk with me in white: for they are worthy. He that overcometh, the same shall be clothed in white raiment; and I will not blot out his name out of the book of life, but I will confess his name before my Father, and before his angels. He that hath an ear, let him hear what the Spirit saith unto the churches.

Please pray for me as I travel the world that our Lord will bring people to Him through His Servant.

The Lord Is Calling You to the One and Only Truthful God

I traveled quite a lot as a missionary and spoke with thousands of Mormons all over the country. ***Islam is a cult, just like Mormonism.*** In various cults, members experience myriad events without the heart of understanding why God has put us on this earth. I wish I could speak with each cult member personally and show them the history and facts and have them experience the loving fulfillment and happiness that belonging to a true Christian Church can bring. I hope that if you are a member of a cult, the Holy Spirit touches your heart and allows you to see the true nature of God and what it means to be a Christian. You can know what it took me forty years to realize in one day. Jesus does love you no matter where you came from or what you did.

When I became a Christian, I began to attend Christian conferences. I began to speak in the tongue of the Holy Spirit and to experience many other gifts of the Spirit. I am not perfect. However, I am at peace now, knowing I truly have the answers to my questions concerning the Bible, God, and His true plan for my life and His kingdom.

I remember growing up in the Mormon Church and asking many questions for which I did not receive answers. Now I have the answers to all my questions, and I know the Lord has a plan for me,

> For I know the thoughts that I think toward you, saith the Lord, thoughts of peace, and not of evil, to give you an expected end.
>
> (Jeremiah 29:11 KJV)

> ... "Truly, truly I say to you, unless one is born again he cannot see the Kingdom of God."
>
> (John 3:3 ESV)

As a member of a cult, it is difficult to have true fellowship with God—to know Him and walk and talk with Him… person to person. There are over 2,000 mentions in the Old Testament where God speaks directly to humans. A few examples are…

> Come unto me, all ye that labour and are heavy laden, and I will give you rest.
>
> (Matthew 11:28 KJV)

> But as many as received him, to them gave he power to become sons of God, even to them that believe on his name:
>
> (John 1:12 KJV)

> Then the Lord put forth his hand, and touched my mouth And the Lord said unto me, Behold, I have put my words in thy mouth.
>
> (Jeremiah 1:9 KJV)

Think about your life now. Do you have a personal relationship with God right now? Do you know that the Bible tells you not just everything you need to know to live right before God but also gives you many great and precious promises? God is reaching out to you with a deeper and more profound love than you might ever imagine. No rules, no regulations. Just God and you. Forever.

A Challenge to You, the Reader

While citizens in the modern world seek medical, therapeutic, and homeopathic remedies for healing, we can ask God directly for healing, and throughout history, God has used the discovery of medicine and specialized physicians for healing as well.

Read the account from the Gospel of John in the New Testament (John 9:7, 11). The blind man that was healed and made whole by Jesus wanted to follow Him. But the people that could see did not believe or want to follow Jesus? Which one is really blind? Which one are you?

The Pool of Siloam

> The pool of Siloam is referenced only twice in the Bible. Both of its occurrences are recorded in the gospel of John (John 9:7, 11). Siloam's pool is the famed place where Jesus, walking with His disciples, noticed a man who was born blind. He then decided, out of compassion, to make the man whole even though the man was not asking to be healed.[158]

The Garden of Gethsemane

Just prior to His crucifixion, Jesus was praying in the Garden of Gethsemane (Matthew 26:36–56). How it is with the incredible majesty of our Lord to have Jesus be drawn to the Garden of Gethsemane, which was at the foot of the Mount of Olives, which is an olive tree grove.

The significance of the olive garden is that buckets of olives would be picked during the harvest and put into a stone press, and the olive oil would be used to feed people. Olive oil is also

158 "The Pool of Siloam," Bible Study, 2022, https://www.biblestudy.org/biblepic/the-pool-of-siloam.html.

used for anointing and healing and is the lightest and sweetest of all vegetable oils. The color of olive oil is also a beautiful translucent amber.

An interesting analogy is that it is Jesus Himself who would go to the winepress for the sins of the world. At the last supper in the upper room, Jesus said, "This cup is the new covenant in my blood; do this, whenever you drink it, in remembrance of me" (1 Corinthians 11:25 NIV). The wine is a symbol of His blood (1 Corinthians 11:23–25).

There's an interesting parallel with Jesus' last appearance in the olive orchard of Gethsemane. You see, in an olive orchard, olive trees are harvested, buckets of olives are placed in a stone press, and the olive oil is used to feed people. In the same olive orchard that feeds people, Jesus was frantically praying with all of His mind, body, and spirit. Jesus was praying because he was so pressed from within His soul to take on the world's sins and to be obedient to His Father's will. Jesus willingly died on the cross for you and me to set us free from our sins and to feed our spirit and soul just as olive oil feeds our bodies.

When Judas brought the Pharisees, Sadducees, Roman guards, and temple guards to arrest Jesus, most likely, they walked out of the East Gate or Golden Gate of the olive orchard. This gate was eventually sealed in the same way that Jesus' burial spot was sealed to try to prove that Jesus would not be resurrected from the tomb or return in His second coming through the East Gate or Golden Gate.

The East side of Jerusalem is also where the Garden of Eden and Tree of Life is purported to be. If Adam and Even did not partake of the forbidden fruit of the Tree of Knowledge, our human experience would be radically different. We can only imagine.

Let's connect the East Gate from the very beginning in the Garden of Eden to Jesus's tomb and His imminent return. This is what I remember from a tour of Israel in March 2018.

There are eight gates (8 is the number for new beginnings in the Bible) in the Old City of Jerusalem. The Eastern Gate, Golden Gate, or Beautiful Gate (Acts 3:2) is called the Sha'ar Harahamim in Hebrew or the Gate of Mercy. The East Gate is the oldest gate in Old City Jerusalem, which was built in the 6th to 7th century AD. The East Gate is where Jesus Christ will enter the Old City of Jerusalem. Christ returns on the Second Coming after the 'Tribulation," and the East Gate is the closes direct access to the temple mount.

In Matthew 21, when Jesus Christ was on earth the first time He entered the Mount of Olives, Christ used the same gate as He will use when He comes again. The Eastern Gate was closed in around 1540/41 AD by Sultan Suleiman the Magnificent, the leader of the Ottoman Empire.

Thus, an Islamic Muslim Sultan sealed the East Gate over 500 years or so ago to prevent Jesus Christ's prophecy from happening in the future and Christ from walking through the East Gate. The Sultan also put a small cemetery there and 16 ft of cement in the Gate to prevent Jesus Christ from walking over the graves (Ezekiel 10:18–19, 11:23, 43:1–5, 44:1–2, 46:12).

There are many important things to point out. This is just one that stands out at this moment. Adam's (the first man) life before sin was 35 times 360 equals 12,593. Jesus Christ's life was 12,585, so 12,593 minus 12,585 equals an 8-day difference.

Jesus Christ is signifying that Christ (God) is reversing what Adam and Eve did in the Garden of Eden and taking off sin to all mankind if you receive Him (John 14:6) and repent.

Not only are there eight gates, but the earth was created in seven days (7 means divine perfection, which is also tied into the Hebrew Shmita Feast of every seven years (explained in another chapter) and on the eighth Jewish day of creation and with the Second Coming of Christ, He has taken all sin of all of mankind and opened the door or East Gate to the temple or Heaven for all mankind to enter—with their free will or choice to follow the things of Heaven or Hell.

Every Islamic Muslim, young or old, who does not receive Christ as their Lord and Savior will not go to Heaven—but end up in Hell. I am just trying to be real with you and am putting everything on the line so that not even one soul should perish, your soul included. Now, let's look at how it was discovered that Jesus' tomb was empty after He was laid there following the crucifixion.

Within the Jewish culture, it would take at least two men to move a 4 to 8 feet in diameter, 1 to 3 inch thick, and weighing 1 to 2 tons or 2,000 pounds stone (Matthew 27:6; John 19:38–42). Moving the stone that covered the entrance of a tomb was no easy task. This tomb was also excavated and originally prepared for someone other than Jesus, someone with great wealth (see Joseph of Arimathea John 19:38–42).

I had the privilege to visit these places in March 2018, and I assure you that in the same way that Jesus rose from the sealed tomb—He will surely walk through the East Gate if He so chooses when He returns.

CHAPTER 17

End Game Unfolding

An update of end-time world events happening right before our very eyes...

As Russia continues its assault on Ukraine and the world looks on in support of Ukraine, the headline news is like pieces of ancient prophesy coming to pass. It is barely Spring of 2022, and the U.S. shipping ports have been awaiting the arrival of items deemed in short supply—high-tech equipment, parts for automobiles—cars, trucks, motorcycles, appliances, cell phones, etc. In terms of global warming, climates around the globe are slowing the supply chain for copper, steel, iron, lumber, cardboard boxes, etc. Additionally, we may not be able to purchase corn, soybeans, and coffee readily.

In more sobering news, U.S. President Biden is avoiding boots on the ground with Ukraine to avoid WWIII. However, those that know what the Holy Scripture says know that, if anything, this would be a precursor to WWIII because the end-game war would involve Israel, Russia, and the Middle East.

Corruption Perceptions Index

Two years into the devastating COVID-19 pandemic, this year's Corruption Perceptions Index (CPI) reveals that corruption levels have stagnated worldwide.[159] Despite commitments on paper, 131 countries have made no significant progress against corruption over the last decade, and this year twenty-seven countries are at historic lows in their CPI score.[160]

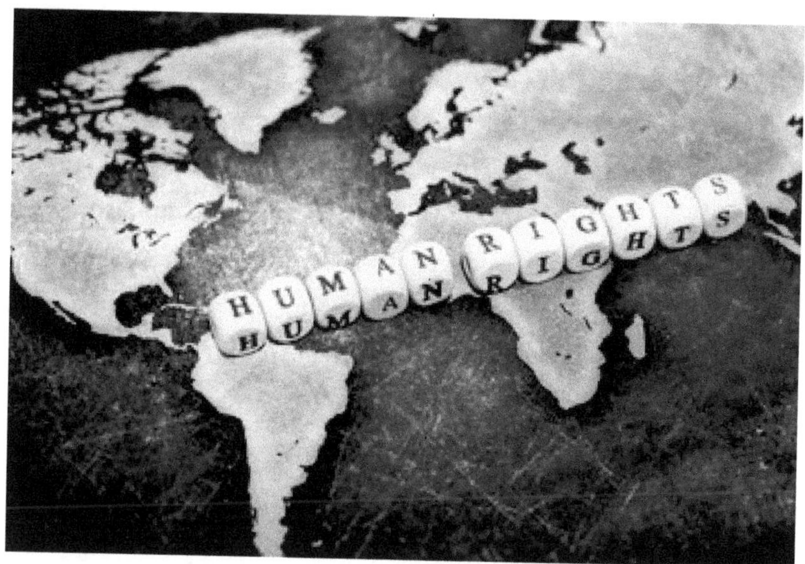

Human Rights[161]

Are Human Rights overriding God's Plan for Humanity?

Meanwhile, human rights and democracy across the world are under assault. This is no coincidence. Corruption enables human rights abuses, setting off a vicious and escalating spiral. As rights and freedoms are eroded, democracy declines, and authoritarianism takes its place, enabling higher levels of corruption. The past year has brought disturbing examples of this, from the killing of human rights defenders and the clos-

159 "Economic Data for the Benefit of Investors," World Economics, 2022, https://www.worldeconomics.com/.
160 Ibid.
161 © by Sean J — adobestock.com

ing of media outlets to government spying scandals like the Pegasus Project.

Increasingly, rights and checks and balances are being undermined not only in countries with systemic corruption and weak institutions but also among established democracies. Respecting human rights is essential for controlling corruption because empowered citizens have the space to challenge injustice. The global COVID-19 pandemic has also been used in many countries as an excuse to curtail basic freedoms and sidestep important checks and balances. And despite the increasing international momentum to end the abuse of anonymous shell companies, many high-scoring countries with relatively "clean" public sectors continue to enable transnational corruption.

There is an urgent need to accelerate the fight against corruption if we are to halt human rights abuses and democratic decline across the globe. Ethnic (Muslim) groups are fighting ethnic (Hebrew) groups. Nations (Russia) are fighting other nations (Ukraine).

The current governments around the world are falling apart, like in the days of Hitler; the people of Germany voted him into office. Also, Fidel Castro (Cuba) the people of Cuba voted him into office. Both were bad choices, as history has shown. Soon, the world will get tired of these rogue governments and ask for a "one world" government. This is where the antichrist and the false prophet appear on the scene to rule the world.

Major Points Concerning Shmita (Rosh Hashanah) With Respect to the Signs of the Times (the End Game)

Please read Daniel 12:4 and Leviticus 25:1–5

Code Red

- Ukraine War (notice Russia will be attacking Israel for its natural gas, oil, gold, silver, and other booties soon).
- COVID-19 and other variants such as Delta, Omnicron B1, B2, and Monkey Pox.
- I had a vision of a washing machine (shaking). This is explained in another chapter in this book. As we celebrate the seventh Year of the Shmita (September or October of 2021–2022), will the pouring out of God's Spirit occur between now and the next or the eighth Shmita year? A radical change from God, Jesus, and the Holy Spirit will go through to August (20) of 2028–2029.
- The Shmita cycle ends on August 20, 2029, and on October 1, 2029. China celebrates its eightieth anniversary. I don't feel that God would want His holy day or a huge and significant event of the Christian Church (such as the Rapture) coincide with China's eightieth celebration. [162]
- Shmita dates, according to the Jewish Calendar, originally occurred in September and October, and our Triune God (God the Father, Jesus, and the Holy Spirit) has allowed the Shmita month of 2028 to begin in August or one month before the communist eightieth anniversary.[163] Explaining the Shmita in its entirety would be worthy of an entirely separate book, but if you do your research about Shmita, you will find the information

162 "Jubilee 2022? - Whiteboard Animation (Plus Bonus Content)," YouTube: RockIslandBooks, 2022, https://www.youtube.com/watch?v=9-j8YpZH9yk.
163 Ibid.

relevant and surprising to where we are in the course of humanity today.

- Soon the world will reach 7,000 years from the earth being created by God, Jesus (also God), and the Holy Spirit (also God). Notice all the 7s in God's calendar or 7 in the Bible, meaning "perfection" or "divine completion". The number 7 is one of the sacred numbers in the Bible. The number 7 is found in 7 trumpets, 7 bowls, 7 year Tribulation, 7 years Jacobs trouble, 70th jubilee (October 5th, 2022), 7 stars, 7 candle stands—Menorah, 7 seals, 7 eyes, 7 plagues tribulation, 7 thunders, 7 hills and kings, 7 horns, 7 churches, Earth's Creation in 7 days, 7 day week, a bride circles her future husband 7 times during the Jewish marriage ceremony, Joshua circles the city 7 times, 7 angels, 7 visions, 7,000 years of mankind on earth and much more. Seven the biblical numeral for perfection, is incredibly astounding! The next biblical number, 8, is symbolic of new beginnings. We will begin to see the number 8 as a significant number to watch for and embrace in terms of new beginnings.
- Notice the number 40. The Israelites spent 40 years in the desert looking for the promise land, Jesus fasted and prayed 40 days and nights, Jesus spent 40 days doing ministry before His resurrection, and there are many more events and concepts with the numeral 40.
- In Judges 6:1–8:35, we find that the enemies of Israel were defeated, and the land had rest for forty years. Throughout the whole Bible, we find numbers have a spiritual and physical meaning. For example, the num-

ber forty is used 159 times in the Old and New Testaments of the Bible with a deep and specific meaning. Jesus fasted for forty days. Moses spent forty years in the desert wandering with his 2–3 million people. There are also forty suggested days for a woman to rest after giving birth to a child. God flooded the earth for forty days and nights with Noah. Moses fasted for forty days and sought God on the mountain for forty days.

- This is important in the end game or end times because, on May 14, 1948, Israel became a state or a nation. Now in 2028, it will be eighty years and Israel's eightieth anniversary. This is numerically 2 times 40 equals 80, which also means 8 (new beginning) or 8 times 10; ten meaning judgment or completion or fulfillment towards the "rapture of His Christian Church," and the number 888 is the number for Jesus Christ.
- Yes, I get it, ***no one*** knows the day or the hour as to when the rapture of the Christian Church will take place, but forty and eight and ten mean something? What do you think?
- One year after this, in 2029, China will have its eightieth anniversary as a "Communist" Nation.
- Again, on May 14, 2028, Israel will reach its eightieth anniversary as a modern state or nation. I believe that on May 14, 1948, when Israel became a state, the countdown began toward the "rapture of the Christian Church". I feel that God, through His grace of a nation's emergence, survival, and thriving, said, "For 40 years you have suffered, yet I am still desiring that people on earth come to

know me and accept me [Jesus] as their Lord and Savior so I [our Triune God] will give you another 40 years as my abundant "Grace" and "Mercy" to receive me [Jesus] so that you could be in Heaven with me and not suffer the other eternal existence—Hell."

- The number 40 is mentioned 146 times in the Bible, representing testing, trial, and probation (Exodus 24:18, 24:1--28; Numbers 13:25, 14:34). A good example is the Prophet Jonah warned the leaders of Ninevah for forty days. The Prophet Ezekiel laid on his right side for forty days to symbolize Judah's sins (Ezekiel 4:6); the Prophet Moses spent forty days and nights on Mount Sinai—and the list goes on where the number forty is used throughout the Bible.
- Looking at 80 years, the number 8 in the Bible means "new beginnings". The number 10 in the Bible means "judgment" or "completion". So, 80 equals 8 x 10.
- If you type in 888 in the search bar from your phone, Google will return countless sites which contend that the number 888 stands for "Jesus". My question to God, which I pose right here in this book: Is 2028 the year that something big will happen?
- Jesus lived 12,585 days on earth, and Adam lived 12,593 days before he sinned. I said before he sinned, so 12,585 minus 12,593 equals 8 days difference. Considering that everything God, Jesus, and the Holy Spirit does have a hidden meaning, and the Bible has many hidden meanings. Followers of Christ are compelled to pray and fasting order to enter into an intimate relationship with

our Lord, calling upon the Holy Spirit. Convening with the Holy Spirit allows you to dig deep. In my heart and mind (my soul), I'm wondering—is the 8 days difference the last number in 2028, the year of the Shmita? And yet no one knows the day or hour. Jeremiah 33:3 (NIV) says, "Call to me and I will answer you and show you great and unsearchable things that you do not know."

- If the Shmita is followed by following God's laws or principles and there is a blessing after six years of work, we are going into the seventh year of rest. If God's commandments are not observed or followed and disobeyed in the previous years, then there can be a curse for disobedience. When we try to teach our kids certain family principles, such as when to go to bed and wake up and eating well and choosing friends wisely, etc., and they rebel or don't listen—do they sometimes get punished and have privileges (like staying up late on Friday or Saturday taken away) taken away, or they may be grounded for a period of time. God is very much like Father God, who teaches us certain principles in hopes that we will follow these with our own free will. Scholars say that when "sin" entered mankind or the world from 4005 BC to 3970 BC, it was some thirty-five years.
- Every seven years, the Shmita takes place, and then another seven year-cycle of Shmita begins. However, will the next Shmita cycle usher in the "Tribulation"?
- The ending of the Shmita on God's calendar goes to the "Elul" or the twenty-ninth of the month, and the "Tishri" or the first of the month, or the beginning. With the Ro-

man calendar, the months are beginning (September) and ending (October). However, keep in mind that October 1, 2029, is the eightieth anniversary of Communist China. I do not think the Lord God will coincide His important date with Communist China. Remember also that May 14, 2028, is Israel's eightieth anniversary for Israel a Shmita year.

- No one knows the day or the hour (of the rapture), but interestingly, the tribulation timeline can be determined with major events occurring every seven years. Consider what happened every seventh year since 2001:
  - 9/11 of the World Trade Center occurred on September 1, 2001.
  - Sub-prime market fallout in 2008.
  - 2014–2015: February—The West African Ebola virus epidemic begins, infecting at least 28,616 people and killing at least 11,310 people, the most severe both in terms of numbers of infections and casualties. February 7–23—The XXII Olympic Winter Games are held in Sochi, Russia.
  - What crisis happened in 2015?

    Syria refugee crisis. Syria's descent into conflict has resulted in the deaths of more than 220,000 people, according to the United Nations, with millions displaced from their homes as President Bashar Assad and his opponents have waged a bitter, bloody war.
  - 2021–2022 Unprecedented, worldwide COVID-19 and variants pandemic, and the Russian-Ukraine War...

Year of the Jubilee—God Has a Divine Purpose and Plan for Mankind

Living in the "Church Age" and getting ready for the "Rapture of the Christian Church" and the year of the Jubilee or God's fifty year or 5 meaning "Grace" and 10 meaning "judgment" or "completion" or 5 times 10 equals 50 or Jubilee year.

Please read Ezekiel 40:1–3.

- A Jubilee year is very special on God's calendar.
- Jubilee (Leviticus 25:10) is separated from the previous forty-nine years.
- Jubilee is about rest and restoration.
  Please refer to 1 Kings 6:1.
- Some scholars and rabbis believe that September 26 – October 5, 2022, is the seventieth Jubilee year of mankind on earth.
  Please see John 5:43.
- Many scholars and rabbis are looking at God the Father, not Jesus the Son, coming to redeem them during the month of "Tishri" on the day of atonement, October 5, 2022, in the "7-year Shmita cycle". Again, I believe that God, Christ, and the Holy Spirit want to give these last five years (2023 to 2028/2029) of additional "grace" upon mankind as a window of opportunity for each person on earth to receive Jesus Christ as their Lord and Savior. As saints (believers of Christ), we have the responsibility of fulfilling the Great Commission (Matthew 28:16–20). Jesus calls on His followers to make disciples of and baptize all nations in the name of the Father, the Son, and the Holy Spirit.

- It is all important for a new Believer (or Believer who hasn't done so) to be baptized, find a church, and build an intimate relationship with Christ.
- The rest of the people in the world will receive the false Christ or the antichrist as their messiah and receive the mark of the beast—666. They will do this to stay alive on the so-called earth with remaining humanity. They will do this to have food to eat, a place to live and avoid martyrdom.

  Please read John 10:9.

CHAPTER 18

Ask God for a Dream or Vision

Did you know God's plan for humanity includes pouring His Spirit on ***all*** people (on all flesh)?

Acts 2:17 (NIV) in the Bible says:

> In the last days, God says, I will pour out my Spirit on all people. Your sons and daughters will prophesy, your young men will see visions, your old men will dream dreams.

Therefore I believe with all my heart that asking God for a dream or vision to allow you confirmation in your life or to speak a prophetic word into someone else's life is a game changer.

For example, suppose you ask God to give you a prophetic word for someone or ask Him for a dream or vision to clarify a dilemma in your life, such as showing you who the true God is or convicting you of the validity and truth of Christianity, God may cause you to have a dream.

In Acts 16, the Apostle Paul had a dream of a man pleading with him to come to Macedonia and help them. Paul had never been to Macedonia, but he followed the dream and went to Macedonia. Macedonia today is a region that includes six Balkan countries larger parts of Greece, North Macedonia, Bulgaria, and smaller parts of Albania, Serbia, and Kosovo. It covers approximately 67,000 square kilometers (25,869 sq. miles).[164] So Paul went to Macedonia, preached the Word of God, and revival broke out!

Similarly, Apostle Peter had a vision of a sheet coming down from Heaven of unclean animals that represented unclean nations—Gentiles (Acts 10:9–23). Immediately following the vision, God sent a messenger from the house of the Roman centurion Cornelius to Peter. The messenger asked Peter to go with him to Cornelius' house.

Arriving there, Peter preached, and the Spirit of God fell on all who were in the house (Acts 10:44). They began to speak in tongues, and all of a sudden, the floodgates opened.[165]

My prayer is that you ask God for a dream or vision and that the floodgates of faith, hope, love, and truth. Amen

Testimonials of the Holy Spirit at Work

I mentioned that I would share some stories of how God has been working in my life as a Christian. This is one of those stories. Here's the story involving the life of a four-month-old baby whom I will call Baby N. This testimony was mailed to

164 "Macedonia (Region)," Wikimedia Commons, 2022, https://en.wikipedia.org/wiki/Macedonia_(region).
165 Eckhardt, 2021.

Terry MacAlmon, who is a Christian praise and worship leader with the World prayer center.

> *"I am not sure if I should email this story to you, but I do it to Praise My Lord & Savior Jesus Christ (2 Thes. 1:11–12). I tried to type this a couple of times and had a hard time, but the Lord just allowed me to finish it today. Praise God!*
> *My name is Constantine Nightingdale, and I have been born again since December of 1999. I have been listening to Hawaii's Christian radio since receiving Christ as my Lord. My spirit was not satisfied with the Christian music that was being played. My spirit yearned for music that would touch the deepest part of my soul. One day I was visiting the "The Prayer Center of the Pacific," and I heard Terry MacAlmon's music playing. I asked Pastor Virginia for the name of that music; it was touching my spirit. She said that is the only music that they play at the Prayer Center of the Pacific at the time.*
> *A couple of days later, I called Logo's, the local Christian bookstore, and they said they only had two left, "I Came To Worship You" and "Live Worship". I told them to put them on hold. The next day I picked them up. I played them in the house and usually in my CD player before I go to bed. A month or two passed by, I knew I needed a CD from Terry to listen to in my car; thus, I could listen to God's anointed music wherever I am. So on 4/20/04, Tuesday, I went to pick up Terry's new CD "The Sound of Heaven" at Logo's bookstore.*
> *On Friday, 4/16/04, Mom J went to pick up her three-month-old daughter, Baby N, after work. My former wife at the time worked with Mom J's mother-in-law (L).*

L loved her grandchild, Baby N, so much that she would have her baby grandchild next to her when they took naps after she came home from work. (You see, they all live together in what we consider extended ohana living here in Hawaii. That Friday evening L left to go to the mainland to visit friends and family, and she mentioned to her daughter that she felt guilty because she always took care of little Baby N and never left her side, except to go to work.

Mom J needed a babysitter since the baby's grandmother would be on a trip, so she went to the State of Hawaii Child-care Providers list. She found a babysitter that was taking care of five kids, Mom J's child being the youngest at three months. When Mom J dropped off her child on Friday, the baby was crying and moving as usual. On Friday afternoon, after she picked up Baby N from the babysitter, she noticed that her baby was very lethargic. Baby N was not moving, even when she tried to pinch her just to check if she would respond, she didn't cry at all. Julie taught that her baby was just feeling sick or sleepy.

When Mom J awoke in the morning, she noticed that her baby was still not responding to any type of stimulation, so Mom J took her to the Emergency room at Kapiolani Hospital the next day.

The doctor said the child was shaken so badly or dropped. The doctor went on to say that little Baby N would not cry again or talk in her life, as the nerves and muscles in the back of her eyes were also damaged, and she would be blind for life. She would be handicapped for the rest of her life and would end up in a nursing home or local care home.

My wife relayed this story to me, which I believe was on Sunday. Immediately the Holy Spirit put a burden on my heart. I asked my wife to call Mom J so I could pray for the baby. She responded, "Don't worry, a few pastors and family members have already prayed for her." So I felt it was a good thing that the baby had been prayed over by elders in the Church. However, on Monday, the Holy Spirit continued to place a burden on my heart to pray for her, and on Tuesday, the Lord warns me again. On Wednesday, the Holy Spirit fell upon me a couple of times, and I kept on crying out of nowhere. I prayed to the Lord to give me direction as to what time he wanted me to be at the hospital (in my mind, I said I'd be there at 5:00 p.m.), but the Lord told me to be there at 4:00 p.m.

I said to my wife, "You really need to call Mom J so I can pray for the baby." (This is the first time this is happening to burden on my heart was so strong, so I wasn't sure how to have access to pray over the baby). I called the hospital, but no one answered. My wife finally called L for Mom J's cell phone. We learned that Mom J had gone home from the hospital to take a shower but that she would be heading back to Kapiolani hospital.

I ended up arriving at Kapiolani Hospital at 3:00 p.m. after I dropped my wife off at work. This is my first time I had been inside Kapiolani hospital so I'm not sure where to go. I only know I am going to PDICU (intensive care unit).

As soon as I reached the entrance of the hospital, I saw a man dressed in blue, walking at the same pace as me. I asked him where PDICU is, and he said, "Follow me." (It was as if God sent me an angel to guide me). After going through the maze of doors & halls, I reached the PDICU, and he pointed to the door and left. I proceeded to the front desk and asked to see Mom J and her three-month-old Baby N (the nursing staff is quite cautious about anybody coming to visit the baby because, at present, the police is doing an investigation on this child abuse).

I learned that the Honolulu Police Department and the Hawaii Child Protective Agency had put the babysitter under investigation, and Mom J and her husband, Dad L, were also under investigation. They were also required to take a lie detector test. Mom J and Dad L's two-year-old son (D) was taken by the Child Protect Agency and put in a Foster Home until the investigation was completed.

The nursing station is in the middle of the unit with a circular formation of beds with emergency patients. I saw Mom J, and in the Hawaiian custom, I gave her a kiss on the cheek and shared with her of my experience with the Holy Spirit throughout the week. I also had a vision of what to bring and what to do when I arrived at the hospital. I knew I needed to bring my Bible, Terry's CD The Sounds of Heaven, which the Lord just had me purchase the day before (not knowing I would be playing this for Baby N the next day), and I knew I had to borrow my Father-in-law's purple CD player to play Terry's music.

Mom J was sitting on the side of the bed with the baby in her arms. The baby was hooked up to all kinds of apparatus and, sadly, seemed lifeless. I asked if I could get assistance setting up the CD player because I didn't want to mess up the emer-

gency outlets, so we called the nurse. The nurse came in and plugged in the CD player. I asked Julie to ask the Lord for forgiveness for anything that she may need forgiveness for and begin to praise the Lord. The music started playing, and the recording artist said, "Get ready for a miracle." I begin worshipping the Lord for what He was about to do. I noticed the clock on the wall; it was 3:04 pm.

All of a sudden, I started to cry uncontrollably, and at that moment, Mom J's sister came in with another baby in her arms. I looked up with tears rolling down my cheeks, and Mom J introduced me to her sister. I continued praising the Lord with thanksgiving. Mom J's sister left. I remember the Lord telling me to be there at 4:00 p.m., but I got there at 3:00 p.m., and I knew I needed to praise Him before the miracle, for praise and worship prepares the heart and soul). I remember the Lord telling me to put my left hand on the mother and my right hand on the baby.

It was 3:45 p.m., and the time is getting close. My heart was beating faster and faster in anticipation of how God was about to use me as a vessel in healing this baby. The nurse came in to check on the baby, and she asked Mom J, "What is that sweet smell?"

Because of all the medications administered throughout the day, along with diaper changes, the hospital room smelled of blood, urine and feces.

But as soon as we played the "Sounds of Heaven" on the CD player, a sweet aroma came to that spot. The sweet aroma was not on the hospital bed or to the right or left, or any other spot in PDICU. I learned later that the occurrence of a sweet aroma has happened before with Terry's music. I knew that the Holy Spirit was in the room with us.

The nurse asked again, "What is that sweet smell? Is it you, Mom J?" Remember when I first came in, I kissed Mom J on the cheek and did not notice any perfume. The nurse was puzzled for a few minutes about the sweet smell. She continued to check on the baby. She turned to ask me, "Are you meditating?" and I replied, "Yes, I am praying." She then stepped behind me to fill out her paperwork.

"OH LORD, THE TIME IS GETTING CLOSE. WHAT IS IT THAT I AM SUPPOSED TO DO?"

I remember visiting men and women of God and sharing the experience of a warmth or tingling on the arm when the Holy Spirit abound.

The clock showed 3:55 p.m.; I'm thinking, "Lord, I feel NO warmness or tingling in my arms. LORD, USE ME AS A VESSEL RIGHT NOW TO HEAL THIS BABY WITH SUPERNATURAL PRAYER. The time is getting close to the time YOU told me to be here."

Suddenly I heard the baby making a sucking sound with her lips—the baby continued with the sound again and again at a fast pace as if something was about to happen (before this, the baby was silent and listless).

My watch shows 4:00 p.m., and I remember crying out to the LORD, "LORD, LORD, HELP ME!" and at the same time, the music was continuously playing a sweet melody, Heavens are Opening. I closed my eyes and asked God, "Is it now, Lord?"

Then I heard a whisper, "Put your hands on them and say what I told you to say '"Heal in the name of Jesus Christ.'"

After praying at a feverish pace, I felt at peace when it was done. I remember telling Julie that whatever happens, give ALL the praises to God. Then I left.

I was told by my wife a few days later that the baby was crying and talking (not consistent with the prognosis given by the doctor that she would be mentally and physically handicapped for the rest of her life); and that she would be on a tube feeding through the abdomen, but she did not need that.

The baby was also supposed to go to a nursing home, but she went home to the grandparents' & parents' home upon leaving the hospital. The last report was that the baby was moving more and more each day. At the time of this writing, we were hoping that God would restore the baby's sight."

It's All about a Personal Relationship with God

You see, the God I know is the God of Abraham, Isaac, and Moses. I have never encountered God as a Mormon because Joseph Smith set up the Mormon religion, and it did not align with God's nature—which is clearly defined in the Bible. Because I was indoctrinated as a Mormon from a small child, I wish to reach out to those who may have been indoctrinated into a cult or false religion—and share how true Christianity transformed my life to walk with the Lord and have fulfillment in life like never before.

> Delight yourself in the Lord and He will give you the desires of your heart.
>
> (Psalm 37:4 ESV)

I would like to take this time to help you get to know Jesus and build a personal relationship with Him. This is the most important thing that God wants for you. Not your money, not your church tasks, not religious tasks—but a loving relationship with Him who created you.

I have included a Salvation Prayer to our Lord in Heaven, Jesus Christ, and the Holy Spirit, so you may begin to build a personal relationship with the Holy Trinity of God (Matthew 28:19). I encourage you to pray the Salvation Prayer. "This is a decision you will make now for all eternity. This is the most eternal decision you will ever make.

When you accept Jesus Christ as your Lord and Savior, there's only one way to go, and that's UP! No other way but down, otherwise. What would you choose?

I love all Muslim people in this world (I view Islam religion as separate from the person), and I hope and pray that you, too, can find Jesus Christ in your heart when He died on the cross for your sins, was resurrected in three days, and is now sitting at the right hand of God.

I pray that you will visualize how one day, when you pass from this earth and enter the heavenly realm, you will see yourself standing at the right hand of God. It is my sincere prayer that the information in this book has influenced you to seek God in a deeper way and understand His plan for your life (Jeremiah 29:11; Proverbs 16:9; Romans 8:28).

To God be all the Glory and Honor for this book!

~SALVATION PRAYER~

Say this prayer with an open heart and see what God does!

Dear Father God, Creator of all of Heaven and Earth;
I am praying this prayer right now, out loud, in Jesus' Holy Name to ask for forgiveness of my sins. When I say Jesus' Name out loud, the enemy of my soul, satan, must flee from me.
My life has not been perfect or easy, but I understand by accepting Jesus Christ as my Lord and Savior right NOW; that when I pass from this earth, I will open my eyes in eternity with You in the Heavenly Places which you have prepared for those who believe in You.
I ask that You pour out Your Holy Spirit upon me and within me so that I will have a heart that yearns to know and understand Your Word, Will, and Way; and by Your Spirit, I shall understand Your nature as well as my own to draw closer and closer to You each day.
Your great commission is that every knee shall bow, and every tongue shall confess that Jesus Christ is Lord, to the glory of the Father.
I submit this heartfelt prayer to You, In Jesus' Holy and Powerful Name, Amen!

"Then you will know the truth, and the truth will set you free."
(John 8:32 NIV)

Appendix

Bible Study Tools

Bible Translations:

There are two types of Bible translations:

1. "Formal equivalence" —a word-for-word rendering of the original language into whatever language the reader needs, i.e., English. Every effort is made to retain both the word order and sentence structure of the original Hebrew or Greek.
2. "Functional equivalence" —more of a 'thought for thought' rendering of the original text. Also referred to as 'dynamic equivalence'. The goal here is to produce in the reader's language (i.e., English) the closest equivalent in both meaning and style of the original Hebrew and Greek (and Aramaic).[166]

For example, below is 1 Kings 2:10 written out in different versions.

KJV: "So David slept with his fathers and was buried in the city of David."

166 Madelon Maupin, "Types of Bible Translations," Bible Roads, 2021, https://bibleroads.com/bible-resources/bible-translations/.

NIV: "Then David rested with his fathers and was buried in the City of David."
NLT: "Then David died and was buried in the City of David."
As in many other specific verses, the NLT ('functional') more accurately conveys the meaning in English than the KJV and NIV (both 'formal' equivalence).
The point is to find a contemporary translation that you find 'speaks' to you and touches your heart and thought in a way that awakens them to the spiritual meaning within.[167]

Below is a list of some of the more popular Bible Translations used by various denominations:

- New International Version (NIV)
- King James Version (KJV)
- New Living Translation (NLT)
- Christian Standard Bible (CSB)
- Reina Valera (RV) (Spanish Translation)
- New International Reader's Version (NIrV) (NIrV for those for whom English is a second language)

Note that the different translations are not the same as adding or subtracting from the Word of God with each translation. Think of the different translations as saying the same thing to an individual in their own language, even if the language is English.

Recall what Deuteronomy 4:2 says:

167 Maupin, 2021.

> You must not add to or subtract from what I command you, so that you may keep the commandments of the LORD your God that I am giving you.
>
> (BSB)

> Do not add to what I command you and do not subtract from it but keep the commands of the LORD your God that I give you."
>
> (NIV)

Ask the Holy Spirit for guidance as to which translation is best for you. If you are a Bible scholar, you will likely have many translations in your library.

> The Old Testament consists of 39 different books originally written in the Hebrew and Aramaic languages and can be divided into four categories, including the Torah (or Pentateuch), the historical books, the prophetic writings, and the poetic or wisdom literature.[168]
>
> The New Testament was originally written in Greek, the commonly used language in Palestine well before the first century AD. As the universal language of commerce and trade, Koine Greek was the primary language of Jesus, the apostles, and the early New Testament Church.[169]

---

168 Timothy Andrew," A Complete List of Old Testament Books in Order: Bible Summary GuideLord's Library," Lord's Library, 2021, https://www.lordslibrary.com/old-testament-books-in-order-bible/.
169 "Appendices D - The New Testament Was Originally Written in Greek," A Faithful Version, 2022, https://afaithfulversion.org/appendices-d.

Five Crowns in Heaven

There are five heavenly crowns mentioned in the New Testament that will be awarded to believers. They are the imperishable crown, the crown of rejoicing, the crown of righteousness, the crown of glory, and the crown of life. The Greek word translated "crown" is *stephanos* (the source for the name Stephen the martyr) and means "a badge of royalty, a prize in the public games or a symbol of honor generally." Used during the ancient Greek games, it referred to a wreath or garland of leaves placed on a victor's head as a reward for winning an athletic contest. As such, this word is used figuratively in the New Testament of the rewards of heaven God promises those who are faithful. Paul's passage in 1 Corinthians 9:24-25 best defines for us how these crowns are awarded.

1. The Imperishable Crown – (1 Corinthians 9:24-25) "Do you not know that those who run in a race all run, but one receives the prize? Run in such a way that you may obtain it. And everyone who competes for the prize is temperate [disciplined] in all things. Now they do it to obtain a perishable crown, but we for an imperishable crown" (NKJV). All things on this earth are subject to decay and will perish. Jesus urges us to not store our treasures on earth "where moth and rust destroy, and where thieves break in and steal" (Matthew 6:19). This is analogous to what Paul was saying about that wreath of leaves that was soon to turn brittle and fall apart. But not so the heavenly crown; faithful endurance wins a heavenly reward which is "an inheritance incorruptible and undefiled and that does not fade away, reserved in heaven for you" (1 Peter 1:4).

2. The Crown of Rejoicing – (1 Thessalonians 2:19) "For what is our hope, or joy, or crown of rejoicing? Is it not even you in the presence of our Lord Jesus Christ at His coming?" The apostle Paul tells us in Philippians 4:4 to "rejoice always in the Lord" for all the bountiful blessings our gracious God has showered upon us. As Christians we have more in this life to rejoice about than anyone else. Luke tells us there is rejoicing even now in heaven (Luke 15:7). The crown of rejoicing will be our reward where "God will wipe away every tear . . . there shall be no more death, nor sorrow, nor crying. There shall be no more pain, for the former things have passed away" (Revelation 21:4).
3. The Crown of Righteousness – (2 Timothy 4:8) "Finally, there is laid up for me the crown of righteousness, which the Lord, the righteous Judge, will give to me on that Day, and not to me only but also to all who have loved His appearing." We inherit this crown through the righteousness of Christ, which is what gives us a right to it, and without which it cannot be obtained. Because it is obtained and possessed in a righteous way, and not by force and deceit as earthly crowns sometimes are, it is an everlasting crown, promised to all who love the Lord and eagerly wait for His return. Through our enduring discouragements, persecutions, sufferings, or even death, we know assuredly our reward is with Christ in eternity (Philippians 3:20). This crown is not for those who depend upon their own sense of righteousness or of their own works. Such an attitude breeds only arrogance and pride, not a longing, a fervent desire to be with the Lord.

4. The Crown of Glory – (*1 Peter 5:4*) "And when the Chief Shepherd appears, you will receive the crown of glory that does not fade away." Though Peter is addressing the elders, we must also remember that the crown will be awarded to all those who long for or love His appearing. This word "glory" is an interesting word referring to the very nature of God and His actions. It entails His great splendor and brightness. Recall Stephen who, while being stoned to death, was able to look into the heavens and see the glory of God (*Acts 7:55-56*). This word also means that the praise and honor we bestow to God alone is due Him because of who He is (Isaiah 42:8, 48:11; Galatians 1:5). It also recognizes that believers are incredibly blessed to enter into the kingdom, into the very likeness of Christ Himself. For as Paul so eloquently put it, "For I consider that the sufferings of this present time are not worthy to be compared with the glory which shall be revealed in us" (Romans 8:18 NKJV).
5. The Crown of Life – (Revelation 2:10) "Do not fear any of those things which you are about to suffer. Indeed, the devil is about to throw some of you into prison, that you may be tested, and you will have tribulation ten days. Be faithful until death, and I will give you the crown of life." This crown is for all believers, but is especially dear to those who endure sufferings, who bravely confront persecution for Jesus, even to the point of death. In Scripture the word "life" is often used to show a relationship that is right with God. It was Jesus who said, "I have come that they may have life and that they may have it more abundantly" (John 10:10).

Just as things such as air, food, and water are vital for our physical lives, Jesus provides us what is required for our spiritual lives. He is the One who provides "living water." He is the "bread of life" (John 4:10, 6:35).

We know that our earthly lives will end. But we have the amazing promise that comes only to those who come to God through Jesus: "And this is the promise that He has promised us—eternal life" (1 John 2:25).

James tells us that this crown of life is for all those who love God (James 1:12). The question then is how do we demonstrate our love for God? The apostle John answers this for us: "For this is the love of God, that we keep His commandments."

James tells us that this crown of life is for all those who love God (James 1:12). The question then is how do we demonstrate our love for God?

The apostle John answers this for us: "For this is the love of God, that we keep His commandments. And His commandments are not burdensome" (*1 John 5:3*). As His children we must keep His commandments, obeying Him, always remaining faithful. So, as we endure the inevitable trials, pains, heartaches, and tribulations—as long as we live—may we ever move forward, always "looking unto Jesus, the author and finisher of our faith" (Hebrews 12:2) and receive the crown of life that awaits us.[170]

170 Rhonda Ballance, "Question: 'What Are the Heavenly Crowns That Believers Can Receive in Heaven?'" Yesterday's Prophecy, Today's News, 2017, https://yesterdaysprophecy.com/question-heavenly-crowns-believers-can-receive-heaven/.

Current Events

No other generation has seen more prophecies than this generation. 2 Timothy 3:1–5 (KJV) says:

> This know also, that in the last days perilous times shall come. For men shall be lovers of their own selves, covetous, boasters proud blasphemers, disobedient to parents, unthankful, unholy, Without natural affection, trucebreakers, false accusers, incontinent, fierce, despisers of those that are good, Traitors, heady, high-minded, lovers of pleasures more than lovers of God; Having a form of godliness, but denying the power thereof: from such turn away.

Here is a list of things to give you an idea of how far we've come from the traditional and wholesome values to today's corrupted values:

- Today there are more couples who live together and do not get married for a lifetime commitment.
- Sexual immorality continues to spiral out of control.
- Bestiality (sex with animals) is more widespread, and there are reports of a man who died from trying to have sex with a horse.[171]
- Today there is a new version of the Bible, the Queen James Bible, for homosexual-oriented people (gay, lesbian, bisexual, transgender)
- Today people have sex with dead people.

---

171 "Seattle Man Dies after Sex with Horse," NBC Universal, 2005, https://www.nbcnews.com/id/wbna8589349.

- Anal Sex is increasing in popularity. This form of intercourse is unhealthy and causes bacteria transmission and sickness.
- The new trend is for teens to commit suicide on TikTok.[172]
- There are over 5 million children worldwide who are orphaned due to losing their parents to COVID-19.[173]

Every day, the antichrist spirit is prevalent and dominates the TV, news outlets, magazines, newspapers, movie theaters, etc. Satan is essentially trying to *deconstruct the Church*. Read 1 Peter 3:15, 1 Timothy 6:20–21, and Ephesians 6.

What exactly do I mean by this? The enemy of our souls—satan, devil, Lucifer—is out to harm, kill and destroy us (John 12:10; 1 Peter 5:8). By distracting us away from God, the enemy thinks he has won. He's out to get every person on this earth.

By believing and following a false cult such as Islam, Hinduism, Buddhism, Mormonism, or Jehovah's Witness, etc., you will be following a false cult god to that false god's resting place—which is Hell.

If you ask Jesus Christ into your heart for salvation, asking God with an open and humble heart to come into your life while you fast and pray, God will answer you. God will guide you with His Word as to what is right and true. Don't take my word for it; take God's Word. Why, may you ask? Because if you are wrong,

172 Samantha Agate, "19-Year-Old Killed Himself Live On TikTok — Why Aren't More People Talking About It?" Talent Recap, 2021, https://talentrecap.com/19-year-old-killed-himself-live-on-tiktok-why-arent-more-people-talking-about-it/.
173 Mary Van Beusekom, "COVID-19 May Have Orphaned 7.5 Million Kids Worldwide," Center for Infectious Disease Research and Policy [CIDRAP], 2022, https://www.cidrap.umn.edu/news-perspective/2022/09/covid-19-may-have-orphaned-75-million-kids-worldwide.

it will cost you Heaven, and you will be going to Hell for all eternity! This is what is at stake, and I have put my life on the line to try to let as many people as possible in the world know.

It is my hope that when you face Christ and satan, you will not say, "I read this book and that the End Times Apostle from the World, Constantine Nightingdale from Hawaii, tried to warn me but I didn't want to listen."

Age of Accountability

If crowns are literal or symbolic rewards in Heaven, we may wonder: *What is the age of accountability for a woman, man, or child?* The Bible doesn't say specifically when the age of accountability is but tells us in Romans 2:14–15 that those *"having not the law, are a law unto themselves (KJV)."*

Children mature and develop at varying rates in different cultures all over the world. However, because God is perfect, He knows each person's heart, attitude, and disposition in life. Israel holds its children accountable at the age of thirteen. Since I have raised kids from birth until beyond thirteen years, this makes sense to me. These children are in middle school, and they already have a grasp on what is good, bad, or evil.

Remember, we are created in the likeness of God, not just on the outside but on the inside too. Ultimately God knows all, and God can judge all humans fairly!

Here is how Generational theorists Neil Howe and William Strauss identify twentieth-century generations:

- Baby Boomers 2—1955–1964
- Generation X—1965–1980
- Millennials—1981–1996

- Generation Z—1997–2012[174]

The current generation, which is not necessarily by age group, seems to prefer socialism and concepts based on Marxism. See 2 Timothy 3:1–17. Socialism, Marxism, and Communism mean essentially that the government owns everything, pretty much all of the socio-economic and political aspects of society (land, people, places, and things). Within these ideologies, you are made to feel happy and provided for, but your life is not your own, and you will eventually feel empty.

The *Green Initiative* is another ideology that is increasingly being pushed in the U.S. under the current administration. The proponents of this initiative believe that, in some way, they are saving the planet. But what good is that when millions are out of work and the U.S. becomes increasingly dependent upon other sources such as oil and gas?

A construct of the Green Initiative is for consumers to eat less beef because some scientists believe that the emissions from cattle are contributing to the ozone layer. It's almost laughable if it weren't actually devastating and sad when you think of the innocent lives adversely affected by these special interest groups and their one-sided platforms.

174 "Age Range by Generation," Beresford Research, 2022, https://www.beresfordresearch.com/age-range-by-generation/.

Biblical Colors and Their Meanings

- **Amber**—Glory of God, judgment upon sin, endurance
- **Orange**—Fire of God, deliverance, passionate praise
- **Pink/Fuchsia**—Right relationship with God
- **Scarlet**—Royalty, fine linen for the tabernacle
- **Red**—Blood of Jesus, love of God, the blood of lamb, atonement, salvation
- **Blue**—Heaven, the Holy Spirit, authority
- **Purple**—Priesthood, kingship, royalty, mediator, wealth
- **Gold**—Glory, divinity, kingship, eternal deity, foundation, altar, beauty, precious, holiness, majesty, righteousness
- **Wine**—New birth, multiply, overflow
- **Sapphire**—Law, commandments, grace, the Holy Spirit, divine revelation
- **Turquoise**—River of God, sanctification, healing, New Jerusalem
- **Green**—Praise, growth, prosperity, a new beginning, flourishing, restoration
- **Silver**—Word of God, purity, divinity, salvation, truth, atonement, redemption
- **White**—Bride of Christ, surrender, harvest, light, righteousness, conquest, victory, blessedness, joy, angels, saints, peace, completion, triumph
- **Brown**—End of season, rags, people, pride, weary, faint
- **Yellow**—Faith and Glory of God, anointing, joy
- **Black**—Darkness, sin, Earth, affliction, humiliation, calamity, death, mourning[175]

---

175 Jacob Olesen, "Biblical Meaning of Colors," Color Meanings, 2013, https://www.color-meanings.com/biblical-meaning-colors/.

Biblical Numerology

What Is Biblical Numerology?

Biblical numerology is the symbolic use of numbers used throughout the Bible—for example, the three in the *triune* nature of God. The Early Church recognized that the Bible had four layers of interpretation, called the *quadriga*. They are:

1. Literal (*sensus tropologicus*)
2. Allegorical/Symbolic (*sensus allegoricus*)
3. Moral (*sensus moralis*)
4. Anagogical/mystical (*sensus anagogicus*)

In this way, numbers are often used symbolically to reveal the truth in the Bible verses. Understanding the numbers will give you great awareness in your Christian life of the divine perfection of God's Word.[176]

Below is an introduction to what numbers 1–10 *represent* from a Biblical Numerology context. Numerology, which may be practiced in the cult, is apart from and outside of the biblical context of what is provided here, and you must tread very carefully if you study or share Biblical Numerology for yourself or with others.

> The number 1 is only divisible by itself. It is independent of any other numeral yet composes them all. It symbolizes in the Bible the unity and primacy and the oneness of the Godhead.
>
> The number 2 conveys the meaning of a union, division of the verification of facts by witnesses. A man

176 "The Complete Guide to Understanding Bible Numerology," Testimonio LLC., 2022, https://testimon.io/blog/bible-numerology.

and woman, though two in number, made one in marriage

(Genesis 2:23–24). There is also a union between Christ and the church (see 1 Corinthians 12).

The number 3 is used 467 times in the Bible. It pictures completeness, though to a lesser degree than 7. The meaning of this number derives from the fact that it is the first of four spiritually perfect numerals (the others being 7, 10, and 12). The 3 righteous patriarchs before the flood were Abel, Enoch, and Noah. After the deluge there was the righteous "fathers" Abraham, Isaac, and Jacob (later renamed Israel).

The number 4 derives its meaning from creation. On the fourth day of what is called 'creation week' God completed the material universe. On this day he brought into existence our sun, the moon, and all the stars (Genesis 1:14–19). Their purpose was not only to give off light, but also to divide the day from the night on earth, thus becoming a basic demarcation of time. They were also made to be a type of signal that would mark off the days, years, and seasons.

The number 5 symbolizes God's grace, goodness and favor toward humans and is mentioned 318 times in Scripture. Five is the number of grace and multiplied by itself, which is 25, is 'grace upon grace' (John 1:16). The Ten Commandments contains two sets of 5 commandments. The first five commandments are related to our treatment and relationship with God, and the last five concern our relationship with other humans.

In the Bible, the number 6 symbolizes man and human weakness, the evils of Satan and the manifestation of sin. Man was created on the sixth day. Men are appointed 6 days to labor.

A Hebrew slave was to serve six years and be released in the 7th year. Six years were appointed for the land to be sown and harvested. The number 6 is also associated with Satan in his temptation of Jesus. The bringing together of three 6's is the number and mark of the end time Beast of Revelation. As such, it represents the very best system of governance that mankind can produce without God and under the constant influence of his chief adversary.

Used 735 times (54 times in the book of Revelation alone), the number 7 is the foundation of God's word. If we include with this count how many times 'sevenfold' (6) and 'seventh' (119) is used, our total jumps to 860 references.

Seven is the number of completeness and perfection (both physical and spiritual). It derives much of its meaning from being tied directly to God's creation of all things.

According to some Jewish traditions, the creation of Adam occurred on September 26, 3760 B.C. (or the first day of Tishri, which is the seventh month on the

Hebrew calendar). The word 'created' is used 7 times describing God's creative work (Genesis 1:1, 21, 27 three times; 2:3; 2:4). There are 7 days in a week and God's Sabbath is on the 7th day.

In the Book of Revelation there are a) 21 judgements; b) seven seals—which bring plagues upon the earth when unsealed; c) seven trumpets, when blown also bring plagues upon the earth; and d) seven bowls of wrath.

The number seven (7) means perfection, and the number two (2) in 21 represents two witnesses, and number one (1) represents oneness in the Godhead.

The number 8 in the Bible represents a new beginning, meaning a new order or creation, and man's true 'born again' event when he is resurrected from the dead into eternal life.

Like the Old Testament Passover lamb, Jesus was selected as the Lamb to take away man's sins on the Hebrew day of Nisan 10 (April 1, 30 A.D. – John 12: 28 – 29). He was crucified on Nisan 14 (Wednesday, April 5 in 30 A.D.). His resurrection occurred, exactly as he stated, three days and three nights after he was buried, which was at the end of the weekly Sabbath day that fell on Nisan 17 (seventeen symbolizes victory). Nisan 17 was also the eighth day, counting inclusively, from the time Christ was selected as man's sacrificial Lamb. All this bears record of Jesus' perfect sacrifice and His complete victory over death.

Used 49 times in Scripture, the number 9 symbolizes divine completeness or conveys the meaning of finality. Christ died at the 9th hour of the day, or 3 p.m., to make the way of salvation open to everyone. The Day of Atonement (Yom Kippur) is the only one of God's annual Feast days of worship that requires believers to fast for one day. This special day, considered by many Jews to be the holiest of the year, begins at sunset on day 9 of the seventh Hebrew month (Leviticus 23:32).

The number 9 also represents the fruits of God's Holy Spirit, which are Faithfulness, Gentleness, Goodness, Joy, Kindness, Long suffering, Love, Peace and Self-control (Galatians 5:22–23).[177]

The number 10 in the Bible is used 242 times. The designation "10th" is used 79 times. Ten is also viewed as a complete and perfect number, as are 3, 7, and 12. It is made up of 4, the number of the physical creation, and 6, which is symbolized. As such, the meaning of 10 is one of testimony, law, responsibility, and the completeness of order. We find, in Genesis 1, the phrase "God said" 10 times, which is a testimony of His creative power. God gave the Ten Commandments to man. Ten, therefore, represents man's responsibility to keep the commandments. A tithe is a

177 "Biblical Numerology," Numberology Toolbox, 2020, https://numerologytoolbox.com/biblical-numerology/.

10th of our earnings and is a testimony of our faith in the Lord.[178]

About Tefillin

Tefillin are two black leather cubes (boxes) that are worn by many Jewish men while at morning prayer. One of the cubes is called "Shel Rosh" and is placed on the forehead. The second is termed "Shel Yad" and is worn on the upper right or left arm. The cubes have long straps of leather attached to it, which enable the man to wrap the tefillin on his head and arm. The straps of the Shel Yad are wound seven times down the arm and three times down the middle finger. Within the cubes are four sections of the Bible written on parchment paper. These sections declare the existence and unity of God and recall the liberation from Egypt. Once a man has had his Bar Mitzvah, he may wear the tefillin during weekday prayers. Tefillin are not worn on the Sabbath (day of rest) nor on the Jewish holidays. The putting on of tefillin is like a ceremony in itself, for as the man puts on his tefillin, he recites a prayer. The use of tefillin stems from the biblical commandment: "And thou shalt bind them for a sign upon thy hand, and they shall be as frontlets between thine eyes" (Deut. 6:8). Today some women are reclaiming tefillin as part of their Jewish ritual.[179]

---

178 "Meaning of the Number 10 in the Bible," Bible Study, 2022, https://www.biblestudy.org/bibleref/meaning-of-numbers-in-bible/10.html.

179 "Choosing Tefillin," Ajudaica, 2022, https://www.ajudaica.com/jewish-guides/tefillin.

Tefillin Straps[180]

Satan's tactics are that he does what God does as a counterfeit. He copies God's true doctrines and replaces the truth with lies and false doctrines. This is why satan uses the mark of the beast, 666 (Revelation 13:16–18), which will be placed on the forehead or hand. This is a counterfeit of God's mark on humans, such as the Tefillin.

God has a mark on Believers when we are baptized with the Holy Spirit. We do this with our free will, and God sees the mark of the Holy Spirit upon those who love and follow Him. We are not forced to have a mark as satan will force people to take the mark of the beast 666 in the end times. However, we can lose the Holy Spirit if we blaspheme against the Holy Spirit.

180 © by Marcela Ruty Romeo — adobestock.com

The Book of Enoch

The reason why I include the Book of Enoch here is that many Christians and non-Christians alike are not sure if the fallen angels could actually mate with humans, which would result in half-human, half-angel entities. Theologians are not certain whether angels carry DNA that can be shared. To dispel many other misconceptions, reading this excerpt and discussing the Book of Enoch will prove very helpful.

> The Book of Enoch is any of several pseudepigraphal (falsely attributed works, texts whose claimed authorship is unfounded) works that attribute themselves to Enoch, the great-grandfather of Noah; that is, Enoch son of Jared (Genesis 5:18). Enoch is also one of the two people in the Bible taken up to heaven without dying (the other being Elijah), as the Bible says, "And Enoch walked with God, and he was not; for God took him." (Genesis 5:24; see also Hebrews 11:5). Most commonly, the phrase "Book of Enoch" refers to 1 Enoch, which is wholly extant only in the Ethiopic language.
>
> The biblical book of Jude quotes from the Book of Enoch in verses 14–15, "Enoch, the seventh from Adam, prophesied about these men: 'See, the Lord is coming with thousands upon thousands of his holy ones to judge everyone, and to convict all the ungodly of all the ungodly acts they have done in the ungodly way, and of all the harsh words ungodly sinners have spoken against him.'" But this does not mean the

Book of Enoch is inspired by God and should be in the Bible.

Jude's quote is not the only quote in the Bible from a non-biblical source. The Apostle Paul quotes Epimenides in Titus 1:12 but that does not mean we should give any additional authority to Epimenides' writings. The same is true with Jude, verses 14–15. Jude quoting from the book of Enoch does not indicate the entire Book of Enoch is inspired, or even true. All it means is that particular verse is true. It is interesting to note that no scholars believe the Book of Enoch to have truly been written by the Enoch in the Bible. Enoch was seven generations from Adam, prior to the Flood (Genesis 5:1–24). Evidently, though, this was genuinely something that Enoch prophesied—or the Bible would not attribute it to him, "Enoch, the seventh from Adam, prophesied about these men" (Jude 1:14). This saying of Enoch was evidently handed down by tradition, and eventually recorded in the Book of Enoch.

We should treat the Book of Enoch (and the other books like it) in the same manner we do the other Apocryphal writings. Some of what the Apocrypha says is true and correct, but at the same time, much of it is false and historically inaccurate. If you read these books, you have to treat them as interesting but fallible historical documents, not as the inspired, authoritative Word of God.[181]

181 "What Is the Book of Enoch and Should It Be in the Bible?" Got Questions Ministries, 2022, https://www.gotquestions.org/book-of-Enoch.html.

The Book of Enoch is an unfounded text, much like the Book of Mormon, Quran, etc. The Bible warns us of false prophets and not adding to or subtracting from the Word of God.

You may wonder about the popularity of this book on the internet and from various booksellers. This is another ploy of the enemy to use popular culture as a way to deceive many. Even Christians may wonder whether a text such as the Book of Enoch is valid. Most Christian or Bible Study sites seem to agree that the Book of Enoch is unfounded and, therefore, not an *inspired* or *valid text*.

Simply put, this is another scheme (deception) satan uses to misguide people away from Christ, even more so in these end times. The following scripture verses refer to angels and the spirit of man and angels.

- Genesis 6:1–2—The sons of God are Christians, not fallen angels.
- Mathew 22:30—Angels *do not* and cannot marry because angels are spirits with no flesh and bones. One must have flesh and bones to have sexual or intimate relations with one another.
- Hebrews 1:13–14—Angels are ministering spirits.
- Luke 24:39—A spirit has *no* flesh and bones (angels or fallen angels).
- John 3:6—Flesh is born of the flesh, and spirit is born of the spirit. Men and women are born of flesh as babies. Angels or spirits are not born as babies.
- Genesis 6:1—Men are not angels.
- Genesis 6:3—God will not confront humans indefinitely because humans are mortal.

- Genesis 6:5–6—Man's wickedness is of man, not angels.
- Hebrews 1:5—God never calls angels His sons. The only one He calls His Son is Jesus.
- Job 38:4–7; Ephesians 2:20; 1 peter 2:6—Foundations of the earth is Jesus. He is the chief cornerstone.
- John 1:12—The sons of God are Christians in Heaven.
- Genesis 2:1—God created the heavens, angels, earth, and man and woman in six days.

What Are the Dead Sea Scrolls, and Why Are They Important?

The first of the Dead Sea Scroll discoveries occurred in 1947 in Qumran, a village situated about twenty miles east of Jerusalem on the northwest shore of the Dead Sea. A young Bedouin shepherd, following a goat that had gone astray, tossed a rock into one of the caves along the sea cliffs and heard a cracking sound: the rock had hit a ceramic pot containing leather and papyrus scrolls that were later determined to be nearly twenty centuries old. Ten years and many searches later, eleven caves around the Dead Sea were found to contain tens of thousands of scroll fragments dating from the third century B.C. to A.D. 68 and representing an estimated eight hundred separate works.

The Dead Sea Scrolls comprise a vast collection of Jewish documents written in Hebrew, Aramaic, and Greek, and encompassing many subjects and literary styles. They include manuscripts or fragments of every book in the Hebrew Bible except the Book of Esther, all of them created nearly one thousand years earlier than any previously known biblical manuscripts. The scrolls also contain the earliest existing biblical commentary, on the Book of Habakkuk, and many other writings, among them religious works pertaining to Jewish sects of the time

The legends of what was contained in the Dead Sea Scrolls are far beyond what was actually there. There were no lost books of the Bible or other literature that there were not already other copies of. The vast majority of the Dead Sea Scrolls were simply copies of books of the Old Testament from 250–150 B.C. A copy or portion of nearly every Old Testament book was found in Qumran. There were extra-biblical and apocryphal books found as well, but again, the vast majority of the scrolls were copies of the Hebrew Old Testament. The Dead Sea Scrolls were such an amazing discovery in that the scrolls were in excellent condition and had remained hidden for so long (over 2000 years). The Dead Sea Scrolls can also give us confidence in the reliability of the Old Testament manuscripts since there were minimal differences between the manuscripts that had previously been discovered and those that were found in Qumran. Clearly this is a testament to the way God has preserved His Word down through the centuries, protecting it from extinction and guarding it against significant error.[182]

182 "What Are the Dead Sea Scrolls and Why Are They Important?" Got Questions Ministries, 2022, https://www.gotquestions.org/dead-sea-scrolls.html.

Texts from the Hebrew Bible found at Qumran Torah (The Law)[183]

Book Title	Scroll Copies
Genesis	20
Exodus	16
Leviticus	12
Numbers	6
Deuteronomy	30

NEVI'IM (The Prophets)

Former Prophets	Scroll Copies
Joshua	3
Judges	4
Samuel (1 and 2)	4
Kings (1 and 2)	3

Latter Prophets	Scroll Copies
Isaiah	21
Jeremiah	6
Ezekiel	6
Twelve Minor Prophets	8

183 Ibid.

KETUVIM (The Writings)

Book Title	**Scroll Copies**
Psalms	34
Proverbs	4
Job	4
Song of Songs	4
Ruth	4
Lamentations	4
Ecclesiastes	2
Esther	0
Daniel	8
Ezra	1
Nehemiah	1
1-2 Chronicles	1

In March 2018, I had the rare and life-changing opportunity to view the display of the Dead Sea Scrolls in the Shrine of the Book at the Israel Museum in Jerusalem.

Are You a Modern-Day Nimrod?

While I was able to view this fascinating copy of the Dead Sea Scrolls, which is the oldest documentation validating the Bible (see the chapter of Dead Sea Scrolls), a thought occurred to me: *Whoa, these ancient texts are very telling*. As I walked where Jesus walked and visited His tomb, and made my way to Golan Heights (which is now occupied by Palestinians) and back down to the Dead Sea of Galilee, this made me realize that

Christianity is 100% true—we must be in alignment with God and that Jesus is sitting at the right hand of God. History tells us how God's people fell away from God, and one such person who has left his indelible mark on society is Nimrod—Noah's great-grandson.

Nimrod and Semiramis

Around 3000 BC (Genesis 9–11; Jeremiah 44), King Nimrod (name meaning rebel), who was Noah's great-grandson, built the tower of babel. God destroyed the tower and confused the people with many languages. Today the modern location of the tower of Babel is Iraq. God did this because the people were proud and wanted to be like God. Nimrod wanted power and built the tower with revenge in his heart against God for the flood.

Nimrod prided himself on being self-sufficient and was very prideful and arrogant. He had incestual relations with his mother, Semiramis (Queen of Heaven), and she gave birth to Tammuz, Nimrod's son. Nimrod died (some Jewish historians claim that Nimrod suffered pain inside his head for forty years before he died), and Semiramis didn't want the people to know that she had sexual relations with her son, so she told them that Tammuz was Nimrod reincarnated from the Sun God.

> Semiramus became Ishtar of Syria, Astarte of Phoenicia, Isis of Egypt, Aprhodite of Greece, and Venus of Rome—in each case the deity of sexual love and fertility. Her son Tammuz also came to be deified un-

der various names and was the consort of Ishtar and god of the underworld.[184]

How did Semiramis affect the church? Judaism was the religion of that day, and church was on Saturday, but Semiramis changed it to Sunday because of the Sun god. This is how Sunday church services originated—from the same man who influenced the Tower of Babel—a symbol of man's efforts to reach God in a very prideful and arrogant manner.

Semiramis became queen, and she and her people were evil, following the Sun god and other gods, which is the same as embracing demonic practices.

Today, you can see many statues of Semiramis (Queen of heaven) around the world, like in front of the CERN corporation. These statues are discussed elsewhere in this book. In New York, the Statue of Liberty is actually a statue depicting the Queen of Heaven. Interesting how this seemingly patriotic symbol of freedom is really a pagan goddess in disguise.

Later, this Babylonian state in ancient Mesopotamia, Iraq, near the Euphrates River, was ruled by King Hammurabi. On November 5, 1990, Iraqi General Georges Sada, under President Saddam Hussein, was ordered to attack and destroy Israel. However, the USA thwarted this attack.

One of the end-time prophecies is that the Euphrates River will dry out. This is happening right now, even as I speak. This will allow Russia, Iran, and their coalitions to cross the Euphra-

184 Bro. Rory "The Judgment of the Great Harlot - Part 1 (Revelation 17:1-6)," First Baptist Church Spur Texas, 2017, https://fbcspur.org/judgment-great-harlot-part-1-revelation-171-6/.

tes River. Their intention is to destroy Israel as soon as possible. However, God has other plans!

Today a modern-day Nimrod would be someone who is characterized by greed, pride, and arrogance. Someone who thinks he is not only above the law but above God. All we need to do is remind ourselves of how Nimrod, in his extreme narcissist view of how he and other men could be closer to God, instituted the Tower of Babel. We recall that after this tower was built, God confused the language of man, and this created a further division within what used to be God's people. Each gathered to his own tongue and nation after the fall of the Tower of Babel.

> So the LORD scattered them from there over all the earth, and they stopped building the city.
>
> (Genesis 11:8 NIV)

End Time Book of Revelation—The Tribulation Period

There are a total of twenty-one special judgments that fall upon the earth during the Tribulation Period. There are three series of sevens described as seals, trumpets, and vials (or bowls). Please read Chapters 6–11 in the Book Revelation.

- 21 Judgments (2 witnesses, 1 new beginning)
- 7 Seals bring plagues (7 is perfection)
- 7 Trumpets bring plagues (7 is perfection)
- 7 Bowls of wrath (7 is perfection)
- Revelation 6—Tribulation
- The mark of the Beast (number 6 means unperfected or the earth wasn't made or perfected until the seventh day).

- Revelation 6:1–2 (God, Jesus, and Holy Spirit)
- 6—unperfected angel satan vs. the 7 Seals.
- 6—unperfected human antichrist vs. the 7 Trumpets.
- 6—unperfected human false prophet vs. the 7 Bowls.

Being left behind to live through the Tribulation means that you will be cursed. You will experience stress, depression, difficulty, aggression, fighting, stealing, killing, rape, assault, battery, trouble, yelling, sorrow, persecution, woe, major suffering, suicides, pain, affliction, loss, and much, much more. We should pay attention to the validity of what the Bible says about end-time events and the coming Tribulation.

Again, I cannot impress upon you, the reader, enough that satan's nature is *always to lie and deceive and copy God*. Despite satan's deceiving nature, God is in *control* of everything. Perhaps as a foretaste of God's rapture of His church, we read in the texts that there were two people who were taken up to Heaven while they were still alive and walking around on earth.

By virtue of this *incredible rapture*, Enoch and Elijah *bypassed human death*. Biblical scholars suggest that Enoch and Elijah (2 Kings 2:11) may be the two prophets mentioned in Revelation 11:3–5, which I also mention in another book I wrote, End Game.

There are two people whom God throws into the fiery pit or lake of fire—the antichrist (a human who has been overpowered by demonic forces) and the false prophet (another human who is controlled by satan).

God's authority doesn't change throughout time, from the beginning of creation. There is hope for those who stand strong in their faith and accept Jesus as their Lord and Savior.

During the tribulation period, God will come back to earth with those in the first resurrection (which includes those who were still alive and raptured). The significance of this passage is that *we don't go up to Heaven—God in His Trinity comes to meet us on earth:*

> Then I saw a "new heaven and a new earth," for the first heaven and the first earth had passed away, and there was no longer any sea. I saw the Holy City, the new Jerusalem, coming down out of heaven from God, prepared as a bride beautifully dressed for her husband.
>
> (Revelation 21:1–2 NIV)

Four Horsemen of the Apocalypse[185]

The Four Horsemen in Revelation 6

> "Now I watched when the Lamb opened one of the seven seals, and I heard one of the four living crea-

185 © [germanjames] — adobestock.com.

tures say with a voice like thunder, "Come!" And I looked, and behold, a **white horse**! And its rider had a bow, and a crown was given to him, and he came out conquering, and to conquer. When he opened the second seal, I heard the second living creature say, "Come!" And out came **another horse, bright red**. Its rider was permitted to take peace from the earth, so that people should slay one another, and he was given a great sword. When he opened the third seal, I heard the third living creature say, "Come!" And I looked, and behold, a **black horse**! And its rider had a pair of scales in his hand.

And I heard what seemed to be a voice in the midst of the four living creatures, saying, "A quart of wheat for a denarius, and three quarts of barley for a denarius, and do not harm the oil and wine!" When he opened the fourth seal, I heard the voice of the fourth living creature say, "Come!" And I looked, and behold, a **pale horse**! And its rider's name was Death, and Hades followed him. And they were given authority over a fourth of the earth, to kill with sword and with famine and with pestilence and by wild beasts of the earth."

(Revelation 6:1–8 ESV)

What Is the Millennial Reign?

Many of us might wonder what the Millennial or One-thousand (1000) year reign is and why Christians who are Heaven bound should be concerned. It's God's Plan to reward His

Children (Church) for their sacrifices for Him (Matthew 25:34; 1 Corinthians 6:2; Isaiah 40:10; 1 Thessalonians 3:13; Matthew 16:27; Revelation 22:12; Matthew 25:23; Colossians 3:24; Revelation 20:4).

Take a quick look at Matthew 6:9–13 (KJV):

> "...Our Father which art in Heaven, Hallowed be thy name.
> Thy kingdom come,
> Thy will be done
> on earth as it is in heaven.
> Give us today our daily bread.
> And forgive us our debts,
> as we also have forgiven our debtors.
> And lead us not into temptation,
> but deliver us from the evil one.

For centuries humanity has been praying this prayer. The millennial is an answer from God to perhaps billions of prayers along this vein.

The old prophets from the Bible prophesied the 1,000 years or *millennial prophecy*, which is coming to pass, and conveying the truth. Remember, God does not lie. Because of the original corruption and sin of Adam and Eve and human nature, satan will be released after a thousand years to tempt those who are still on the earth after the first resurrection, including those who were still alive and simultaneously raptured.

Satan will be released after the millennial reign to tempt the youth who may have been sanctified by their parents rather than their own free will, young adults, and other adults who later confessed at the end of the tribulation that Jesus Christ is Lord and Savior. This group of individuals will be tempted by satan in the final rebellion against God (Revelation 20).

Satan Is Released After 1,000 Years

In the millennial reign, Bible prophecy tells us that thousands will end up following satan. Despite Jesus' laws and guidelines, many do not want to follow Him at the time of satan's 1,000-year captivity release (see Revelation 20). Through satan's lying and deceiving ways, people in the millennial reign at a certain period or time will attack the city of the *millennial Jerusalem* to destroy Christ and Christians for the second time or better known as the "War of Armageddon".

At the end of the millennial reign, Jesus is still reigning on earth, but satan will attack with an army as large as the sand on a seashore. Any further grace being offered to satan and his followers are moot, and with just a *Word* from Heaven (which is God in His Trinity), fire emerges and wipes out satan and his evil demonic army. There is no time for satan to throw any punches, no time for fighting, and no war takes place. With a Word from Heaven and a fiery furnace, satan and his last rebellion are done (Revelation 21).

This sounds reminiscent of Sodom and Gomorrah (Genesis 19:1–28), and the power of the destruction is like the *Noachian deluge*, the water inundation of the earth at the time of Noah. The final post-millennium rebellion may sound far off. A thousand years plus away. But here's the thing: Satan is scheming and fighting God for possession of your soul—all the way up to

Judgment Day, when many will stand before God on the great white throne of judgment. Satan would like none other than to take you to hell for all eternity.

Live as If You Are Standing before God

If you could stand before your maker right this instant, in His eyes, would you say your life is characterized by evil or bad things? Have you been faithful to our Lord Jesus through all your life's battles? Did you overcome your bad habits? Do you have unforgiveness? Did you help people in need, the homeless, etc.? Were you able to witness to your best friends, friends, family members, neighbors, and co-workers about Jesus Christ? Did you read your Bible? Did you pray? Did you pay your tithing? And other good things?

God has kept a record of your life. When you are baptized in a true Christian Church, everything you did before that time is erased. *This is what is meant by a Born-again Christian.* If you belong to a cult like Islam, Hinduism, Buddhism, Mormonism, Jehovah's Witness, etc., according to the Word of God, *you are not yet saved.* This should be a wake-up call, and I pray that the Holy Spirit speaks to your soul about this.

After being baptized, if you should fall away or break one of the ten commandments and you repent of your recognizance, you are immediately forgiven by God. But if you continue in your sin, your repentance is in vain, and you may be playing with fire—you may be in a "red zone," where you can grieve the Holy Spirit, or worse, cause blaspheme of the Holy Spirit (see Mark 3:22–30; Matthew 12:22–32).

To help us be accountable, God forewarns us and keeps a record of what we have done, good and bad. Believers can anticipate that God will bring down from Heaven a 1,500-mile wide by 1,500-mile-high Heaven. In a pure and unadulterated state, we will be living with God, Jesus Christ, and the Holy Spirit—like Adam and Eve at the beginning of the Bible.

I invite you to peer into Revelation 20:6 with me.

> According to this verse, whoever participates in the first resurrection is blessed and holy. "Blessed" is a beatitude that means "happy" or "spiritually prosperous". A blessed person may not be materially rich, but he is happy and spiritually prosperous. All who rise from the dead in the first resurrection, regardless of when or how they died, are blessed, and they are free forever from the second death. The second death. The second death refers to suffering forever in the lake of fire (Revelation 20:14).
>
> Participants in the first resurrection will perform priestly and kingly duties during the thousand-year reign of Christ. The designation "thousand years" occurs six times in Chapter 20, so it would be hard to reject this designation as something other than a literal period of time. Prior to the thousand years, Christ returns to earth and destroys the armies that oppose Him. He throws the Beast and the False Prophet into the lake of fire. Also, before the thousand years begin, an angel incarcerates Satan in the bottomless pit, tribulation martyrs are resurrected, and thrones of judgement are established (Revelation 20:1–4).

> During the millennial period, there are no wars, hate, prejudice, etc. You will have "Peace" (Isaiah 11:6–9; Psalms 72:7; Micah 4:2–3). You will have a certain type of "Purity" (Isaiah 66:23; Zechariah 13:2; Isaiah 11:9, 25:9). You will be "Prosperous" (Ezekiel 36:29–30; Zechariah 8:12; Amos 9:13; Ezekiel 34:36–37; Isaiah 35:1).[186]

We read in Bible that before the flood of Noah, people were living 900-something years or a long time. After the flood, God said,

> ... "I won't let my life-giving breath remain in anyone forever. No one will live for more than 120 years."
>
> (Genesis 6:3 CEV)

However, in the Millennial Reign, we will live longer than we live today (Isaiah 9:3, 12:3, 25:8–9, 65:20, 14:7, 30:29, 42:10–12). Please read Revelation 20:1–6. Your future existence has a stake in this amazing "post-earth" prophecy!

> The millennium (also known as the millennial kingdom) is the 1,000-year reign of Jesus after the tribulation which occurs before the Great White Throne Judgment of the wicked. During the millennium, Jesus will reign as king over Israel and all the nations of the world (Isaiah 2:4, 42:1).[187]

---

186 "What Does Revelation 20:6 Mean?" BibleRef.Com., 2022, https://www.bibleref.com/Revelation/20/Revelation-20-6.html.

187 "What Is the Purpose of the Thousand-Year Reign of Christ?" Got Questions Ministries, 2022, https://www.gotquestions.org/thousand-year-reign-Christ.html.

In Jesus Christ's rapture and eventually the millennial reign of Jesus, together with the Christian Church, the cult will simply cease to exist. There will be no Islam, Hinduism, Buddhism, Mormonism, Jehovah's Witnesses, or other counterfeit gods. The denizens of Heaven will be rejoicing and have the agape love of Christ, joy, gladness, rest, peace, deliverance, and much more.

> The world will live in peace (Isaiah 11:6–9; 32:18), Satan will be bound (Revelation 20:1–3), and, at the beginning, everyone will worship God (Isaiah 2:2–3). The purpose of the 1,000-year reign is to fulfill various promises God made to the world. Some of these promises, called covenants, were given specifically to Israel. Others were given to Jesus, the nations of the world, and creation. Jesus' 1,000-year reign will be a time of promises kept.[188]

What Is the Great White Throne of Judgment?

> The great white throne judgment is described in Revelation 20:11–15 and is the final judgment prior to the lost being cast into the lake of fire. We know from Revelation 20:7–15 that this judgment will take place after the millennium and after Satan is thrown into the lake of fire where the beast and the false prophet are (Revelation 19:19–20; 20:7–10). The books that are opened (Revelation 20:12) contain

188 "What Is the Purpose of the Thousand-Year Reign of Christ?" 2022.

records of everyone's deeds, whether they are good or evil, because God knows everything that has ever been said, done, or even thought, and He will reward or punish each one accordingly (Psalm 28:4; 62:12; Romans 2:6; Revelation 2:23, 18:6; 22:12).

Also, at this time, another book is opened, called the "book of life" (Revelation 20:12). It is this book that determines whether a person will inherit eternal life with God or receive everlasting punishment in the lake of fire. Although Christians are held accountable for their actions, they are forgiven in Christ and their names were written in the "book of life from the creation of the world" (Revelation 17:8). We also know from Scripture that it is at this judgment when the dead will be "judged according to what they had done" (Revelation 20:12) and that "anyone's name" that is not "found written in the book of life" will be "thrown into the lake of fire" (Revelation 20:15).

The fact that there is going to be a final judgment for all men, both believers and unbelievers, is clearly confirmed in many passages of Scripture. Every person will one day stand before Christ and be judged for his or her deeds. While it is very clear that the great white throne judgment is the final judgment, Christians disagree on how it relates to the other judgments mentioned in the Bible, specifically, who will be judged at the great white throne judgment.

Some Christians believe that the Scriptures reveal three different judgments to come. The first is the

> judgment of the sheep and the goats or a judgment of the nations (Matthew 25:31–36). This takes place after the tribulation period but prior to the millennium; its purpose is to determine who will enter the millennial kingdom. The second is a judgment of believers' works, often referred to as the "judgment seat [bema] of Christ" (2 Corinthians 5:10). At this judgment, Christians will receive degrees of reward for their works or service to God. The third is the great white throne judgment at the end of the millennium (Revelation 20:11–15). This is the judgment of unbelievers in which they are judged according to their works and sentenced to everlasting punishment in the lake of fire.[189]

Prayer, Fasting, and Being Humble Before God

There's only one Jesus, and there's only one you. So what does prayer, fasting, and being humble before the Lord have to do with creation (the earth, Sun, Moon, sky, etc.) and the design of our human body? Everything listed below has God's fingerprints on it; for example, the creation of the earth we live in, our galaxy, and the universe, for that matter. 'Here is a quick overview of some of the incredible aspects of God's creation.

The universe has 8,000 plus galaxies. Our own Milky Way Galaxy is 100,000 light-years away with over 100,000 stars and countless planets in our solar system.[190] Our sun, a medium

189 "What Is the Great White Throne Judgment?" Got Questions Ministries, 2022, https://www.gotquestions.org/great-white-throne-judgment.html.
190 Jolene Creighton, "Scientists Map 8,000 Galaxies," Futurism, 2014, https://futurism.com/scientists-map-8000-galaxies.

star, is 15 million degrees Celsius at its core and 6000 degrees at its outer surface.[191] Earth is 12,500 kilometers or 7,800 miles in diameter, with a molten center of iron and nickel at approximately 4,500 degrees Celsius.[192] Our planet earth contains 525 million cubic miles of water, which covers 70% of the earth.[193] We have 300,000 named species of plants and 1.2 million species of animals.[194]

Layers of Soil

As we walk on the earth's surface, we may not always be mindful that our amazing earth has at least four layers of soil. Further, the Bible mentions the importance of being on "good ground" or "good soil" See Matthew 13:23.

Luke 8:15 (KJV) says,

> But that on the good ground are they, which in an honest and good heart, having heard the word, keep it, and bring forth fruit with patience.

Farmers and scientists say the soil for plants like wheat or other critical plants for farm or wild animals to eat and to meet human needs should be moist or wet for four months. In many

---

191 "Why Is the Sun's Atmosphere Hotter than Its Surface?" Earth Sky, 2021, https://earthsky.org/sun/why-suns-atmosphere-hotter-than-its-surface/.

192 "The Importance of Water," Facebook, 2015, https://pt-br.facebook.com/444194128994211/photos/pb.444194128994211.-2207520000../832048370208783/?type=3&eid-ARA9Tp2MMMS3GVpPeWum6WtC-cJJmcj2rrQymuja8orWin7hErmqVtMY1VCfOOH3bI2vrN_HTZGbCHbOY.

193 Loarie, "We Passed 300,000 Species Observed on INaturalist!." INaturalist, 2013, https://www.inaturalist.org/blog/42626-we-passed-300-000-species-observed-on-inaturalist.

194 Kim Rutledge, Hilary Costa, Erin Sprout, Santani Teng, Melissa McDaniel, Diane Boudreau, Tara Ramroop, Jeff Hunt, and Hilary Hall, "Biodiversity | National Geographic Society," Nationalgeographic, 2011, https://education.nationalgeographic.org/resource/biodiversity.

places worldwide, we have climate change refugees for not enough water (like in Africa) to drink or plant or too much water (like in the Philippines and Indonesia). Over a billion people around the world are lacking in essentials for life, and today are climate change refugees.

The four layers of soil (dirt) are called *horizons*. Each layer has its own characteristics, which play a very important role in plant growth.

1. Top layer—made up of living material, and decompressed materials, i.e., leaves, dead plants, bugs, etc. This top layer is a very thin layer and is usually dark in color.
2. Topsoil—this layer is made up of .minerals and decompressed organic matter. This layer is usually darker in color. Plant roots grow at this layer or level.
3. Subsoil—includes mineral deposits and less organic materials than topsoil. This layer is usually lighter in color than the top layer and topsoil.
4. Regolith—slightly unbroken rock with a few organic materials. Roots are not usually found at this layer.[195]

I am sharing this with you so that you can imagine that Hell is somewhere near the core of the earth—far below the layers of soil.

Layers of Atmosphere Which Make up the Sky and Heavens

Not only is the earth so splendidly designed that scientists, geologists, physicists, and other scholars are continually fasci-

195 "Topsoil vs. Garden Soil – What's the Difference?" The Dirt Bag, Accessed October 6, 2022, https://www.thedirtbag.com/topsoil-vs-garden-soil-whats-the-difference/.

nated and astounded by what their research reveals—but our creator had a vision to create great and wondrous elements beyond what we can see, touch, hear and feel from the earth.

The next time you step outside, I would ask that you take a good look at the sky. Try to record in your mind all the details of what you see. Then gaze up at the sky at night when the stars are out and try to comprehend how our creator spoke all of this into existence.

There are five layers of atmosphere surrounding our blue planet.

1. *Exosphere*—a thin, atmosphere-like volume surrounding a planet or natural satellite where molecules are gravitationally bound to that body.
2. *Thermosphere*—is above the mesosphere.
3. *Mesosphere*—is above the stratosphere.
4. *Stratosphere*—is above the troposphere.
5. *Troposphere*—is the closest to earth, 5–10 miles from the surface.[196]

Heaven is way above or beyond the exosphere, the topmost layer of the earth. The Bible verses that mention our atmosphere are found in Judges 5:4, James 5:17, Isaiah 13:10, and Deuteronomy 17:3. The three levels of Celestial Space or Heavens are (Please read 2 Corinthians 12:2):

1. *Heaven of Heavens*—where God lives (Nehemiah 9:6; 2 Corinthians 12:2–3).

196 Alan Buis, "Earth's Atmosphere: A Multi-Layered Cake," Global Climate Change: Vital Signs of the Planet, 2019, https://climate.nasa.gov/news/2919/earths-atmosphere-a-multi-layered-cake/.

2. *Outer space*—galaxy, stars, moon, solar system, and planets.
3. *Atmosphere*—Exosphere, Thermosphere, Mesosphere, Stratosphere, and Troposphere.

A Quick Glance at the Human Body

Our body has 600 muscles, two million optical nerves, and 100 million nerve cells.[197] Every second, our bodies produce 25 million new cells; our hearts beat about 100,000 times a day; our brains produce enough electricity to light a small light bulb, and the mind-blowing facts about the human body could fill a book.

All of these truly amazing and astounding facts are merely discovering the mind of God when He first designed our universe, sun, moon, planets, and earth—then created humans to populate the earth. Although God has created the heavens and the earth, and all the galaxies in the universe—He has created only one Son—*Jesus Christ*.

By believing in Jesus Christ, one becomes the recipient of God's grace—which is extended to all. Eternal life isn't living in Heaven; eternal life is *Jesus Christ and Him alone!* There's no Allah, Buddha, or Joseph Smith—no false prophets in Heaven or eternal life, no one else but *Jesus, Jesus, Jesus!*

I must stress this emphatically. For me, the difference between Heaven and Hell is everything. Everything in your life is at stake (John 1, Acts. 19, Titus 3:2).

197 "Muscles," Better Health Channel, 2012, https://www.betterhealth.vic.gov.au/health/conditionsandtreatments/muscles.

Your Old Men Shall Dream Dreams; Your Young Men Shall See Visions

"The prophet Joel, son of Pethuel, is the author of the *book of Joel*. The book was written from Jerusalem between BC 835–796 to the people of Israel and to *all later readers of the Bible*."[198] Read Joel 2:14–28 to see how God speaks through the prophets who lived hundreds of years *before Christ* and even now in the twenty-first century.

> "Who knoweth if he will return and repent, and leave a blessing behind him; even a meat offering and a drink offering unto the LORD your God?
>
> Blow the trumpet in Zion, sanctify a fast, call a solemn assembly:
>
> Gather the people, sanctify the congregation, assemble the elders, gather the children, and those that suck the breasts: let the bridegroom go forth of his chamber, and the bride out of her closet.
>
> Let the priests, the ministers of the LORD, weep between the porch and the altar, and let them say, Spare thy people, O LORD, and give not thine heritage to reproach, that the heathen should rule over them: wherefore should they say among the people, Where is their God?
>
> Then will the LORD be jealous for his land, and pity his people.

198 "Book of Joel Introduction: The Day of the Lord Is Coming," Learn Religions, 2022.,https://www.learnreligions.com/book-of-joel-701135.

Yea, the LORD will answer and say unto his people, Behold, I will send you corn, and wine, and oil, and ye shall be satisfied therewith: and I will no more make you a reproach among the heathen:

But I will remove far off from you the northern army, and will drive him into a land barren and desolate, with his face toward the east sea, and his hinder part toward the utmost sea, and his stink shall come up, and his ill savour shall come up, because he hath done great things.

Fear not, O land; be glad and rejoice: for the LORD will do great things.

Be not afraid, ye beasts of the field: for the pastures of the wilderness do spring, for the tree beareth her fruit, the fig tree and the vine do yield their strength.

Be glad then, ye children of Zion, and rejoice in the LORD your God: for he hath given you the former rain moderately, and he will cause to come down for you the rain, the former rain, and the latter rain in the first month.

And the floors shall be full of wheat, and the vats shall overflow with wine and oil. And I will restore to you the years that the locust hath eaten, the cankerworm, and the caterpillar, and the palmerworm, my great army which I sent among you.

And ye shall eat in plenty, and be satisfied, and praise the name of the LORD your God, that hath dealt wondrously with you: and my people shall never be ashamed. And ye shall know that I am in the midst of Israel, and that I am the LORD your God, and none else: and my people shall never be ashamed.

And it shall come to pass afterward, that I will pour out my spirit upon all flesh; and your sons and your daughters shall prophesy, your old men shall dream dreams, your young men shall see visions:

(Joel 2:14–28 KJV)Baptism of the Holy Spirit

When you are baptized by a true Christian Church disciple, pastor, bishop, reverend, apostle, evangelist, teacher, priest, etc., with the proper authority in a pool, ocean, under a shower, etc., you will become *born again*. Your *old self* died! Your new self just became clean by the *Holy Spirit!*

Baptism erases your past but not your future. Remember—before baptism, you *must* do the following:

1. **Confess that you are a sinner and in need of a Savior.** Say in your heart, "I know I did this or thought that..."
2. **Repent**—put right what you are doing wrong (i.e., stop adultery, stealing, lying, drunkenness, etc.). Baptism is for the *dirty* and burial for the *dead*. When you come out of the water (*immersion*), you emerge *clean* and *born again*, and when you are baptized in the name of the Father, the Son, and the Holy Spirit, *you are a new creature in Christ* (2 Corinthians 5:17).
3. **Water baptism** (repentance of sins)—Jesus was perfect and sinless, and yet He was baptized by John the Baptist

to set an example for all of us who would decide to follow Him and accept Jesus as our Lord and Savior.

4. **Baptism of the Holy Spirit.** The Holy Spirit is the third person of the Godhead, which only manifested after Jesus was crucified and rose from the deal and ascended to Heaven. Jesus said He would send His Comforter.

> And I will pray the Father, and he shall give you another Comforter, that he may abide with you forever; Even the Spirit of truth; whom the world cannot receive, because it seeth him not, neither knoweth him: but ye know him; for he dwelleth with you, and shall be in you. I will not leave you comfortless: I will come to you.
>
> (John 14:16–19 KJV)

Speaking in tongues is the gift of the Holy Spirit, and If You Ask God, He Will Give You This Gift.

> And when the day of Pentecost was fully come, they were all with one accord in one place. And suddenly there came a sound from heaven as of a rushing mighty wind, and it filled all the house where they were sitting. And there appeared unto them cloven tongues like as of fire, and it sat upon each of them. And they were all filled with the Holy Ghost, and began to speak with other tongues, as the Spirit gave them utterance.
>
> (Acts 2:1–4 KJV)

God moves in a village, tribe, community, location, city, state, province, wherever He needs to be on this planet Earth, wherever there are people. God will move His Spirit among the people with signs, wonders, and miracles! Man moves people with ceremonies, rituals, and traditions, which sometimes douses God's movement of the Holy Spirit, much like water from a firehose will douse a fire and put it out. The Holy Spirit Fire of the Lord is the kind of fire you want under your feet and surrounding you as much as possible in these times.

If you are following your own ways and not God's ways, please read Isaiah 55:8 and Romans 8:28.

Bringing Others to Christ

Bringing someone like a best friend, co-worker, family member, friend, neighbor, or anyone you talk to and meet to Christ. Building a relationship first is the critical part of today's end times. First, get to know them, their likes, dislikes, family, work, goals in life, are they divorced, single, married, etc.

Here are ten steps to follow when bringing others to Christ Jesus:

1. Pray
2. Fast
3. Empathy
4. Ask open questions
5. Be an example
6. Define their faith
7. Expose incompatibles
8. Teach the Gospel of Christ

9. Clarify the message
10. Pray

Cross-references in this book:

- Pray—see page 89 of this book.
- Fast—see page 91 of this book.
- Empathy—John 7:53–8:11.

A Woman Caught in Adultery

> Jesus returned to the Mount of Olives, but early the next morning he was back again in the temple. A crowd soon gathered and he sat down and taught them. As he was speaking, the teachers of the religious law and the Pharisees brought a woman who had been caught in the act of adultery. They put her in front of the crowd.
>
> "Teacher," they said to Jesus, "this woman was caught in the act of adultery. The law of Moses says to stone her. What do you say?"
>
> They were trying to trap him into saying something they could use against him, but Jesus stooped down and wrote in the dust with his finger. They kept demanding an answer, so he stood up again and said, all right, but let the one who has never sinned throw the first stone! Then he stooped down again and wrote in the dust.
>
> When the accusers heard this, they slipped away one by one, beginning from the oldest, until only Jesus

was left in the middle of the crowd with the woman.
"Where are your accusers? Didn't even one of them condemn you?"
"No Lord," she said.
And Jesus said, "Neither do I. Go and sin no more."
(John 8:1–11 NLT)

As you relate this parable to the person you're talking to, maybe you might ask how you would have responded if you were in Jesus' position.

1. Ask open questions, Matthew 8:27.
   Jesus and His disciples left Galilee and went up to the villages near Caesarea Philippi. As they were walking alone, He asked, "Who do people say I am?" (Matthew 16:13).
   You might ask the person you're talking to about their religion and what they believe.
2. Be an example 1 Peter 2:13–17 (NLT):
   For the Lord's sake to all human authority—whether the king as head of state or the officials he has appointed. For the king has sent them to punish those who do wrong and honor those who do right.
   It is God's Will that your honorable lives should silence those ignorant people who make foolish accusations against you. For you are free, yet you are God's slaves, so don't use your freedom as an excuse to do evil. Respect everyone, and love the family of the believers Fear God, and respect the king.
   Ask how do you feel about obeying local or state, or federal laws?

3. Define their faith—Acts 7.
   In your religion, what does (for example, heaven or hell or something else) mean?
4. Expose incompatibles.
   Ask questions about their perception of their religion or false issues of their religion compared to Christ. An example is in Buddhism. Since Buddha is not a god, he cannot take you to heaven for your sins.
5. Teach the Gospel of Christ—Acts 4.
   Read Acts 4, Genesis 1–2, John 3:16, and Matthew 28. Ask what your viewpoint of salvation in Christ's plan for you is?
6. Clarify the message—Acts 17:22–25 (NIV):
   Paul then stood up in the meeting of the Areopagus and said: People of Athens! I see that in every way you are very religious. For as I walked around and looked carefully at your objects of worship. I even found an altar with this inscription: to an unknown god. So you are ignorant of the very thing you worship—and this is what I am going to proclaim to you.
   "The God who made the world and everything in it is the Lord of Heaven and earth and does not live in the temples built by human hands. And he is not served by human hands, as if he needed anything. Rather, he himself gives everyone life and breath and everything else."
   1 Corinthians 9:19–23 (NLT):
   Even though I am free man with no master, I have become a slave to all people to many to Christ. When I was with Jews, I lived like a Jew to bring the Jews to Christ.

When I was with those who follow the Jewish law. I too under that law. Even though I am not subject to the law, I did this so I could bring to Christ those who are under the law. When I am with the gentiles who do not follow the Jewish law, I too live apart from the law so I can bring them to Christ, but I do not ignore the law of Christ.

When I am with those who are weak, I share their weakness, for I want to bring the weak to Christ. Yes, I try to find common ground with everyone, doing everything I can to save some. I do everything to spread the good news and share in the blessings.

You can address any issues of shame, honor, etc. in receiving Jesus.

7. Pray—2 Peter 3:9 (NIV):

   The Lord is not slow in keeping his promise, as some understand slowness. Instead, he is patient with you, not wanting anyone to parish, but everyone to come to repentance.

   Pray for Jesus to reveal Himself to you.

Preparing Your Household for the End Times

Simplicity or simplify your life for the "end times" before it's too late—don't procrastinate!

My Dad passed away on August 16, 2020, at the age of eighty-three, from *stage 4 renal cancer with a stoma,* and my Mom passed away on February 23, 2021, at the age of eighty-three, with *stage 4 renal and vaginal cancer*. They were married for sixty-four years. My Mom was a *hoarder* and kept all items stored and stashed around the house. It occurred to me that she was a shopaholic when I encountered item after item. It took me literally two and a half plus years to clean their three-story condo with two storage rooms. I took care of my Dad for eight years and my Mom for one and a half years. I was completely drained after all those years. My tank was empty, just fumes. I realized the only way to deal with the aftermath of both my parents' death was to compartmentalize everything and do one step at a time. Here's the actual process that I went through to take care of what my parents left behind after they passed.

First Step. I looked at everything and decided if I needed the item at present or if I may need it in six months. If I didn't need it, I would give it to family members, military homeless shelters, local homeless shelters, Salvation Army, Goodwill, or friends.

Second Step. I looked at all the bills, legal issues, and outstanding debt and balanced everything. I went over my parents' will, power of attorney, and health care directives with their attorney. Mr. Ito, the attorney, was so very helpful.

Third Step. Set up a trust. There are two types of trusts. The first is a revocable trust. This is a state and federal document that spells out what happens to your estate after you are gone. The trust ensures that when you pass from this earth, your estate, especially your home, doesn't go through government probate. Probate takes time and can cost you a lot without the trust.

Why do you need a trust? Because when you are dead or can no longer decide (for example, if you have dementia and are in a Nursing home or hospital or in-home care, they (your kids will fight among themselves about your estate).

As a previous nursing home assistant administrator of the second-largest nursing home in Hawaii, I've seen the best and most well-behaved kids fight over money, assets, and the house. Don't put yourself, assets, or kids in this position. Incidentally, studies show that Women are more likely than men to be providing primary care to an aging parent (13% vs. 7%). And those who are not married (15%) are more likely than those who are married (7%) to provide most of the care to a parent.[199]

The second type of trust is an irrevocable trust. Once you do this type of trust, you cannot add an addendum for any changes you might want to make. You must pay the full price to do the trust all over again.

Will

I would suggest you use a certified attorney, but you could do this yourself. Some people type up their *will* on a computer, but it could be challenged in court. Best to use your handwriting. Usually, a will have the small details, such as "this jewelry will go to... or this picture will go to..., or the furniture will go to..." and so on.

Power of Attorney (POA)

A power of attorney is tricky because if you don't choose the right person or child, the rest of your kids or family will suffer the consequence. That person or family member can either be trustworthy, loving, grateful, conscientious, caring, fair—or do

199 Kim, Parker and Eileen Patten, "Caregiving for Older Family Members," Pew Research Center, 2013, https://www.pewresearch.org/social-trends/2013/01/30/caregiving-for-older-family-members/.

less than what others feel should be done throughout the entire process.

I've seen the outcome many times where the person who had the power of attorney did not carry out the parents' estate in a way that the parents might have been happy or proud of. I suggest again that you choose a succession of three who are named in the power of attorney document. Never make anyone equal (reason above). The person designated with the power of attorney will have the authority to use your banking account, checking account, pay bills, etc. If you can no longer make decisions about the affairs of your healthcare or estate because you have dementia or are very ill in a Nursing home, hospital, or hospice—think of whom you would trust to carry out all your affairs. Think wisely!

Health Care Directive

The doctors' mission statement and nurses' mission statement are to keep you alive. Because of my experience as an assistant nursing home administrator, I've seen many cases where a patient or resident is kept alive by machines. I'll give you an example of someone. He was a construction worker in his forties to fifties. He fell off the thirtieth floor. He survived the fall but was completely paralyzed. He was in a *vegetative state*—unable to speak, look around, or move.

Someone in that unfortunate state will usually have a feeding tube feed put into their stomach. The doctor makes a small incision, and through the tube, you are fed your daily supplements (like *Ensure*). An alternative way to feed you is through your nose, where the tube feeding system goes through your nose, down your esophagus, and into your stomach.

The point I'd like to make about this patient in a vegetative state is that he lived like this at the nursing home for many years. Why? Because the insurance paid the bills, and the doctors' and nurses' mission are to keep life going. This is a bad quality of life. Would this patient have chosen this for himself if he knew there was an alternative? We cannot say because he did not have a choice. *But it's your choice* while you are still alive, well, and able to make decisions on your own behalf.

With my health care directive, I have *no* tube feeding to prolong my life and no CPR to resuscitate me. When God calls me, I want to go be with Him and not suffer or have my life prolonged by a feeding tube!

Once your attorney gives you the trust documents, I suggest you obtain a fireproof safe and, as a safety measure, let your power of attorney know the combination and/or have the duplicate key. If they die before you go, the key or combination goes to the second person.

I also suggest you get an attorney who specializes in these documents only, as they usually keep up with current federal and state laws, vs. getting an attorney that just wants your money, someone who doesn't keep up with current laws and may be quite distracted with other legal cases, such as assault and battery, divorce settlements, etc. All these documents must be legally notarized. Usually, in Hawaii, these fourplex documents cost $1,500 per person or $3,000 per couple.

Please, I urge you to take care of your estate before it's too late, please.

Fourth Step. Make sure you have a burial plot and plan. In Hawaii, land is very expensive. The burial plots and plans (casket, headstone, hearse limousine, memorial services cost such as facility rental and food costs, etc.) go up every year.

So, put the funds away now to take care of your funeral expenses when you are gone. Don't put this burden on your kids. The other option is being cremated. Some people choose beforehand to be cremated. This cost less than a traditional burial, and some choose to have their ashes scattered in the ocean or on land.

I'm not against this, as I feel we were born of dust, and to dust, we shall return. I believe God allows human remains to be cared for either way—in a casket or cremated. God will make you whole in Heaven. No worries, the main thing is that you repent and receive Jesus in your heart and be water baptized if you can. If you're at a hospital, nursing home, or somewhere else and 'are unable to be water baptized, you can say Romans 10:9, and to Heaven, you will go after death.

I have a family plot in the Mililani mortuary, and because I am a USA Navy veteran, I will be fortunate to receive a free plot and headstone, but I would have to pay for other items, such as the casket, services, food, hearst limousine, etc.

Fifth Step. Make sure you have a financial planner who is educated, reputable, and has a good track record. They can help you set financial goals and objectives for retirement.

Sixth Step. *Jeremiah 29:11* says that God has a plan and purpose for your life. How do I know that? How can I find out what God wants for me in my life? First, pray about it! Ask God with a sincere, open, and honest heart. God says He has called the apostles, prophets, evangelists, pastors, and teachers.

Which one are you? You also go to www.chosenbooks.com and click on "finding your spiritual gifts." Fill out the easy-to-use, self-guided questionnaire by C. Peter Wagner, or go to your local Christian bookstore or your church to see what gifting questionnaires or tests are available. Then you will discover what your gifting means.

Seventh Step. I have markers all over my house to remind me of Christ (i.e., praying hands, framed scripture verses, crosses, pictures of the Dead Sea Scrolls, Ark of the Covenant model, etc.) I also bless every room in my house with oil from Israel. You can buy Blessed Oil at your local Christian bookstore or use any oil (i.e., vegetable oil, olive oil, coconut oil, etc.) and bless the oil in the Name of Jesus Christ. I bless each room over the doorframe and make a cross by dipping my finger in the oil and drawing a cross. I do the same with my truck.

Eighth Step. Since we are in the end times now and Jesus can come any second for His Church, or the Rapture can occur at any minute, I just buy enough food for one week.

Ninth Step. If Jesus gave me seven days to prepare for the Rapture of His Church or the rapture of myself or my family, I would think of everything to get ready for this. Who will take over my house, apartment, or condo? Who will take over my car, truck, or motorcycle? Who will take over my checking account? Who will take over my bank account? Who will feed my animals? Who will water my plants? You might ask yourself many of these same questions for you and your family to answer.

The reality is that those left behind are left behind because they lack a relationship with Jesus Christ.

Tenth Step. Each new year in January, I celebrate a different way. I go through my house and get rid of everything that I had not used for six months to a year. If I didn't use the item(s) within that time period, I probably don't need it. I give these items away to others who may need them.

Nine Spiritual Gifts

We can count at least nine spiritual gifts that we may use in our life—whenever we *think* about something or someone, do something, or say something.

Think:
Word of wisdom
Word of knowledge
Gift of faith

Do:
Working in miracles
Gift of healing
Prophecy

Say:
Speaking in tongues
Distinguishing between spirit
Interpreting tongues

As Christians—do not allow *fear, pride,* and *embarrassment* to hinder you from growing and practicing or exercising these nine gifts.

Virtues of a True Christian

There are elements of the human spirit called *virtues*, which work hand in hand when operating within your spiritual gifts, including prophetic and healing gifts. According to the Oxford dictionary, *virtue* is behavior showing high moral standards.[200] Virtue is also a quality considered good or desirable in a person.

1. Virtues of the human spirit.

Humility	Courtesy
Meekness	Forgiveness
Honor	Diligence
GenerosityCourage	Gentleness
Frugality	Equity
Temperance	Truth
Kindness	Mercy
Patience	Peaceable was
Fortitude	Godliness
Steadfastness	Cleanliness
Tolerance	Orderliness
Prudence	Loyalty
Modesty	Faithfulness
Compassion	Charity
Reverence	Integrity
Honesty	Gratitude
Chastity	Sincerity
Hope	Joy
Faith	Goodness
	Hospitality

Virtues of the Human Spirit

200 "Virtue," Oxford Online Dictionary, Lexico. Com., 2022, https://www.oxfordlearnersdictionaries.com/us/definition/english/virtue.

As an "End-Time Apostle," I attend church weekly, pray daily, fast, attend a small group, serve in the Church, serve in other ministries, serve homeless veterans and homeless organizations, and am involved in many other community outreaches. Step by step, God will provide a clear path for me to accomplish what He wants me to accomplish for His Kingdom.

Now, I will give my life to serve Him around the world and will give or sell everything I have once I die (via trust and will) to New Hope Church Oahu or New Hope International to plant home churches around the world even after I die. Again, I plan to give 10% tithing plus everything else I own to build God's kingdom on earth.

It's important for me to say this to you, the reader—because there may have been times when it's easier said than done and a concept that looks good only on paper. I am convinced that the Lord had me write this book, sixteen years in the making, and other books to come—which the Holy Spirit puts upon my heart and leads me to write—are all part of serving God and obeying the plans He is laying out for me (Jeremiah 29:11).

A scripture verse in the Bible tells us not to store up treasure on earth where moths and rust can destroy (Matthew 6:19–21). To me, this means worldly goods and staying clear of the love of money (1 Timothy 6:10). Of course, we need funds to pay our bills and to bring in the tithe. Money in itself is neutral. It is the love of money that the Lord warns against because *it is the root of all evil.*

For myself, I strive to save up things for my bank account that is in Heaven. Even if I end up with nothing but a grass shack or tent, I would be happy—as long I don't go to Hell. Even though I know I really deserve it! Thank you, Lord, for your Mercy and Grace.

In Hawaii, when someone dies, the POA will decide to publish a paragraph about your death in the Obituary section of the local newspaper. I believe this is the case if no debtors or persons, family members, kids, etc., challenge the death. You can move on with the will, trust, etc., immediately if your death is not published in the local paper; otherwise, you have fourteen months for any debtors to arise or make claims.

Four Questions Which Have the Power to Change Your Eternal Destiny

1. Did Jesus rise from the dead?
2. Is the resurrection true or false?
3. Was Jesus' tomb empty after three days?
4. Why should I follow only the "real" Jesus?

Are Movie Theatres Taking the Place of the Church?

One look at the line-up for *Coming Soon* or *Now Showing* at the movie theaters makes us wonder whether movie theatres are taking the place of churches. Worldly ideas and prevalent violent or sexual themes in the movies are influencing Christians and young people to seek things other than God (witchcraft, spiritualism, false religions, such as Islam, Buddhism, Hinduism, etc.

In just about every movie, you will hear someone use God's name in vain, and this profanity will continue to increase so that not only are we getting used to it, but we will also be *immune* to it. If you are wondering why I'm making such a big deal about using God's name in vain, please ask yourself if perhaps you are already immune to the deviant things of pop culture.

End Time Corruption

In these last days, many companies will use fraud, deception, and greed to cheat people around the world for their bottom-line money. Unfortunately, a good example is Volks Wagon (VW), based in Germany. The company's CEO, Martin Winterkorn, is making 17 million euros a year.[201] In September 2015, he cheated, lied, and misled millions of VW car owners around the world, saying VW had new diesel cars that could improve emissions.[202] This turned out to be the biggest case involving industrial fraud in Germany's history.

Prompting of the Holy Spirit

I heard the Holy Spirit saying to me, *"So here we go!"* Again, it's not about only going to church, attending a midweek service or a small group, etc. Jesus, God, and the Holy Spirit want you to have a *personal relationship* with them. *How do I do this?* How do you have a personal relationship with family members, neighbors, co-workers, friends, and best friends? First, you get to know them. I explain their characteristics throughout this book but read the Bible; you will learn everything about God, Jesus, and Holy Spirit.

---

201 Charles Riley, "Martin Winterkorn Pays $14 Million to VW for His Role in the Diesel Scandal," CNN Business, 2022, https://amp.cnn.com/cnn/2021/06/09/business/volkswagen-martin-winterkorn-dieselgate/index.html.
202 Riley, 2022.

Next, talk to any of three persons of the Godhead in the morning, afternoon, evening, at work, at home, riding in your car, truck, or motorcycle. *Why, Constantine? I've tried that, but I don't hear any of them talking to me.* Is your heart right with God? Are you doing what the Bible says to do and not doing what it says not to do? That's why you must read the Bible daily at least one or two pages.

Where do I start? From the beginning of Genesis. Is your heart clean? Are you humble before the Lord, your spouse, your children, your neighbors, your family, your co-workers, etc.? Are you willing to make the changes once the Holy Spirit tells you? Do you truly want to follow Jesus and make Him the top priority in your life? Do you want to be intimate with Jesus and have Him deal with your sin in your life? Are you worshiping Jesus in your home, workplace, etc.? When reading your Bible, the Holy Spirit can talk to you.

I've mentioned in this book that each of us has three parts. We have a "body" (blood, flesh, and bones, which equals a physical death), "soul" (will, mind, and emotions—out of this comes your pride, disobedience, etc., which equals a spiritual death) and spirit (communion, conscience, and wisdom, which equals an eternal death). All of God's principles in heaven, which are presented throughout the Bible, are relatable to human life. For example, because we are created in God's likeness, He teaches us how to live like you, in turn, teach *your* child. There are certain things you need to do to teach your child, such as protect, educate, and guide, etc., your child. As your child grows older, let's say thirty to forty years old, there are fewer teachable things you will likely impart to your child, and as they become forty to seventy-five, 'there are much fewer things or ideas that you will share.

God is like that with us! Your "spirit" is getting wisdom from attending church, praying, fasting, and small group. Thus because of your "free will," you are choosing to have a personal relationship with Him. In your "spirit," God's DNA or conscience is already in you to commune with or speak to him. God doesn't have to tell you to take a bath, to be clean; you already know that. God doesn't have to tell you to put on certain clothes to go out; you already know that. God won't tell you to brush your teeth; you already know that.

So, the 3rd part of your inner "spirit—communion" is for you to have a personal relationship with Him every second of the day. Give Jesus your burdens and ask Him to help you and guide you with a humble heart. Write down or journal your prayer requests.

As you read the Bible, God will give you a scripture, and you will ponder it and take observation of this scripture. Then you will apply it to your life. For example, if you know you are doing something sinful, God will show you from Scripture, then you need to apply it and stop that sin. God answers you 99% from Scripture through circumstances, church, small groups, friends, family members, coworkers, and even neighbors. The ability to hear God is within you. God is talking, but many of us cannot hear Him simply because we are not listening.

If you need further help... ask your local pastor, bishop, reverend, or priest.

I truly hope that all I've shared from the depth of my heart, mind, and soul will be helpful to you as you not only survive the times we live in but thrive in your life in all things heavenly, Godly, and good. Amen.

God moves in a village, tribe, community, location, city, state, province, wherever He needs to be on this planet Earth, wherever there are people.

God will move His Spirit among the people with signs, wonders, and miracles!

Man moves people with ceremonies, rituals, and traditions—which sometimes douses God's movement of the Holy Spirit, much like water from a firehose

will douse a fire and put it out.

The Holy Spirit Fire of the Lord is the kind of fire you want under your feet and surrounding you as much as possible in these times.

If you are following your ways and not God's ways, please read Isaiah 55:8 and Romans 8:28.

Some Worthy Definitions to Take to Heart

Humble

The meaning of *humble* is:

humble ['həmbəl]

ADJECTIVE

1. having or showing a modest or low estimate of one's own importance.

He was humble about his stature as one of rock history's most influential guitarists."

Synonyms:

meek deferential [more]

2. of low social, administrative, or political rank. "She came from a humble, unprivileged background"
Synonyms: low-ranking low [more]
3. (of a thing) of modest pretensions or dimensions. "He built the business empire from humble beginnings."
Synonyms: unpretentious ·

VERB
4. Lower (someone) in dignity or importance.
"I knew he had humbled himself to ask for my help."[203]

Koine Greek

koi·ne | \ kōi-ˈnā , ˈkōi-ˌnā; kē-ˈnē \ variants: or *less commonly* **koiné**

Definition of *koine*

1: a dialect or language of a region that has become the common or standard language of a larger area

2: *capitalized*: the Greek language commonly spoken and written in eastern Mediterranean countries in the Hellenistic and Roman periods.[204]

Koine is simply the Greek word for "common." Many people may recognize the word *koine* from the word *koinonia*, which means "fellowship." Fellowship is having something in common.[205]

Koine Greek was simply the common language of the Mediterranean world in the first century. As Alexander the Great

203 "HUMBLE," Oxford Dictionary on Lexico.Com., 2022, https://www.lexico.com/en/definition/humble.
204 "Koine," Merriam-Webster Online Dictionary, Merriam-Webster, Incorporated, 2022, https://www.merriam-webster.com/dictionary/koine.
205 Ibid.

conquered the "civilized world" of his time, he spread the Greek language and culture. Much like English has become today, Greek became the most common and pervasive "international language" of the day.[206] Since most people could understand Koine, it was uniquely suited to proclaim the gospel throughout the world.

206 Ibid.

References

"70 AD: Romans Destroy Jerusalem and Temple." n.d. Aboutbibleprophecy.com. Accessed August 21, 2022. http://www.aboutbibleprophecy.com/e30.htm.

"1960 Charismatic Movement - BEAUTIFUL FEET BEAUTIFUL FEET." 2022. Beautiful Feet: Reviving Believers & Churches. 2022. https://romans1015.com/charismatic-movement/.

"2019 Report on International Religious Freedom: Sudan." 2020. U.S. Department of State. 2020. https://www.state.gov/reports/2019-report-on-international-religious-freedom/sudan/.

"Abortion Rates by State 2022." 2022. World Population Review. 2022. https://worldpopulationreview.com/state-rankings/abortion-rates-by-state.

Agate, Samantha. 2021. "19-Year-Old Killed Himself Live On TikTok — Why Aren't More People Talking About It?" Talent Recap. 2021. https://talentrecap.com/19-year-old-killed-himself-live-on-tiktok-why-arent-more-people-talking-about-it/.

"Age Range by Generation." 2022. Beresford Research. 2022. https://www.beresfordresearch.com/age-range-by-generation/.

Allen, Virginia. 2021. "Are These 7 LGBT 'Kids' Books in Your Child's Classroom, School Library?" The Daily Signal. 2021. https://www.dailysignal.com/2021/08/09/are-these-7-lgbt-kids-books-in-your-childs-classroom-or-school-library/.

Andrew, Timothy. 2021. "A Complete List of Old Testament Books in Order: Bible Summary GuideLord's Library." Lord's Library. 2021. https://www.lordslibrary.com/old-testament-books-in-order-bible/.

"Apollyon." 2022. Merriam-Webster Online Dictionary. Merriam-Webster, Incorporated. 2022. https://www.merriam-webster.com/dictionary/Apollyon.

"Appendices D - The New Testament Was Originally Written in Greek." 2022. A Faithfulversion.org. 2022. https://afaithfulversion.org/appendices-d/.

"Armor of God: What Is It?" 2022. Bibleinfo.com. 2022. https://www.bibleinfo.com/en/questions/armor-of-god#shield.

"Assyrian Empire Builders - Israel, the 'House of Omri.'" 2013. History Department, University College London. 2013. https://www.ucl.ac.uk/sargon/essentials/countries/israel/.

"Asylum Grants in Europe 2020." 2022. Statista. 2022. https://www.statista.com/statistics/293350/asylum-grants-in-europe/.

Ballance, Rhonda. 2017. "Question: 'What Are the Heavenly Crowns That Believers Can Receive in Heaven?'" Yesterday's Prophecy, Today's

News. 2017. https://yesterdaysprophecy.com/question-heavenly-crowns-believers-can-receive-heaven/.

Bassist, Rina. 2022. "Israel Draws Closer to NATO." Al-Monitor: Independent, Trusted Coverage of the Middle East. 2022. https://www.al-monitor.com/originals/2022/06/israel-draws-closer-nato.

Basuga, Allan. 2019. "Lesson 6 Islam." SlideShare. 2019. https://www.slideshare.net/AllanBasuga/lesson-6-islam-168855759.

Beusekom, Mary van. 2022. "COVID-19 May Have Orphaned 7.5 Million Kids Worldwide." Center for Infectious Disease Research and Policy [CIDRAP]. 2022. https://www.cidrap.umn.edu/news-perspective/2022/09/covid-19-may-have-orphaned-75-million-kids-worldwide.

"Biblical Numerology." 2020. Numerology Toolbox. 2020. https://numerologytoolbox.com/biblical-numerology/.

"Book of Joel Introduction: The Day of the Lord Is Coming." 2022. Learn Religions. 2022. https://www.learnreligions.com/book-of-joel-701135.

Bro. Rory. 2017. "The Judgment of the Great Harlot - Part 1 (Revelation 17:1-6)." First Baptist Church Spur Texas. 2017. https://fbcspur.org/judgment-great-harlot-part-1-revelation-171-6/.

Bruner, Rachel. 2019. "The Many Names and Titles of Jesus Christ." Learn Religions. 2019. https://www.learnreligions.com/names-of-jesus-christ-2159232.

Buis, Alan. 2019. "Earth's Atmosphere: A Multi-Layered Cake." Global Climate Change: Vital Signs of the Planet. 2019. https://climate.nasa.gov/news/2919/earths-atmosphere-a-multi-layered-cake/.

"Canada Province Allows Possession of Some Drugs | BTS Visits White House." 2022. YouTube: Wion News TV. 2022. https://www.youtube.com/watch?v=Z8GoOwEEFDE.

Cawthorne, Andrew, and Catherine Bremer. 2010. "U.S. Pours Aid into Haiti, Survivors Fight for Food." Reuters. 2010. https://www.reuters.com/article/us-quake-haiti/u-s-pours-aid-into-haiti-survivors-fight-for-food-idUSTRE60B5IZ20100116.

"China's Great Leap to Wallet-Free Living | Moving Upstream." 2018. YouTube: Wall Street Journal. 2018. https://www.youtube.com/watch?v=75AXINUL47g.

"Chinese New Year Celebrations." 2022. KING-TV: King5.Com. 2022. https://www.king5.com/gallery/news/nation-now/chinese-new-year-celebrations/465-6d54bda5-a755-400b-a858-ed4f226b5660.

"Choosing Tefillin." 2022. AJudaica. 2022. https://www.ajudaica.com/jewish-guides/tefillin.

"Christians in the Holy Land: Under (Israeli) Siege." 2012. Institute for Middle East Understanding [IMEU]. 2012. https://imeu.org/article/christians-in-the-holy-land-under-israeli-siege.

Clark, D. 2020. "Muslim Populations in European Countries Statistic." Statista. 2020. https://www.statista.com/statistics/868409/muslim-populations-in-european-countries/.

CLEARIAS Team. 2022. "World Economic Forum (WEF)." ClearIAS. 2022. https://www.clearias.com/world-economic-forum/.

"Core." 2022. National Geographic Society. 2022. https://education.nationalgeographic.org/resource/core?_gl=1*1vblqcu*_ga*NjI5NDQxMzIuMTY2NTAwNDg1NA..*_ga_JRRKGYJRKE*MTY2NTAwNDg1NC4xLjEuMTY2NTAwNDk2Ni4wLjAuMA..

Creighton, Jolene. 2014. "Scientists Map 8,000 Galaxies." Futurism. 2014. https://futurism.com/scientists-map-8000-galaxies.

Cristobal, Emily. 2022. "With Loved Ones Stuck in Ukraine, Maui Residents Call for an End to the War." HawaiiNewsNow. 2022. https://www.hawaiinewsnow.com/2022/02/27/with-loved-ones-stuck-ukraine-maui-residents-call-an-end-war/.

"Cult." 2022. WordHippo Thesaurus. 2022. https://www.wordhippo.com/what-is/another-word-for/cult.html.

Curry, David. 2022. "PayPal Revenue and Usage Statistics (2022)." Business of Apps. 2022. https://www.businessofapps.com/data/paypal-statistics/.

Dahir, Abdi Latif. 2021. "Fresh Violence in Darfur Adds to Sudan's Crises." The New York Times. 2021. https://www.nytimes.com/2021/11/26/world/africa/sudan-darfur-violence-protests.html.

"Date and Founders of Christian Faith Groups." 2019. Religious Tolerance. 2019. http://www.religioustolerance.org/chr_den1.htm.

"Demographics of Israel: Population of Jerusalem (1844-Present)." 2022. Jewish Virtual Library: A Project of AICE. 2022. https://www.jewishvirtuallibrary.org/population-of-jerusalem-1844-2009.

"Describe the Kaaba: What Is the Black Stone." 2022. Precious Link. 2022. https://www.precious-l.com/btvhtd/describe-the-kaaba-what-is-the-black-stone.

Durst, Rodrick K. 2015. *Reordering the Trinity: Six Movements of God in the New Testament*. Kregel Academic & Professional.

Eckhardt, John. 2021. *Activate Heaven*. Charisma House.

"Economic Data for the Benefit of Investors." 2022. *World Economics*. 2022. https://www.worldeconomics.com/.

"Eliezer Ben Yehuda." 2022. *Your Dictionary*. 2022. https://biography.yourdictionary.com/eliezer-ben-yehuda.

"Evangelist Nathan Morris, Guest Speaker at King's Chapel in Honolulu, HI." 2022.

Fairchild, Mary. 2019. "Who Is the Holy Spirit? Third Person of the Trinity." *Lear*. 2019. https://www.learnreligions.com/who-is-the-holy-spirit-701504.

"Federal HIV Budget." 2022. HIV.Gov. 2022. https://www.hiv.gov/federal-response/funding/budget.

Forbes, Steve, and Forbes Staff. 2022. "Biden Says U.S. Must Lead New World Order: What America Needs If He's Serious." *Forbes*. 2022. https://www.forbes.com/sites/steveforbes/2022/03/25/biden-says-us-must-lead-new-world-order-what-america-needs-if-hes-serious/?sh=63b4c4691640.

Francis, Ian. 2017. "Kathryn Kuhlman – A WARNING TO 21ST CENTURY CHARISMATICS -." YouTube. 2017. https://www.youtube.com/watch?v=QUVg6vyXH3o.

Frangoul, Anmar. 2015. "Major Global Events That Shook 2015." CNBC World News. 2015. https://www.cnbc.com/2015/12/31/major-global-events-that-shook-2015.html.

Frank, Robert. 2013. "Millionaires Give Nine Percent of Income to Charity." CBNC. 2013. https://www.cnbc.com/amp/id/49596515.

Frynas, Jedrzej George, and Manuel Paulo. 2007. "A New Scramble for African Oil? Historical, Political, and Business Perspectives." *African Affairs* 106 (423): 229–51. https://doi.org/10.1093/afraf/adl042.

Hagee, John. 2013. *Four Blood Moons*. Brentwood, TN: Worthy Publishing.

Hass, Ryan. 2021. "Assessing China's 'Common Prosperity' Campaign." The Brookings Institution. 2021. https://www.brookings.edu/blog/order-from-chaos/2021/09/09/assessing-chinas-common-prosperity-campaign/.

"Heaven: A Place to Imagine" 2010 by C. K. Davis. Excerpts from this book used by permission.

Heinrich, Bill. 2016. "03.02.04 Israel Falls to the Assyrians; Israelites Deported to the East; 723 B.C. Israel Ends." *Mysteries of the Messiah*. 2016. https://www.mysteriesofthemessiah.net/2016/01/03-02-04-israel-falls-to-the-assyrians-israelites-deported-to-the-east-723-b-c-israel-ends/.

"History of Technology." n.d. History of Technology. Accessed August 21, 2022. https://historyoftechnologyif.weebly.com/.

Hodge, Bodie. 2007. "How Old Is the Earth?" Answers in Genesis. 2007. https://answersingenesis.org/age-of-the-earth/how-old-is-the-earth/.

———. 2010. "From Genesis to the Gospel." Answers in Genesis. 2010. https://answersingenesis.org/jesus/from-genesis-to-the-gospel/.

"How Cash Is Becoming a Thing of the Past | DW Documentary (Banking Documentary)." 2020. YouTube. 2020. https://www.youtube.com/watch?v=GbECT1J9bXg.

"HUMBLE." 2022. Oxford Dictionary on Lexico.com. 2022. https://www.lexico.com/en/definition/humble.

"Information Age." 2014. History of Technology. 2014. https://historyoftechnologyif.weebly.com/information-age.html.

"Jerusalem's Christian Population Dwindles Further." 2021. Al Monitor. 2021. https://www.al-monitor.com/originals/2022/04/jerusalems-christian-population-dwindles-further.

"Jewish Holidays in 2022." 2022. Chabad Jewish Center of Oakland Inc. 2022. https://www.jewishoakland.org/holidays/jewish-holidays-in-2019/.

"Jewish Population by Country 2022." 2022. World Population Review. 2022. https://worldpopulationreview.com/country-rankings/jewish-population-by-country.

Jones, Jeffrey M. 2022. "LGBT Identification in U.S. Ticks Up to 7.1%." Gallup, Inc. 2022. https://news.gallup.com/poll/389792/lgbt-identification-ticks-up.aspx.

Jones, Timothy. 2018. "Jewish Immigration to Israel Increases in 2018." Deutsche Welle (DW) News. 2018. https://www.dw.com/en/jewish-immigration-to-israel-increases-in-2018/a-46905719.

"Jubilee 2022? - Whiteboard Animation (Plus Bonus Content)." 2022. YouTube: RockIslandBooks. 2022. https://www.youtube.com/watch?v=9-j8YpZH9yk.

Kaplan-Zantopp, Max. 2022. "How Israel Used Innovation to Beat Its Water Crisis. *Israel*. 2022. https://www.israel21c.org/how-israel-used-innovation-to-beat-its-water-crisis/.

Kathryn, Reid. 2014. "2014 Ebola Virus Outbreak: Facts, Symptoms, and How to Help." World Vision. 2014. https://www.worldvision.org/health-news-stories/2014-ebola-virus-outbreak-facts.

Kershner, Isabel. 2021. "How Israel Became a World Leader in Vaccinating Against Covid-19." The New York Times. 2021. https://www.nytimes.com/2021/01/01/world/middleeast/israel-coronavirus-vaccines.html.

Kessler, Glenn. 2011. "Did Ahmadinejad Really Say Israel Should Be 'Wiped off the Map'?" The Washington Post. 2011. https://www.washingtonpost.com/blogs/fact-checker/post/did-ahmadinejad-really-say-israel-should-be-wiped-off-the-map/2011/10/04/gIQABJIKML_blog.html.

Kharpal, Arjun. 2022. "China Launches Digital Currency App to Expand Usage." CNBC LLC. A Division of NBC Universal. 2022. https://www.cnbc.com/2022/01/04/china-launches-digital-currency-app-to-expand-usage.html.

"Koine." 2022. Merriam-Webster Online Dictionary. Merriam-Webster, Incorporated. 2022. https://www.merriam-webster.com/dictionary/koine.

Laan, Ray Vander. 2022. "That the World May Know | Jewish Feasts." Focus on the Family. 2022. https://www.thattheworldmayknow.com/jewish-feasts.

"List of 27 European Union Member Countries." 2022. Countries of the World. 2022. https://www.countries-oftheworld.com/european-union-countries.html.

"Live: Emergency Arab League Summit Convenes in Mecca." 2019. YouTube. 2019. https://www.youtube.com/watch?v=J7gFfVxXUJU.

Loarie. 2013. "We Passed 300,000 Species Observed on INaturalist!" INaturalist. 2013. https://www.inaturalist.org/blog/42626-we-passed-300-000-species-observed-on-inaturalist.

LONAS, LEXI. 2022. "10 Things to Know about Ukraine." *The Hill*. 2022. https://thehill.com/policy/international/596722-10-things-to-know-about-ukraine/.

"Macedonia (Region)." 2022. Wikimedia Commons. 2022. https://en.wikipedia.org/wiki/Macedonia_(region).

Madar, Daniel. 2020. "Israel Not yet World Power in Renewable Energies." The Jerusalem Post. 2020. https://www.jpost.com/opinion/israel-not-yet-world-power-in-renewable-energies-634747.

Maki, Sydney. 2022. "Why Developing Countries Are Facing a Debt Default Crisis." Bloomberg Business Week. 2022. https://www.bloomberg.com/news/articles/2022-07-07/why-developing-countries-are-facing-a-debt-default-crisis?leadSource=uverify wall.

Maupin, Madelon. 2021. "Types of Bible Translations." Bible Roads. 2021. https://bibleroads.com/bible-resources/bible-translations/.

McNamara, Robert. 2020. "Six-Day War in 1967 Reshaped the Middle East." ThoughtCo. 2020. https://www.thoughtco.com/1967-six-day-war-4783414.

"Meaning of the Number 10 in the Bible." 2022. Bible Study. 2022. https://www.biblestudy.org/bibleref/meaning-of-numbers-in-bible/10.html.

"More than 100,000 Russian Troops Placed on Ukraine's Borders." 2022. YouTube: Voice of America. 2022. https://www.youtube.com/watch?v=qjyCjxSIcuM.

"Most Educated Countries 2022." 2022. World Population Review. 2022. https://worldpopulationreview.com/country-rankings/most-educated-countries.

"Muscles." 2012. Better Health Channel. 2012. https://www.betterhealth.vic.gov.au/health/conditionsandtreatments/muscles.

Myers, Meghann. 2018. "Army Wants More Iraqi and Egyptian Language Experts, but That Could Affect Pay for Some Arabic Linguists." Army Times. 2018. https://www.armytimes.com/news/your-army/2018/03/13/army-wants-more-iraqi-and-eqyptian-language-experts-but-that-could-affect-pay-for-some-arabic-linguists/.

"National Debt Clock: What Is the National Debt Right Now?" 2022. Peter G. Peterson Foundation. 2022. https://www.pgpf.org/national-debt-clock.

"NATO - Topic: NATO-Russia Relations: The Facts." 2022. NATO. 2022. https://www.nato.int/cps/sn/natohq/topics_111767.htm.

"Nero as the Antichrist." n.d. U Chicago Education. Accessed October 4, 2022. https://penelope.uchicago.edu/~grout/encyclopaedia_romana/gladiators/nero.html.

Norris, Liam. 2015. "Compulsory Dog Micro-Chipping... Do You Agree?" Medium. 2015. https://medium.com/@liamnorris/compulsory-dog-microchipping-do-you-agree-30e13aa7641e.

Olesen, Jacob. 2013. "Biblical Meaning of Colors." Color Meanings. 2013. https://www.color-meanings.com/biblical-meaning-colors/.

"On Ukraine-Russia Border, Baptists and Pentecostals Endure as Invasion Looms." 2022. BCNN1 WP. 2022. https://bcnn1wp.wordpress.com/2022/01/05/on-ukraine-russia-border-baptists-and-pentecostals-endure-as-invasion-looms/.

O'Neill, Aaron. 2022. "Gross Domestic Product of the MENA Countries in 2021." Statista. 2022. https://www.statista.com/statistics/804761/gdp-of-the-mena-countries/.

"Our Mission | CERN." 2022. CERN. 2022. https://home.cern/about/who-we-are/our-mission.

Pant, Himani. 2017. "Russia's Demographic Trajectory: Dimensions and Implications." Observer Research Foundation (ORF). 2017. https://www.orfonline.org/research/russias-demographic-trajectory-dimensions-and-implications/.

Parker, Kim, and Eileen Patten. 2013. "Caregiving for Older Family Members." Pew Research Center. 2013. https://www.pewresearch.org/social-trends/2013/01/30/caregiving-for-older-family-members/.

"Prosecuting Human Traffickers." 2018. National Conference of State Legislatures [NCSL]. 2018. https://www.ncsl.org/research/civil-and-criminal-justice/prosecuting-human-traffickers.aspx.

"Quantum Dots Deliver Vaccines and Invisibly Encode Vaccination History in Skin." 2019. Genetic Engineering & Biotechnology News. 2019. https://www.genengnews.com/topics/drug-discovery/quantum-dots-deliver-vaccines-and-invisibly-encode-vaccination-history-in-skin/.

Reals, Tucker, and Alex Sundby. 2022. "Russia's War in Ukraine: How It Came to This." CBS Interactive Inc. 2022. https://www.cbsnews.com/news/ukraine-news-russia-war-how-we-got-here/.

Reid, Kathryn. 2020. "2014 Ebola Virus Outbreak: Facts, Symptoms, and How to Help." World Vision. 2020. https://www.worldvision.org/health-news-stories/2014-ebola-virus-outbreak-facts.

Riley, Charles. 2022. "Martin Winterkorn Pays $14 Million to VW for His Role in the Diesel Scandal." CNN Business. 2022. https://amp.cnn.com/cnn/2021/06/09/business/volkswagen-martin-winterkorn-dieselgate/index.html.

Rodriguez, Salvador. 2021. "TikTok Insiders Say Chinese Parent ByteDance Is in Control." CNBC. 2021. https://www.cnbc.com/2021/06/25/tiktok-insiders-say-chinese-parent-bytedance-in-control.html.

Rosenburg, Matt. 2020. "Non-Member Countries of the United Nations." ThoughtCo. 2020. https://www.thoughtco.com/non-members-of-the-united-nations-1435429.

"RS-28 Sarmat | Missile Threat | CSIS Missile Defense Project." 2021. Center for Strategic and International Studies. 2021. https://missilethreat.csis.org/missile/rs-28-sarmat/.

Russell, Walt. n.d. "Playing With Fire."

"Russia Becomes to Most Sanctioned Country After Invading Ukraine (Has More Sanctions Than Iran and North Korea)." 2022. LatestNGnews. 2022. https://latestngnews.com/russia-becomes-to-most-sanctioned-country-after-invading-ukraine-has-more-sanctions-than-iran-and-north-korea/.

"Russia Builds More than 8,000 Mosques, Islamic Schools in 20 Years." 2015. TASS. 2015. https://tass.com/society/821145.

Rutledge, Kim, Hilary Costa, Erin Sprout, Santani Teng, Melissa McDaniel, Diane Boudreau, Tara Ramroop, Jeff Hunt, and Hilary Hall. 2011. "Biodiversity." National Geographic. 2011. https://education.nationalgeographic.org/resource/biodiversity.

Sawe, Behjamin Elisha. 2019. "How Many Times Was Jerusalem Destroyed?" WorldAtlas. 2019. https://www.worldatlas.com/articles/how-many-times-was-jerusalem-destroyed.html.

"Seattle Man Dies after Sex with Horse." 2005. NBC Universal. 2005. https://www.nbcnews.com/id/wbna8589349.

"Sermons by Pastor Wayne Cordeiro| New Hope West." 2022. New Hope West. 2022. https://newhopewest.com/sermon/seeing-things-up/.

Sharma, Palki. 2021. "Gravitas LIVE with Palki Sharma| China's Debt Bomb Explodes: How Defaults Worth Billions Impact You - YouTube." YouTube: Wion News TV. 2021. https://www.youtube.com/watch?v=2SpKxDV6Qog.

Shields, Michael. 2022. "U.N. Reports at Least 240 Civilian Casualties, 64 Deaths in Ukraine." Reuters. 2022. https://www.reuters.com/world/europe/un-reports-least-240-civilian-casualties-64-deaths-ukraine-2022-02-27/.

Skene, Gordon. 2019. "Contemplating NATO - Worries Over Cold War - 1949 - Past Daily Reference Room – Past Daily: News, History, Music And An Enormous Sound Archive." Past Daily. 2019. https://pastdaily.com/2019/09/24/contemplating-nato-worries-over-cold-war-1949-past-daily-reference-room/.

Smalley, Gary. 2004. *The DNA of Relationships*. Tyndale House Publishers.

Smith, Chuck. 2009. "Excerpts Taken from Sermons of Pastor Chuck Smith: Sermons T4261 and T4262." *The Word for Today.*

Snelling, Andrew. 2022. "Geology | The New Answers." Answers in Genesis. 2022. https://answersingenesis.org/geology/.

"Sodom and Gomorrah." 2022. Amazing Bible Timeline with World History. 2022. https://amazingbibletimeline.com/blog/sodom-and-gomorrah/.

"South Africa: An Ongoing Battle with HIV." 2021. Open Access Government. 2021. https://www.openaccessgovernment.org/south-africa-hiv/119993/.

Staff, CNA. 2022. "Vatican: Number of Catholics Worldwide Rose by 16 Million in 2020." Catholic World Report: Catholic News Agency. 2022. https://www.catholicworldreport.com/2022/02/11/vatican-number-of-catholics-worldwide-rose-by-16-million-in-2020/.

"State of Israel Proclaimed." 2022. History Channel: A&E Television Networks, LLC. 2022. https://www.history.com/this-day-in-history/state-of-israel-proclaimed.

Stromberg, Joseph. 2013. "What Is the Anthropocene and Are We in It?" Smithsonian Magazine. January 2013. https://www.smithsonianmag.com/science-nature/what-is-the-anthropocene-and-are-we-in-it-164801414/.

"Swarm Of Locusts Threaten Livelihood Of Millions In African, Asian And Middle Eastern Countries." 2020. YouTube: NBC News. 2020. https://www.youtube.com/watch?v=2PVkVv7XRVk.

"The Complete Guide to Understanding Bible Numerology." 2022. Testimonio LLC. 2022. https://testimon.io/blog/bible-numerology.

"The European Union in Prophecy | Is the EU the Revived Roman Empire?" 2022a. Seeking Truth. 2022. https://seekingtruth.co.uk/the-european-union-in-prophecy/.

"The European Union in Prophecy | Is the EU the Revived Roman Empire?" ———. 2022b. Seeking Truth. 2022. https://seekingtruth.co.uk/the-european-union-in-prophecy/.

"The Greater Sum Presents 7000 Languages." 2020. YouTube: The Greater Sum Foundation. 2020. https://www.youtube.com/watch?v=WI9h_cJof7c.

"The Harmony of Faith and Science. Real Science. Stronger Faith." 2016. True Creation. 2016. https://truecreation.org/#chapter5.

"The Hidden Side of World War II: Last Secrets of Nazis." 2022. YouTube: Best Documentary. 2022. https://www.youtube.com/watch?v=unN7e---Mbg.

"The Importance of Water." 2015. Facebook. 2015. https://pt-br.facebook.com/444194128994211/photos/pb.444194128994211.-2207520000../832048370208783/?type=3&eid-ARA9Tp2MMMS3GVpPeWum6WtCcJJmcj2rrQy-muja80rWin7hErmqVtMY1VCfOOH3bI2vrN_HTZGbCH-bOY.

"The Pool of Siloam." 2022. Bible Study. 2022. https://www.biblestudy.org/biblepic/the-pool-of-siloam.html.

"The World Bank Warns of a Global Recession, So Is It Inevitable? | Counting the Cost." 2022. YouTube: Al Jazeerza. 2022. https://www.youtube.com/watch?v=VbQEMsioXxM.

"The Yom Kippur War: Background & Overview." 2022. Jewish Virtual Library: A Project of AICE. 2022. https://www.jewishvirtuallibrary.org/background-and-overview-yom-kippur-war.

Thomas, Brian. 2010. "30 Years Later, the Lessons from Mount St. Helens." The Institute for Creation Research. 2010. https://www.icr.org/article/a-30-years-later-lessons-mount-st-helens.

Thomas, G.P. 2012. "Israel: Mining, Minerals and Fuel Resources." AZO Mining. 2012. https://www.azomining.com/Article.aspx?ArticleID=234.

Tilburg, Kristin van. 2018. "What Joshua's Sun Stand Still Prayer Means For You." Medium. 2018. https://medium.com/publishous/what-joshuas-sun-stand-still-prayer-means-for-you-88cc9af09f50.

"Topsoil vs. Garden Soil – What's the Difference?" n.d. The Dirt Bag. Accessed October 5, 2022. https://www.thedirt-bag.com/topsoil-vs-garden-soil-whats-the-difference/.

Totenberg, Nina, and Sarah Mccammon. 2022. "Supreme Court Overturns Roe v. Wade, Ending Right to Abortion Upheld for Decades." NPR. 2022. https://www.npr.org/2022/06/24/1102305878/supreme-court-abortion-roe-v-wade-decision-overturn.

Tress, Luke. 2019. "Israel Has 131,000 Millionaires, and Its Wealth Is Growing Quickly, Report Finds." The Times of Israel. 2019. https://www.timesofisrael.com/israel-has-131000-millionaires-and-wealth-is-growing-quickly-report-finds/.

"Virtue." 2022. Oxford Online Dictionary. Lexico. com. 2022. https://www.oxfordlearnersdictionaries.com/us/definition/english/virtue.

"What Are the Dead Sea Scrolls and Why Are They Important?" 2022. Got Questions Ministries. 2022. https://www.gotquestions.org/dead-sea-scrolls.html.

"What Are the Essentials of the Gospel Message?" 2022. Got Questions Ministries. 2022. https://www.gotquestions.org/gospel-message.html.

"What Does Revelation 20:6 Mean?" 2022. BibleRef.com. 2022. https://www.bibleref.com/Revelation/20/Revelation-20-6.html.

"What Does Revelation Mean." 2022. Oxford Online Dictionary. Lexico.com. 2022. https://www.google.com/search?q=what+does.revelation.mean&ie=UTF-8&oe=UTF-8&hl=en-us&client=safari#crs=q:revelati on characters,stick:H4sIAAAAAAAAONgfcRYwC3w8s-c9YanoSWtOXmNM5OLozCtJLSpOTS4RUuJi9y9ILUr-MSxESFxLlEnbLTC7JzM9LzHHOSCxKTAYpEzJAqFE-VUubiDErNSSx.

"What Does the Bible Say about Abortion?" 2022. GotQuestions.org. 2022. https://www.gotquestions.org/abortion-Bible.html.

"What Is the Book of Enoch and Should It Be in the Bible?" 2022. Got Questions Ministries. 2022. https://www.got-questions.org/book-of-Enoch.html.

"What Is the Great White Throne Judgment?" 2022. Got Questions Ministries. 2022. https://www.gotquestions.org/great-white-throne-judgment.html.

"What Is the Purpose of the Thousand-Year Reign of Christ?" 2022. Got Questions Ministries. 2022. https://www.got-questions.org/thousand-year-reign-Christ.html.

"What Is the Seven Year Tribulation Period?" 2020. BibleSprout. 2020. https://www.biblesprout.com/articles/bible/seven-year-tribulation/.

"What Is the Seven Year Tribulation Period?" n.d. Accessed July 17, 2022. https://www.biblesprout.com/articles/bible/seven-year-tribulation/.

"What the Bible Says about IMF." 2022. Bible Tools. 2022. https://www.bibletools.org/index.cfm/fuseaction/Topical.show/RTD/CGG/ID/9769/IMF.htm.

"Why Are So Many People Leaving the Church?" 2020. YouTube: Belief It Or Not. 2020. https://www.youtube.com/watch?v=FdU2Bol04tI.

"Why Do Most Jewish People Not Believe in Jesus?" 2021. Jews for Jesus. 2021. https://jewsforjesus.org/learn/why-do-most-jews-not-believe-in-jesus.

"Why Is the Sun's Atmosphere Hotter than Its Surface?" 2021. Earth Sky. 2021. https://earthsky.org/sun/why-suns-atmosphere-hotter-than-its-surface/.

Wikipedia Contributors. 2022a. "Agriculture in Israel." Wikipedia, The Free Encyclopedia. 2022. https://en.wikipedia.org/wiki/Agriculture_in_Israel.

———. 2022b. "Apostle." Wikipedia, The Free Encyclopedia. 2022. https://en.wikipedia.org/wiki/Apostle.

———. 2022c. "History of the Church of the Nazarene." Wikipedia, The Free Encyclopedia. 2022. https://en.wikipedia.org/wiki/History_of_the_Church_of_the_Nazarene.

———. 2022d. "Libya." Wikipedia, The Free Encyclopedia. 2022. https://en.wikipedia.org/wiki/Libya#Independence,_Kingdom_and_Libya_under_Gaddafi_(1951–2011).

———. 2022e. "List of Israelis by Net Worth." Wikipedia, The Free Encyclopedia. 2022. https://en.wikipedia.org/wiki/List_of_Israelis_by_net_worth.

Williams, Helen. n.d. "Ancient India Currency?" Kerala Travel Tours. Accessed July 17, 2022. https://kerala-travel-tourism.com/india/ancient-india-currency.html.

Wilson, Lorimer. 2020. "IMF Plans to Force a Cashless Society On World Unfolding - Here's How (+8K Views)." MunKNEE. 2020. https://munknee.com/imf-plan-to-force-a-cashless-society-on-world-unfolding-heres-how/.

"World Health Organization: More Than 1.2M Abortions Have Been Performed World Wide In First 10 Days Of 2021." 2021. Ventura Broadcasting Company. 2021. http://www.venturabroadcasting.com/world-health-organization-more-than-1-2m-abortions-have-been-performed-world-wide-in-first-10-days-of-2021.

"World Population to Reach 8 Billion on 15 November 2022." n.d. United Nations. Accessed September 28, 2022. https://www.un.org/en/desa/world-population-reach-8-billion-15-november-2022.

Worrall, Patrick. 2015. "FactCheck: How Many of the World's Muslims Are Radicalised?" Channel 4 News. 2015. https://www.channel4.com/news/factcheck/factcheck-worlds-muslims-radicalised.

Wright, David. 2012. "Timeline for the Flood." Answers in Genesis. 2012. https://answersingenesis.org/bible-timeline/timeline-for-the-flood/.

Endnote Call to Action

Aloha Readers:

I have written twelve books in the last year (2021–2022), which could only have been done with the guidance of the Holy Spirit:

- *The End Game*
- *The Danger of Islam*
- *Mormonism Debunked*
- *The Truth of Hinduism*
- *Buddhism Debunked*
- *What It Means to be Jehovah's Witness*
- *The Army of the Lord—5 Distinct Roles*
- *How to Recognize Cults and Witchcraft (Black Magic) in the Modern World*
- *Scientology and the Illuminate: Facts and Fiction*
- *The Role of Gangs and Victory in Jesus*
- *How to Effectively Share Jesus with an Atheist*
- *The Truth About Horoscopes, Astrology, and Gnostic Beliefs*

My heart is to fulfill the Great Commission found in Matthew 28:16–20 (ESV).

> Now the eleven disciples went to Galilee, to the mountain to which Jesus had directed them. And when they saw Him they worshipped Him, but some doubted. And Jesus came and said to them, all authority in heaven and on earth has been given to me. Go therefore and make disciples of all nations, baptizing them in the name of the Father and of the Son and of the Holy Spirit, teaching them to observe all that I have commanded you. And behold, I am with you always, to the end of the age.

If you and your network of friends, family members, neighbors, co-workers, etc., could please assist in fulfilling the Great Commission by writing a review on Amazon, Barnes & Noble, customer reviews, book clubs, etc. You can also pre-order these books through Amazon and Barnes & Noble.

Remember:
Your Gifting = Your Ability
Your Calling = Your Identity
Your Anointing = Your purpose in life for Christ.

—Apostle Constantine I. Nightingdale
The End Times Apostle to the World from Hawaii

Disclaimer

The views and content expressed in this book are those of the author and may not necessarily reflect the view of New Hope Oahu, Foursquare Churches, or New Hope International.

Contact Us:

1. As the author, I would like to suggest that if you are not attending a church in your country, nation, state, town, city, etc., you view the online church at enewhope.org and register online to start a small group in your home. New Hope currently has 19,000 to 20,000 people in 200 locations (countries) on seven continents watching every weekend service.
2. I would like to find out what Jesus Christ is calling me to serve in the Fivefold Army of the Lord in Ephesians 4:6–11. Am I called to be an apostle, prophet/prophetess, evangelist, pastor, or teacher? Go to enewhope.org and go to the search bar on the top right. Type in "spiritual gifting test". Then fast and pray about this.
3. Next, contact "The Fivefold Army of the Lord" at: P.O. Box 1983, Aiea, HI 96701, and we will get back to you. Be sure to include your full name, address, email, phone number, and your spiritual gifting from test or test results.

You can also tell us your story or testimony if you'd like. We love hearing testimonies from around the world.

4. You can also email the Army of the Lord—5 Distinct Roles Team by going to www.armyofthelord5dr.org
General Administrator: Rae Fujioka at P.O. Box 1983, Aiea, HI 96701
Apostle Constantine I. Nightingdale at
cnightingdale@yahoo.com
Prophetess/Editor General Char D. at
alohastagedinteriors@hawaii.rr.com
Prophetess/Prayer General Cynthia Silver at
godngood@hawaii.rr.com
Evangelist General TBA
Pastor Generals Chris & Roxy M. at
chrisnroxymadayag@yahoo.com
Teacher General TBA

GATHERING OF SAINTS for Corporate Prayer
If you need prayer, please log on to:
NewDayPrayerline.com for current times
New Day Prayerline: (559) 671-2028

The Army of the Lord—5 Distinct Roles has monthly training; please go to *www.armyofthelord5dr.org* and mail three copies of the application with three photos to General Administrator Rae Fujioka at P.O. Box 1983, Aiea, HI 96701

Suggested books that you can order for your personal library to share with your best friends, friends, family members, neighbors, co-workers, dentists, doctors, bank tellers, store clerks, etc. can be purchased at Amazon.

Lightning Source UK Ltd.
Milton Keynes UK
UKHW011406100223
416600UK00009B/135